# *If These* **WALLS**
## *Could* **TALK:**
### DENVER BRONCOS

Stories from the
Denver Broncos Sideline,
Locker Room, and Press Box

Dave Logan with Arnie Stapleton

## TRIUMPH
### BOOKS

Library of Congress Cataloging-in-Publication Data available upon request

This book is available in quantity at special discounts for your group or organization. For further information, contact:

**Triumph Books LLC**
814 North Franklin Street
Chicago, Illinois 60610
(312) 337-0747
www.triumphbooks.com

Printed in U.S.A.

ISBN: 978-1-62937-771-1

Design by Amy Carter

Page production by Patricia Frey

All photos courtesy of AP Images

*To my family, for all their love and support: Tonya, Cassidy, Etha, Gunner, Jazzie, and Sadie.*

*—D.L.*

*For my life partner, Kate, and our athletic, artistic, and accomplished daughters, Jordyn, Ashlyn, and Miquela, and of course my forever puppy-at-heart, Choco, my loyal companion who kept me company every step of the way during this thoroughly enjoyable project.*

*—A.S.*

# CONTENTS

# FOREWORD

**W**hen the final seconds of Super Bowl 50 ticked away, I couldn't help but think back to our first Super Bowl victory 18 years earlier.

On the night we finally put to rest so many demons and disappointments from Super Bowl letdowns, Pat Bowlen took the Lombardi Trophy following our 31–24 win over the mighty Green Bay Packers, thrust it into the air, and hollered, "This one's for John!"

Looking back, that was the greatest moment of my playing career.

Nearly two decades later, I had the chance to return the favor after Von Miller led one of the greatest defensive performances in team history and Peyton Manning capped a Hall of Fame career, going out as a champion just like I had done after the '98 season.

Following our 24–10 win over the Carolina Panthers on a cool Northern California night, they handed me the Lombardi Trophy, and I couldn't wait to hold it high and holler, "This one's for Pat!"

The chance to say those four words had been my motivation ever since I returned to work for Mr. B. on January 5, 2011, as the Broncos' vice president of football operations.

Playing for Mr. B. was one of the greatest joys of my life, and working for him proved just as thrilling. He was a tremendous mentor and an incredible friend.

During the 15 seasons I played for him, Pat Bowlen always gave us everything we needed to fulfill his mantra of being the best at everything. Twice we won it all for him when I was the Broncos' quarterback.

There's nothing like leading the team onto the field. But bringing home a third Lombardi Trophy to Mr. B. was very special, too. It was a way of thanking the man who helped make my playing career and my post-playing career so fulfilling.

Although Mr. B. has left us, his organizational philosophies still guide us. Outside the locker room is a large picture of Mr. B and his guiding principle: "I want us to be number one in everything."

That includes Broncos broadcasts.

Dave Logan has been a mainstay behind the microphone at Denver Broncos games for the past 30 years, describing the action in the hot summer days of the preseason through some freezing nights deep into the playoffs. Year after year. Decade after decade.

Dave has a unique perspective and unmatched insight into the game as a former NFL wide receiver and current voice of the Broncos. (Even though I had to redo my pre–Super Bowl show with him before Super Bowl XXXII because of technical glitches with the first taping, which Dave shares with you in Chapter 8!)

I'm glad to see Dave team up with the AP's Arnie Stapleton, whom I've known since my playing days and who's always been fair, accurate, and informative in his coverage of the NFL and the Broncos.

Enjoy the book, Broncos fans!

—John Elway

# INTRODUCTION

On September 25, 1984, Dave Logan jumped into his red Jeep Cherokee and peeled out of the Denver Broncos team parking lot, his nine-year NFL career and four-game cameo with his hometown team in the rearview mirror.

The 6'5", 230-pound wide receiver who had averaged better than 16 yards a catch and scored two dozen touchdowns as a pro, mostly with the Cleveland Browns, reached for the radio dial—and, unknowingly, his future.

Logan played at a time when the NFL was truly a blood sport, glorified by all those greatest hits compilations of tackles and tactics in the rough-and-tumble '70s that would get today's players ejected, fined, and more than likely suspended. Training camp was a survival of the fittest with two-a-day (if not three-a-day) practices in full pads interspersed with a half hour in an ice tub. Those who survived then had to get through a week's worth of hard-hitting practices every week during the season just to get the chance to suit up on game days.

R&B always helped Logan unwind on his drive home. "I was a music guy," Logan said. "I never listened to talk radio."

Earlier that year, Robert Plant's "In the Mood" topped out at No. 39 on the Billboard Top 100, but unlike the popular English recording artist, Logan was in no mood for a melody on this autumn day. A few months earlier, Logan's wish had been granted when the Browns agreed to trade him to his hometown Broncos, giving him the chance to live out his lifelong dream.

On this day, an early morning phone call had roused him from bed, summoning him to team headquarters. "Coach wants to see you," confirmed the voice on the other end. Logan knew exactly what it was about; head coach Dan Reeves was cutting him.

Other teams were interested in signing him, but Logan was now in his thirties. Despite having broken both ankles, he felt pretty good, but he wasn't fond of the idea of subjecting his body to more beatings. After nine seasons and 121 games, his NFL playing career was over.

Football, however, was far from done with Dave Logan. He would find not one, but two second careers in football, sharing his insights and talking football on one hand and teaching it on the other.

Logan would go on to win a record eight state titles coaching at four different high schools in Colorado's highest classification, including the 2019 title with Cherry Creek High School, and serve more than three decades as the voice of the Denver Broncos, giving him front-row access to one of the NFL's most storied franchises and its iconic players, coaches, and characters.

On that day back in 1984, though, Logan didn't know what his future held. He'd probably follow in his father's footsteps and get into estate planning, maybe help out with some high school football as a volunteer, coaching the wide receivers or quarterbacks. Fiddling with the radio dial as he drove out of the Broncos' parking lot and away from the job he had dreamed of all his life while growing up in Denver, Logan stopped when he heard a familiar voice on KRXY-AM 1600. It was Irv Brown, the baseball coach at the University of Colorado when Logan was a multisport star for the Buffaloes in the 1970s.

Rare is the professional athlete who doesn't specialize in one sport but who excels at whatever sport is in season. Logan was among the very best of that elite group, having joined Dave Winfield and Mickey McCarty as the only athletes ever drafted by teams in the National Football League, the National Basketball Association, and Major League Baseball. (Another, Noel Jenke, was drafted by the NFL, MLB, and the Chicago Blackhawks of the National Hockey League.) After starring in football, basketball, and baseball at Wheat Ridge High School, where he won the *Denver Post*'s Gold Helmet Award as the state's top senior football player, scholar, and citizen, Logan was drafted in 1972 by the Cincinnati Reds as a shortstop and a pitcher.

But he wanted to go to college and continue playing all three sports, so he turned down the Reds and instead accepted a scholarship offer from the University of Colorado in Boulder, where he would star in both basketball and football but where his baseball dream would die because his football coach wanted him to play spring football instead. As versatile as ever, Logan played guard and forward on the Buffaloes basketball team, and on the football field he did duty at wide receiver, running back, and punt returner. After lettering in both sports, he was selected in 1976 in both the NBA and NFL drafts by the Kansas City Kings and Cleveland Browns, respectively.

Logan says now he chose football in "a moment of insanity." Playing eight seasons in Cleveland beginning in 1976, Logan ranked among the top five in franchise history in almost every receiving category by the time he was traded to the Broncos in 1984.

Like Logan, Irv Brown was a multitalented sports personality in Colorado. Besides coaching baseball, Brown was a big-time college basketball referee who worked six Final Fours, and he was a television commentator who was part of the first college football game broadcast by a fledgling network named ESPN. He was also a local radio show host whose most famous pairing was with another Denver radio icon, Joe Williams. *Irv and Joe* bantered like old drinking buddies, and on this day they were livid about Logan's dismissal from the Broncos after just four games and a single catch.

"They were really giving it to Dan," Logan recounted. "'What the hell's he thinking about? They trade for Dave Logan and Dan cuts him in the middle of the year?'" Logan listened to them the rest of the way home. "And I'm thinking, *Well now, that's an interesting talk show,*" he said. "First time I had ever listened to talk radio." He was hooked.

Brown reached out and interviewed Dave Logan a couple of times on the air during that 1984 season, and he really liked what he heard from the well-spoken, cerebral ex-player who was so adept at deciphering defenses that he even spent one summer playing quarterback for the Browns.

Logan may have been big for a wide receiver, but he was prototypical quarterback size and nearly got to play the position in the pros, too. "It's funny. I weighed myself; I was 227 today," Logan said in 2019. "At the combine, I ran a 4.52 and I weighed 228 my senior year. So, I was a big wide receiver. With the Browns, my playing weight was anywhere between 228 to 232. I would say back probably in that era, the only receiver who was bigger than me would have been Harold Carmichael. Harold was like 6'8", real thin, but yeah, I don't think they could really figure out what to do with me."

Logan towered over most of his teammates. "I remember going to my second training camp. I was sitting there playing catch. My number was 85, and Blanton Collier, who had been the head coach of the Browns and was then a consultant, a little bitty older fella, walked up with hearing aids," Logan said. "He was standing by me and he said to me, 'Son, are you a wide receiver or a quarterback?' I said, 'I'm a wide receiver.' He just nodded.

"I thought that was a weird question. After that workout, I got summoned to head coach Forrest Gregg's office. He said, 'Blanton Collier seems to think you throw better than some of our quarterbacks.' I said, 'Well, I was a quarterback in high school for a while and then there was talk of moving me to quarterback at CU to run the wishbone.... And he said, 'We'd like to bring you to training camp as a quarterback.'

"So, I thought he was kidding, but I quickly realized he was serious. They flew me back in the off-season to get work at quarterback. And I actually spent most of training camp at quarterback until Paul Warfield, in what would turn out to be his last year, got hurt. Paul was the starting X receiver, and he pulled a hamstring at the end of training camp. Raymond Berry, the Hall of Fame receiver for the Baltimore Colts and my receivers coach in Cleveland, approached me and said, 'Listen, we play Cincinnati in the opener in like 10 days. We're going to bounce you back to X.' So, after not having any training camp reps at receiver, I started at X against the Bengals."

Logan caught four passes for 78 yards from quarterback Brian Sipe in a 13–3 win over the Bengals.

Brown liked the way Logan broke down plays and schemes, formations and coverages, and at season's end, he asked Logan to come in and do an hourlong show previewing Super Bowl XIX between Joe

Montana's San Francisco 49ers and Dan Marino's Miami Dolphins. The gig didn't pay a dime, but it was a chance for Logan to talk about football, share his insights, break down the matchups, and give his prediction.

"Come do it," said Brown, "see if you like it."

Logan gladly took Brown up on his offer and headed into the radio studio the day before the Super Bowl, sharing his thoughts with the audience. "I enjoyed it because I love the game of football," Logan said. "I always was a student of the game. I love the game. I wasn't one of those guys that just played at the top level. I mean, if it was on, I was watching. I was always watching. So, it was Marino and Montana. I really thought San Francisco would win that game."

He was right. The 49ers ran away with a 38–16 win.

"The boss heard the show and loved it," Brown told Logan a few days later, then made him an offer that would prove as pivotal as Logan's decision to choose football over basketball and baseball.

Brown, who was often on the road working television broadcasts for Denver Nuggets games, suggested Logan come work as his fill-in on *Irv and Joe* during the basketball season. He could even name his salary—well, sort of. Instead of a paycheck, he would earn money by selling time slots on the show to local businesses advertising their goods and services.

"Oh, that will be easy," Brown told Logan. "Just go out and sell."

Logan gave it a shot. "It might have been easy for Irv," Logan chuckled, "but it wasn't for me."

Logan had succeeded at everything he'd ever set out to do, combining talent with technique, skills with savvy, and diligence with a dogged determination, a formula that certainly seemed foolproof.

So, he set out with three minutes of advertising slots to sell and quickly enlisted a Denver men's clothier to buy some air time for the show. "I don't even remember how many spots," Logan said. "I just remember driving back and thinking, *Damn, I just got $680. It's a pretty* *good deal just to be talking about their company on the radio. This is going to be great."*

Just as quickly, he realized it wasn't. "Looking back, that first sale might have been a mercy buy," Logan concluded after finding a second sale so very elusive. "I think they remembered me from CU. That was the last thing I sold."

Selling just wasn't in his DNA. "It's hard, because you've got to be able to deal with, 'No thank you,'" Logan said. "But you've also got to be able to overcome objections. And the way that I was always sort of wired and brought up was that when I heard, 'No thank you,' I said, 'Okay, no worries. Thank you.'"

Logan would soon find broadcast jobs on radio and television that did offer regular paychecks, which he parlayed into bigger and better jobs until he landed at 850 KOA Radio in Denver, where he's now in his 24th season as the Denver Broncos' play-by-play announcer after serving seven years as a color analyst on the team's broadcasts. Since 1990, he's brought insights to listeners from coaches and quarterbacks on his pregame shows, chronicled the Hall of Fame careers of John Elway, Gary Zimmerman, Shannon Sharpe, Terrell Davis, Pat Bowlen, Champ Bailey, and Steve Atwater, all while calling the iconic plays so cemented in franchise lore.

There was Elway, who would lead the Broncos to glory from both the huddle and the front office, helicoptering his way into NFL immortality against the Green Bay Packers in Super Bowl XXXII for the Broncos' first title after four flops, three of them with Elway at quarterback.

There was Rod Smith catching an 80-yard touchdown pass a year later against the Atlanta Falcons in Super Bowl XXXIII, a successful title defense that allowed Elway to retire a Super Bowl MVP and a two-time champion, something that cemented his stature among the greatest quarterbacks ever to play the game.

There was Tim Tebow's 80-yard touchdown pass to Demaryius Thomas on the first play of overtime that stunned the Pittsburgh Steelers in the playoffs, the most magical moment in a season full of miracles that defied explanation.

There were Von Miller's two strip sacks of Cam Newton in Super Bowl 50 that allowed Peyton Manning to go out a champion on a spectacular note four years after being released from the Indianapolis Colts following a series of neck fusion surgeries.

Logan brought his insight and voice to all these moments while also serving as a head football coach, beginning in 1993 at Arvada West High School and continuing at Chatfield High School in 2000, J.K. Mullen High School in 2003, and Cherry Creek High School in 2012. He's won Class 5A state championships at every school he coached.

Logan hated two-a-day practices as a player, and he makes a deal with his players every year during summer ball. "What I tell them is I've got to have 85 percent attendance during the summer," Logan said. "I don't miss days. I don't take vacation. If we get 85 percent participation, I tell my players we won't have two-a-days. We've never had two-a-day padded practices in my 27 years as a head coach. I've always thought there was a smarter way to do that. And we've seen the NFL sort of adopt that in the last decade or so."

Logan still shudders to think about those old two-a-days in his era. "I remember one time I lost 11 pounds in one afternoon practice," Logan said. "After practice, they put me on an IV, which isn't all that unusual nowadays, but back then it was. We trained at Kent State; the temperatures could be in the mid-90s with humidity in the high 60s or 70s. Man, it was brutal. And you're in full friggin' pads and you're taking guys to the ground. I remember putting on my shoulder pads one afternoon and they were still soaked from the morning practice. Fast-forward to when I started coaching, and I just always thought I'd try to do it a little differently."

Nowadays, one hard-nosed practice is plenty. "We work 'em now," Logan said. "They're really challenged in those summer workouts. But you have to get them ready physically for the season. I've always believed there's a law of diminishing return for athletes whether you're in high school, college, the pros.... Working smarter makes more sense."

What Logan takes a lot of pride in is having never cut a single player in tryouts. "I make sure we find a role they can be good at, whether on special teams or maybe even a particular group of plays," Logan said. Because he wants all of them to get the same thing he did out of the game: learning about teamwork, striving toward common goals, being unselfish, and working for something greater than oneself.

"It's a beautiful game," Logan said.

To play.

To coach.

To cover.

To study.

To interpret.

To explain.

To share.

"I've loved every minute of it," Logan said.

# CHAPTER 1

## BACK IN THE DAY

**T**oday's NFL players have it easy in their luxurious locker rooms and fantastic facilities where cryogenic chambers have replaced the metal ice tubs of Dave Logan's time in the league back in the 1970s and '80s.

"When I first went to the Saints in the mid-80s, we had an 80-yard grass field, okay?" Broncos head coach Vic Fangio said when he opened his first training camp in 2019. "We had no cafeteria. Guys would go to a greasy deli for lunch right across the street."

It was that way just about everywhere. Most teams back then held training camp at college campuses because universities already had the cafeterias, classrooms, and dormitories to accommodate the teams' expanded rosters before attrition and Oklahoma drills whittled down the rosters to the regular-season limit of 53.

Fans flocked to watch them practice, then lined up for autographs afterward. For many people, this was as close as they'd ever get to both the behemoth players and a real game—and they were hooked for life.

Those days may have been great for business, but few look back on them as the good ol' days.

Nutrition is a much bigger deal today than it used to be, said Chad Brown, a former University of Colorado linebacker who played for the Pittsburgh Steelers, Seattle Seahawks, and New England Patriots during a 13-year NFL career. When Brown began his pro career, the Steelers only provided players lunch. Now, teams have gourmet chefs and nutritionists on staff providing three square meals a day. When players get to work they grab a shake with their name on it—literally. The shakes are tailored to each player's nutritional needs and blended with a unique mix of ingredients. "So, to go from…the Steelers barely providing us a completely awful, terrible lunch to what these guys have now, it's not light years, it's galaxies different," Brown said.

Limits on hitting has also played a role in better athletes making it onto rosters. "Von Miller's an amazingly great player and I think he could play great football in any era," Brown said. "But to have Von Miller pass rush twice a day in pads and do that over a full training camp over all those practices? At some point, he's a smaller man going against a much bigger man. That's going to wear him down. That's going to make him less explosive. I know it certainly did me. I came into the league at 225 pounds. I was an edge rusher and an inside linebacker, and over the course of practices I got physically worn down because I just wasn't as big and as strong as the guys I was going against."

Brown believes we see better athleticism nowadays in the NFL because those players are no longer dropping out during arduous training camps that were more like survival tests; they're making it to cutdown day healthy.

Of course, progress still brings problems. Logan said the limits on live hitting have led to poor tackling, bad offensive line play, and spotty special teams in today's NFL, while also making it much harder for players to get primed for the regular season. "One of the advantages we had back in the '70s and '80s—and we didn't have many—is that training camp was a bitch," Logan said, "so your body got used to the pounding."

The NFL's efforts to reduce concussions and make the game safer have also affected the quality of play. With fewer padded practices and less live hitting, offensive lines are at a disadvantage, because it takes so much time for the beefy men up front to learn to work together, especially with the spread-out college game no longer producing plug-and-play draft picks such as Ryan Clady or Ryan Harris. Tackling on defense and special teams has also become an issue with so few padded practices allowed and the league cracking down on helmet hits.

"Those are the two biggest things I've seen, and I think both of these are byproducts of rules changes," Logan said. "You can put your team in full pads in practice only 14 times during the entire regular season. So, the two areas I've seen that have been hit hardest by some of these rules changes: offensive line play and tackling. You see a bunch of missed tackles, you see guys trying to come up and really deliver a big shot. Even as great as NFL players are, if you're going to be really good at something, you have to be able to practice it over and over.

"Now, with league rules being the way they are, coaches have to be really smart about, *How many times do I want to put my guys through a live session where we're taking players to the ground? How many times do I want my running backs or receivers hit and taken down to the ground?* The answer is not many. So you can practice with thud tackling. They've changed the way they want you to tackle, where you used to put your head across the front of a guy. Now, with hawk tackling, your head goes to the backside. We're talking about some of the best athletes in the world who can break a lot of tackles. Defenders cannot lead with their helmet when tackling, which at face value is a good rule. But it's made it much more difficult for guys to tackle well," Logan said.

"Now, the league's been able to overcome that, right? It's structured to where the offense has every advantage in the world because the NFL wants scoring. They want big plays, they want chunk plays. They want the kinds of plays that make fans stand up and get excited. I just think it's much harder today to play good, solid defense than it was back in the day. It's just what it is, and I think the league's okay with that."

Safety is paramount, and that has made for a sloppier game in some ways. "We used to go live a lot in practice. And I'm not advocating teams do that today, but it just stands to reason that if you go live on certain drills, you're going to get better at them. They've negated a lot of the big hits, right? I'm glad to see that; my former self, especially, is happy to see it. But in doing so, you've made it much more difficult for defensive players to tackle within the rules," Logan continued.

"You can practice wrapping up, you can practice head placement; you can practice these things, including the hawk tackle, where you put your head behind the ball carrier, wrap, and roll. But the game is so fast. It was fast even back when I played. It's a lot faster now. So you just try to get a guy on the ground as best you can, right?

"I also think that it's harder today in the NFL for coaches to sort of callous the players' bodies. Back in the day, we were going live a lot and you practiced twice a day in pads. But your body got used to the pounding. You calloused your body. Now, as a coach in the NFL you've got to have a really good plan. Your first and foremost concern is, *I want to make sure I get guys through this training camp healthy. How do I do that? Well, I limit how much they play in the preseason.*

"We certainly limit all of their contact in training camp. We limit how much time we're hitting. So, players can't callous their bodies, to get used to pads and contact. There's very little hitting going on."

Nowadays, starters are only making cameos in the preseason, if they're playing at all. That's turned September into the new August, when teams ramp up during the first month of the regular season and really don't establish their identity until they've played a number of games.

"It takes a lot. You can be in the greatest shape. These guys all have off-season trainers. They work hard in the off-season. We used training camp to get back into shape, to get back into football shape," Logan said. "These days, guys come into camp in football shape. So that's not an issue. Their cardio and their overall strength, those two things are not a concern. But what is an issue is developing an ability to play—let's say for a wide receiver to play 60 snaps. That conditioning where you're running a deep comeback and the ball goes the other way and then you trot back to the huddle, that might be a 10-play drive. Then, you sit and then you come back for an eight-play drive, and you get hit twice, once on a slant, once on a basic route…. Developing that for your body, they can't do that with how camp is set up these days. So they do that in September instead of August."

Take Emmanuel Sanders, who played six seasons in Denver before being traded to the San Francisco 49ers just before the deadline in 2019. Sanders was coming back from surgery on both ankles—he tore his left Achilles' tendon in practice in December 2018, and after having that repaired he had what's known as "tightrope" surgery on his troublesome right ankle, too. Tightrope surgery helps speed up the healing of a high ankle sprain. Sanders had a terrific preseason performance in 2019 but he was gassed after playing just a dozen snaps in August against the 49ers—who would trade third- and fourth-round picks in the 2020 draft to the Broncos in exchange for Sanders a couple of months later.

"He was dying," Logan said. "Dying. And that's exactly my point. There's nothing like game speed and game conditioning, no matter what. And Emmanuel, a voracious worker in the off-season—I mean, these guys put themselves through it. I don't care what you do. You can't duplicate a game tempo, get in pads, get hit every third play running a deep-9 route, and jog back and then run it again. You just can't."

Sanders was going into his 10th season in the league. It's even harder for rookies who are not only getting used to the longer NFL season but acclimating to professional football. "The game is a lot different than it is in college," Logan said. "You're playing the best athletes in the world, you're playing against teams whose coaches and coordinators have all the time in the world to game plan specifically against you. These guys look for subtle things that tip them off. *You can tell when the ball's coming his way, you can tell it's a pass route by the way he comes off the line of scrimmage as opposed to a running play.* I mean, those are all basic tenets of being a good receiver. Some of those things have never changed."

# CHAPTER 2
## A BEAUTIFUL GAME

In his youth, Dave Logan didn't necessarily see himself spending the better part of four decades in the NFL as a player and broadcaster or more than 25 years as a high school football coach. He just as easily could have envisioned a long career in basketball or baseball.

"I loved them all, honestly," Logan said. "I really enjoyed whatever I was doing at the time. I never really gave serious thought to, *Which one of these, if any, am I going to make a career out of?* Had I played basketball and not had a football season before where I'm pretty beat up, I think I could have played because I could shoot the ball. The competitive part of me says I think I could have made the team and contributed no matter which direction I chose.

"I was a fastball hitter, probably needed a lot of work staying back on off-speed stuff. But they all do. I mean, I love baseball—still do— and I loved basketball. Basketball was probably my favorite sport. But I loved football, too. Football, I played it my whole life. I just loved whatever I was doing at the time."

Logan figures he got some of his athletic traits from his parents: his father, Maury, who died in 1993, and his mother, Etha. Maury played basketball and football at North High School in Denver and then spent a year on the University of Utah's football team. His mother "was probably the best athlete, but back then they didn't have sports for girls," Logan said. "We'd shoot free throws and she'd knock down seven or eight out of 10. She was like five-foot-eight."

Their son would reach a tad over 6'4" and 232 pounds, and whether posting up under the basket, toeing the rubber on the mound, or running a skinny post at Wheat Ridge High School in Denver, Logan was such a star multisport student-athlete that he was afforded the rarest of opportunities: the chance to actually choose which professional sport to play.

"At that time, if you signed a professional contract in a sport, you were ineligible to play any other sport in college," said Logan, who had his heart set on attending the University of Colorado. "So I had told the major league teams that I would not be signing because I wanted to go to college to play sports."

Logan had hopes of resuming his three-sport career at CU but ended up playing just football and basketball in college. "I was going to play baseball after my sophomore football season…but my football coach, Eddie Crowder, got fired, and Bill Mallory took over. He nixed that idea real quick," Logan said with a smile. Instead, Logan played spring football at Mallory's suggestion.

Basketball and football kept him plenty busy, however. "I literally would start playing basketball whenever the football season ended. I'd stop playing football and then I'd go play basketball," Logan said. "In fact, my senior year we played Earl Campbell and the University of Texas in the Blue Bonnet Bowl. I caught a touchdown in that game and then the next day flew to Kansas City, where they had the Big Eight preseason tournament, and suited up.

"I had a big wrap on my leg for some reason. Coach [Russell "Sox"] Walseth put me in the game early. We wound up losing to Kansas State, but I shot the ball pretty well," said Logan, who finished with 18 points. "It was pretty crazy. The day before, I was playing football. But it was always basketball for me as soon as football was done."

Not only was Logan a multisport star, but he was versatile at both. "I was actually a 2 or 3, a shooting guard. I was strong enough at that point I could play some 3 [small forward]. We weren't real big at CU but I played with Scott Wedman, who played a long time in the NBA and was a great shooter. We finished second in the Big Eight one year. All of our guys were like 6'4½" to 6'7½" but everybody could shoot it; a pretty physical team with good athletes. So we had Lee Haven, Pat Kelly, Bobby Hofman, who later became a head coach…. We had a good run."

At 6'5" and nearly 230 pounds, Logan was not only a towering figure on campus but he was colossal by wide receiver standards at the time— not to mention a gigantic punter and punt returner. "I was a split end, and Coach Mallory moved me to wing back," Logan said. "I returned punts a little bit. Steve Haggerty was the punt returner. He got hurt and they put me back there. It was a challenge for me, but I really enjoyed it." Logan wound up with a couple of punt returns for touchdowns in his CU career, one against Air Force and another against Iowa State. After his return against the cadets, longtime Falcons coach Ben Martin quipped, "He's got to be the biggest punt returner in the country."

Although he loved every sport he played, by 1976 it came time to choose one. The Kansas City Kings selected him in the ninth round of the NBA draft. "And then right after the Kings drafted me, the Browns drafted me" in the third round, Logan recounted. "I had broken an ankle playing basketball just before the NFL draft, and my agent sent letters out to all the NFL teams with my orthopedic surgeon stating that I would make a full recovery. But, looking back, I think it probably cost me a little bit." The Kings urged Logan to reject the Browns and return to Colorado for his final season of basketball eligibility.

Logan chose football. Or, rather, football chose him. The building blocks to this unique career path had all been there in his youth: a dogged determination to succeed, a love of details, and a deep desire to outsmart, outwork, and outmaneuver his opponents.

"Yeah, you've got to have that. The greatest players I've ever been around as a player and now as a broadcaster are the most competitive. They're going to do whatever it takes, they're totally committed to the process," Logan said in what doubles as a description of one Peyton Manning. "If they get hurt, they want to know what they have to do to get completely well and whatever it is, *I'm totally committed to it and I will not miss one workout, one anything.* They're driven almost to the point where people around them would sort of worry about their mental psyche. They're totally driven. And I was always that way. I loved it. I wanted to go out, shoot the ball—whatever the weather, didn't matter. Whatever season it was I wanted to be out playing."

Logan said he even enjoyed the tedium of practice and really loved breaking down film. "Very much so. I've always enjoyed it—especially in football there's a real strategy to the game. To me, you can break the game of football down to angles—angles you have to understand at every position—certainly as a receiver, getting into and out of your breaks and the angle, the looks from quarterbacks," Logan said. "I always was fascinated by the strategy of it. I always loved to watch film. Now coaching high school football, I watch a ton of NFL film, look at concepts, stuff that makes sense, and can I use some of that with what we do. I've always been a film guy, always."

Figuring out strategy is something Logan thrives on. "Football to me is a game of chess. You have the first move and then your opponent has a move and you have to counter his move and he'll try to counter your move," Logan said. "And then you'll spend a lot of time thinking ahead, not just one move, but the next two or three moves. *If I do that, that, and that, can I get them to do this? And if they do this, what will that mean for the overall game?* I've always thought of football like chess in that manner," Logan said.

You have to decipher intentions and deceptions alike, because your opponent is trying to set you up, too. "Listen, the game is a game of reaction, and sometimes you're going to get beat; that guy across from you is going to get the best of you on that play," Logan said. "The great ones then can make a split-second adjustment after they've lost that snap. I mean, even great players lose snaps. The best receivers in the world at times get certain coverage or press coverage and that defensive back can get their hands on them. You grade every single play: *Well, that play that DB won, right?*

"So then you have to mentally on the fly be able to process: *Okay, what caused that to happen?* And sometimes you do that walking back to the huddle. So, that's what I love about football: you can break it down to its most simplistic form and it's a still a game of blocking and tackling and I get that.

"But there are so many intricacies in a football game, so many things that people, when they watch the game, more than likely don't fully appreciate from a receiver's standpoint in terms of, *Hey, if I cut my split three yards here on this, maybe it's a running play.* Well, when you cut your split that sort of sounds the alarm for a corner. Because a corner will look at that split, he'll identify, *Okay, this is a cut split, so I'm not sure what I'm looking for.* I mean, film study and game preparation leading up to the game that week will tell him what I'm likely to do. But there's a bell that goes off in his head, *Okay, they split this cut. Are they trying to get me to reduce my leverage point? Do I do that? I've got deep third on this play. Maybe I'm going to stay back out here a little bit so I can sort of diagnose this....* Peyton talked about a game of chess and how he moves and he was so good at identifying coverages. There's just a lot that goes on."

To expand upon Manning's chess example, with 22 players lining up, there are infinitely more strategic moves than in baseball or basketball. "I think it's the greatest team game in the world because everybody is dependent on a lot of other dudes," Logan said. "And they're dependent on good coaching and good scheming and a good game plan and then they're dependent on their coaches' ability to adjust once the game starts and make the right calls.

"And then the quarterback has to depend on the receivers seeing the same thing that he sees. He depends on getting good protection on the offensive line and then, *Oh, by the way, I come out and I see that we've got an issue on the protection, do I change the protection?* You've got to depend on them hearing that you've just changed the protection. And now, *Okay, I changed the protection, my guy I was going to block—it's not him anymore.* There are a lot of moving parts to every single snap of football. It's a beautiful game."

A beautiful game that Logan has been associated with for almost half a century, going back to the Friday night lights of his youth, Saturday afternoons in college, and Sundays in the NFL. Beginning as a rookie wide receiver for the Cleveland Browns in 1976 and continuing through his decades as the voice of the Denver Broncos, Logan has been associated with the NFL for more than 40 years.

The 2020 season marks his 31st year doing play-by-play for KOA 850-AM. Logan is one of only four ex-players, along with Jimmy Cefalo in Miami, Steve Raible in Seattle, and Zach Strief in New Orleans, who have ascended from color commentator to the play-by-play chair on their broadcast team. Logan not only shares his insights on game days and during the week on his radio shows, but he shares his love of the game with new generations in his role as a head high school football coach.

"My dad talked to me about working with kids," Logan said. "I never really thought about the broadcasting. I went to CU my first year, I was in pre-med. With playing football and basketball, I couldn't make that work. So then I switched to business. But I never really thought about the broadcasting thing, honestly, until I got cut that day and I was driving home."

That's when he tuned in to hear Irv Brown and Joe Williams ripping Dan Reeves for cutting Dave Logan, the local kid who'd made a name for himself with the Browns and had just a one catch for three yards in four games for his hometown Denver Broncos.

"Yeah, the same day I got cut, my ears were opened to sports talk radio," Logan remembered.

# CHAPTER 3
# THEY CAN'T PAY YOU

D ave Logan played eight years in Cleveland, his hard-nosed style making him a fan favorite in the "Dawg Pound." After catching five passes for 104 yards his rookie season, Logan had started seven straight seasons in Cleveland and he was coming off another solid season, one in which he'd averaged 16.9 yards a catch, his best as a starter. But his playing career was winding down. He approached Browns coach Sam Rutigliano in 1983 and asked him for a favor.

"I had a really good relationship with Sam, and they had just hired a new offensive coordinator from the Chargers the year before," Logan said. "I'd broken my ankle in a charity basketball game, had surgery with two screws put in my ankle in mid-April. I certainly wasn't completely healthy when training camp started. So, it was a combination of me being limited physically and having a brand-new coordinator. And I think I would be safe in saying I don't think he really liked me all that much as a player and honestly, I didn't really care for him much as a coach. So, after the season, I went to Sam and pretty much said, 'If you can send me somewhere, I'd like to go back to Denver.'"

The Broncos gave Cleveland a fourth-round draft choice for Logan. But Logan had no idea it would end so soon. "It didn't work out for me. I came here and wound up getting cut in the middle of the season."

Head coach Dan Reeves had hired a fresh-faced wide receivers coach in 1984 who had spent the previous three seasons as the offensive coordinator for Charley Pell at the University of Florida. "It was his first year in the league. He picked me up at the airport and I'm thinking, *Who is this guy?*" Logan said. It was Mike Shanahan.

When training camp started at the University of Northern Colorado that summer, Logan reported to the Greeley campus and roomed with fellow wide receiver Steve Watson. Every team has its own verbiage and playbook, and he had to adjust to the Broncos' way of doing things. "It was the Dallas system, where to the right was odd and to the left was even," Logan recalled. It was the opposite of what he'd run in Cleveland. So, he found himself a backup for the first time

Dave Logan with the Denver Broncos as a wide receiver in 1984.

since his rookie season, and he wasn't happy about it. "I'd been a starter for most of my NFL career, so it was really tough not to be on the field very much," Logan said.

Before kickoff against the Kansas City Chiefs at the old Mile High Stadium on September 23, 1984, Shanahan approached Logan in the locker room and informed him he'd be the fifth receiver that day.

*How did that happen?* Logan wondered. Shanahan told him to just hang in there and turned away.

"So I was already ticked off before the game started. Then, one of our wideouts got hurt," Logan said. "So, when they went to the four-wide receiver set, I was the only other active receiver. They had to play me."

On Denver's second series, Logan's number was called on third-and-long from the Denver 31. But free safety Deron Cherry had leverage on him, "and I couldn't get inside," Logan recalled. "So, I catch a ball on third-and-8 for three yards."

It was his first catch for his hometown Denver Broncos. And his last.

"I come off the field and Dan is livid, like wicked pissed. *What are you doing? You've got to get inside him.* So, I stood there and let him get it off his chest. I'm already mad because I wasn't playing very much, and I tried to explain, 'Dan, he had inside leverage.' And Reeves fired back, *I don't give a shit. You've got to get inside.* I said, 'All right,' and I started to head back to the bench."

Reeves wasn't through venting. "At that point, they had the old cable headsets, and he had to pull them with him as he walked to where I was standing. And he just lights into me again about the play and what I didn't do," recalled Logan.

Finally, Logan snapped back at Reeves. They stared at each other for a few uncomfortable seconds before the head coach turned back toward the action on the field.

Logan turned to a teammate and told him, "I'm probably cut." His teammate replied, "I'd have told him what you did sooner."

The Broncos won the game 21–0 to improve to 3–1. Afterward, "I went to dinner with a few of my high school friends and told them I thought it was probably over," Logan recounted. And he was right—48 hours later, Logan's phone rang at 6:15 in the morning.

"Coach wants to see you," said the voice on the other end. Logan drove in, got his walking papers, and drove home.

His agent, Jack Mills, based in Boulder, told him the Seattle Seahawks were interested in bringing him in for a workout to sign him. "But at that point I was pretty discouraged and had lost a step," Logan said. "I didn't want to admit it, but I could see it on film."

Prior to his last season in Cleveland in 1983, Logan's right ankle was broken not by a crushing hit from a linebacker but by a school-teacher who had cut him off during a charity basketball game in Ohio. "I got undercut going in for a dunk," Logan recalled. "I'm sure he didn't mean to. But I had a teacher run under my legs as I was going to dunk the ball with my left hand. And it just sort of flipped my legs and I came down in an awkward way. It sounded like when you take a ruler and just snap it in half across your leg. I didn't fall down. I remember thinking, *I just broke my ankle.*"

He hobbled off to the bench. "We were like four hours out of Cleveland. We were somewhere in southern Ohio, a little bitty town," Logan said.

Judson Flint, a backup safety for the Browns, said, "Man, I'm going to drive you back to Cleveland."

"No, you don't have to," Logan replied. "Because they were playing the next night in some other town down south."

Flint insisted and when they got back to Cleveland, Logan was told he needed surgery.

Just 17 months later, his ankle was feeling fine but he had no more routes to run, no more pads to lace up.

He told the Seahawks thanks but no thanks. "I said, I'm going to just sit out," Logan said, "and that was it."

Dave Logan, star athlete, was now former NFL player Dave Logan, unemployed. "I was kind of deciding that fall what I was going to do. My dad was an estate planner the last few years of his life. So, I actually took the test to go work with New York Life," Logan said.

That's when Irv Brown called.

### Dave Logan's Log

I'd known Irv since he was the baseball coach at CU. I talked with Irv and he said, "Why don't you come and to a Super Bowl preview show?" And Irv and Joe worked on AM 1600, which is the single worst dial position in the history of AM radio. A 5,000-watt station, it was 500 watts at dusk.

So I did an hour on the Super Bowl preview, and the next day, Irv said, "The boss loves you. He wants you to start working." I said, well, okay, but I was taking the test to work for New York Life. He said, "Put that on hold. Just come do this for a while."

I said all right. Then Irv gave me a bit of bad news. "They can't pay you. But they'll give you three minutes to sell." I had no idea what he was talking about, but I quickly learned. The first place I tried to sell was a men's clothing store. And they actually bought a 60-second commercial five days a week for $680. And I got to keep all that money. So, my first sale was for $680 and I was doing men's clothing spots on AM 1600.

And honestly, I'm thinking, *This is going to be all right.* And you know what? It was the last thing I sold in those first six months. So at the six-month mark, I went back in. My daughter had just been born—and I was a single dad—and I'm like, "Irv, I can't do this, I'm making no money." Irv was great about it and said, "Let me go talk to my boss and see what we can do." He came back with a huge grin and said, "The boss loves you, wants to keep you. And I got you $1,000 a month."

I decided to stay. I was enjoying the new gig and really liked working with Irv and Joe.

# CHAPTER 4
## EVERY JOB IMAGINABLE

Dave Logan was working with Joe Williams from 2:00 in the afternoon, when KRXY's signal was strong, to 7:00 in the evening, when it was weak—especially in the winter, when the days end early and the radio's signal was 10 times weaker in the dark.

"It was probably good I learned the business on a station that very few people could hear," Logan chuckled.

"So after that year, I talked to the boss and he gave me a pretty decent contract after a year and a half. And that's how my career started."

Logan learned a lot from Irv Brown and Williams. "Irv was off doing a lot of TV broadcasts, so a lot of it was 2:00 to 7:00 just me and Joe," Logan said.

The first big lesson he learned came courtesy of Brown: just like in the NFL, you have to be prepared for something to happen that you didn't prepare for, that you didn't rehearse in your mind.

Logan and Williams were in the studio one day and their producer was Rich "G-Man" Goins, who once spent 33 days on a billboard 40 feet above West Colfax Avenue in Denver until the Broncos broke a long losing streak.

"Rich writes something on the board and puts it to the glass: Go TO THE HOTLINE. IRV IS IN HOUSTON, where the Nuggets were playing the Rockets that night," Logan recalled. "So I said, 'Hey, we're going to pause for a second, go to the hotline, and talk to my partner who's covering the Nuggets tonight. Irv, it's Dave and Joe, as you know, and he said, 'Hey, guys, great to talk with you. Hey, listen, I've got somebody I want you to talk to. Here's Ralph Sampson.'"

Logan and Williams hadn't been given a heads-up that Sampson would be coming on.

"Hello?" Sampson intoned.

"Hey, Ralph. Dave Logan and Joe Williams here in Denver. How are you?"

"Good."

And so it went with the one-word answers. No insight, no enthusiasm.

"Well, it was good in the sense that it taught me to be prepared for anything. You had to be ready to react quickly to anything going on in the world of sports," Logan said.

Of course, this was long before the Internet and laptops and being able to Google anything you needed to in the spur of the moment. In those days, you had to go to the newsstands and buy a bunch of national newspapers along with the local *Denver Post* and *Rocky Mountain News* to brush up on the big storylines that day before you went on the radio. It's how men like Sandy Klough, one of the most recognizable voices in Denver sports radio, did it.

"It was your knowledge base," Logan said. "I always admired Sandy for how well-read he was in the world of sports. So, I began reading every sports section I could get my hands on. And I'd carry those papers into the studio and have them with me doing a five-hour talk show every day.

"That's how you learned. But it made you develop an ability to think on your feet and come up with something to carry on a conversation instead of panicking. You really had to be a fan of sports and, without a doubt, I was. Clearly, Ralph didn't want to do that interview. We got one- or two-word answers for about six questions and I finally said, 'Ralph, good luck tonight. Thanks for your time.'"

Sampson handed the phone back to Brown; Logan and Williams went to a commercial break.

"And Irv would do stuff like that," Logan said, smiling. "Even though we'd say, 'Irv, give us a heads-up when somebody's coming on, he rarely did."

Radio is show business. That's what Logan learned from Williams.

"Joe, who's one of my best friends to this day, taught me a lot. We were doing the show together in '86 or '87. I said something on the air. Joe disagreed and was really giving me the business. In a way, it felt like he was making fun of me. I've always been really competitive, and he really pissed me off. It went on for about five minutes until we went to a break. I got up, took my headphones off, and went to the bathroom. I think Joe knew that I was pretty hot. I didn't say anything to him when he came into the bathroom and washed his hands. And at one point, I actually thought to myself, *How about I just punch you in the mouth?* Joe looked at me and said, 'That was great radio, kid. Never forget: it's all about making 'em laugh. This is show business.'"

Then Williams spun and walked back into the studio and put his headphones on, awaiting Logan.

"That was his way of saying, 'Hey, what I said to you'—which I don't even remember now—'I'm doing that because you want people to listen and laugh,' even if it was sort of at my expense. Honestly, even at that point, it made sense to me. And Joe and I have been best friends ever since. His son graduated from Columbine High School in '86, maybe. I had a Porsche that I still have, and I let Bert drive it to the senior prom. Joe was like, 'Look, Dave, I'm not sure you want this kid to drive that car.' I said, 'We're good.' So, Bert drove the car to the prom. To put things in perspective, Bert's almost 50 years old now. That's how long Joe and I have been great friends."

Logan worked as hard at his new career as he had on the football field, and he branched into television with CBS affiliate KCNC-TV in Denver and cable outlets. "I took every job imaginable," Logan said. "I started freelancing for Channel 4. I did CU football games with Ron Zappolo. Then I was hosting *The Bill McCartney Show* every Sunday night on Channel 4. I was hosting the basketball coach's show on Channel 4. I started freelancing for Raycom Sports, doing Big Eight basketball games every Friday starting in January. I'd fly to whatever Big Eight town the game was in, Stillwater, Ames, Norman, Lincoln, wherever, doing that. I also did WAC basketball and DU basketball on cable. Every single job that was out there I accepted, because that was the best way to improve and build a career."

## Dave Logan's Log

My Porsche is 33 years old. It has like 21,000 miles on it. Got in a wreck three months before my daughter was born. And I had just put the big harness on. That move saved my life. It was on First and Wadsworth. I was going through a stop light and this older fella in a blue pickup truck—and I know he didn't see me—made a left as I was coming into the intersection and turned right into me. I veered sharply to my right to avoid contact, and the car lifted a bit and dead-ended into a concrete pillar.

I broke the steering wheel in half with my chest. I remember thinking, *Man, that was a jolt.* I looked into the mirror to make sure I had all of my teeth. But I couldn't get out of the car. The floor board had erupted. My knees were up in my chest. The fire department medics got me out of the car and said, "Okay, you've got to come with us." I said, "No, I'm good." They said, "No sir, you've got to get in the back of that rescue unit." I thought I might be able to talk them out of it, and I said, "I'm good. I'm all right." And then one of them responded, "Here's the thing: if you don't get in the back, we're going to handcuff you and put you in the back."

So, I figured I'd better go get in the back. They took me to the hospital. I had nothing broken. But I tell you, the next day I felt like my whole chest had been caved in. The car was totaled, and I got the insurance money. That was 1985, and I was thinking, *I'd better keep this money.* But the car was really the only thing I'd ever spent any of my football money on for almost a decade. So, I went back and replaced the car.

Certain episodes in your life have a big impact on you, and I'm certain had I not put my seatbelt on right before the crash, I would have been dead. So, since that day, every single time I get into a car, that's the first thing I do.

It was all color commentary, and he even worked alongside Brown at high school basketball games. "First one I went to was at Alameda High School and I wore a sport coat... I walked up to the gymnasium door and said, 'I'm here to do tonight's broadcast,' and nobody knew what the hell I was talking about. And the lady at the door asked, 'Where's your ticket?' So, I had to go back to the window and buy a ticket to get in so

I could broadcast the game. Finally, Irv shows up and he's dressed casually, like in a T-shirt and jeans.

"He said, 'Come on, follow me,' and I said, 'Where's the broadcast booth?' Irv responded, 'There's no booth. This is high school.' So, we walk up and we sit in the stands. Irv's got what they call a Marti unit, and he breaks it open and there's one headset for me and one for him. He says, 'Hey, go buy us two programs.' So I did. But high school basketball programs have like, a player's name, his class, and that's it. No stats. No nothing. And that was the first game I ever did on radio with Irv, a high school basketball game where we sat in the stands with fans all around us."

Logan was working with Brown and Williams in the afternoons on KRXY when KNUS-AM called in 1988 wanting to pair him in the afternoon with Jim Turner, a former kicker for the New York Jets and Broncos. KNUS was also home of radio talk show personality Peter Boyles.

"I really loved Irv and Joe, but KNUS offered me a lot more money, and Irv was the first to say, 'Dave, you've got to take that deal,'" Logan recounted.

So, he did. A year later, however, he got a dreaded phone call like the one back in 1984, when he was told Dan Reeves wanted to see him at Broncos headquarters. This time, every employee was summoned to the station.

"The GM who hired me—Craig Cochran—walked in with two guys in suits...and he said, 'As of 1:00 today KNUS is no more. We're going to simulcast with KBPI. For those of you that have contracts, we'll talk to you about those deals. I know this is a lot for you guys to digest. So, we're going to let you think about it for a few minutes, and then we'll come back in.' Then, they turned around and walked out the door.

"I just couldn't believe that they would pull the plug in that fashion. So, I said, 'Hey, this is not going to happen like this. They're going to come back in here and present a huge marketing plan about how we're going after KOA. Everything's going to be okay.' It wasn't. The station went dark. They changed formats and all of us got fired."

Luckily, Logan landed on his feet; he went back to work with Irv and Joe.

A few months after the Broncos' loss to the San Francisco 49ers in Super Bowl XXIV in January 1990, Broncos play-by-play man Bob Martin died. Larry Zimmer called Logan that May asking if he was interested in applying for the vacancy. "Honestly, I hadn't given it any consideration," Logan replied. "I told Larry, 'I'm really not looking for a job. I've already got a good one.' And he said, 'Well, Dave, I think you should apply for this.'... Larry had been Bob's color analyst with the Broncos forever, and I grew up listening to Bob and Larry as a kid."

There was just one thing, though. "When I met with Lee Larsen, the market manager of KOA, about taking the job and saw the offer, it was actually a $17,000 pay cut," Logan said. "And when I mentioned that to Lee, he didn't flinch. He looked right at me and said, 'I know, but this is KOA. And Dave, if you make this move, it will be the absolute best move you make in your broadcasting career.' So I went home, thought about it, and took the job.

"Yeah, Lee was absolutely right," Logan said. "It's been a great foundation for everything I've done in broadcasting, really."

Logan had a noncompete clause in his contract that prevented him from doing a talk show, so KOA had him work with Jeff Kingery on Nuggets broadcasts and teamed him with Zimmer on Broncos broadcasts. After a year, Logan added an evening sports talk show to his plate.

Logan traded his cleats for a career talking football, but he also wanted to teach football. He got into coaching in 1993.

"I actually applied for the Golden High School opening in '92, and I got the job. I was in the process of hiring assistants when I got a call three days later from the A.D. at Golden saying they wanted to bring in a veteran coach. And I said, 'Great. What position do you want him to coach?' And when his response was, 'We want him to be the head coach,' I just went silent. 'Didn't you just give me the job on Monday?'

'We did, but we think we need a coach with high school experience.' So, even though I guess I was the head coach at Golden for four days, I never got to coach a game there," Logan said.

The following June, Brian McGregor retired after a 27-year career coaching Arvada West High School. "By retiring late, a lot of guys that would have certainly loved the opportunity to coach at A-West had already landed jobs. So there were only three who applied: the current offensive and defensive coordinators and me," Logan said. Logan got the job.

The offensive coordinator had no interest in staying and working with Logan.

The defensive coordinator, Jim Zajac, said, "Well, I'm disappointed, but I'm in this for the kids, so Dave, if you want me, I'll stay and help you," Logan recalled. "I said, 'You're hired.' And he's been with me ever since that day as one of my coaches." Zajac is also Logan's spotter for Broncos home games, a gig he's had since 1996.

# CHAPTER 5
## A SPEEDING TICKET

Dave Logan's two former teams, the Cleveland Browns and Denver Broncos, met up in the AFC Championship Game in 1987, 1988, and 1990, and that's when John Elway's legend as late-game hero really blossomed.

On January 11, 1987, the Broncos got the ball at their own 2-yard line trailing 20–13 with 5:43 remaining, and so began "the Drive." Elway drove Denver 98 yards in 15 plays for the game-tying touchdown with 37 seconds left on a five-yard strike to Mark Jackson, whose 20-yard reception on third-and-18 to the Cleveland 28 was the key play of the drive.

Rich Karlis' extra point tied it—he had to make two of them after an illegal procedure penalty negated the first one—and after Cleveland went three-and-out to start the overtime period, Elway drove the Broncos 60 yards to the Cleveland 15-yard line, where Karlis hit the game-winning field goal from 33 yards out for a 23–20 win that sent Denver to its second Super Bowl.

The first had come back in 1977, when the "Orange Crush" defense led the Broncos to Super Bowl XII. The Dallas Cowboys prevailed 27–10 in the Louisiana Superdome.

In Super Bowl XXI at the Rose Bowl in Pasadena, California, Elway led the Broncos to a 10–9 halftime lead over the Giants, only to watch New York score 24 unanswered points to start the second half on their way to a 39–20 blowout.

The following year, the Browns and Broncos met again for the Lamar Hunt Trophy, which goes to the champion of the American Football Conference. This time the game was at Mile High Stadium in Denver. Again, though, Cleveland was considered the better team.

Elway and the Broncos denied Bernie Kosar and the Browns a trip to the Super Bowl, this time via "the Fumble." Elway's touchdown toss to Sammy Winder with just over four minutes left gave Denver a 38–31 lead, but Kosar drove the Browns to the Denver 8-yard line with 1:12 remaining and it looked like the teams were heading for overtime again.

That's when backup cornerback Jeremiah Castille stripped the football from Earnest Byner and smothered it at the 3-yard line with 65

John Elway's legend as late-game hero blossomed in the AFC Championship Games in 1987, 1988, and 1990.

seconds remaining. Denver punter Mike Horan took a deliberate safety on fourth-and-1 from the Denver 12 with eight seconds remaining. After the free kick, Kosar had one play, an incompletion, and Denver was headed back to the Super Bowl.

Just as he had the year before, Elway gave Denver an early lead, 10–0 this time, before Washington's amazing 35-point second quarter led to a 42–10 wipeout of the Broncos in Super Bowl XXII at old Jack Murphy Stadium in San Diego.

Two years later Elway again denied the Browns in the AFC title game, only this time Denver didn't need any last-second heroics because it crushed Cleveland 37–21, with Elway throwing for 385 yards and three touchdowns.

Another Super Bowl and another super blowout followed as Joe Montana and the San Francisco 49ers rolled over Elway and the Broncos 55–10 on January 28, 1990, at the Louisiana Superdome.

Six months later, Dave Logan was hired as the color commentator for the team that he'd rooted for as a kid growing up in Denver and which had fired him six years earlier, ending his NFL playing career.

Dan Reeves, who had cut Logan, was still coaching the Broncos, but Logan said he didn't hold a grudge. "No, you know what? Honestly, when I jumped into the media, even before I went to KOA in '90, I said to myself, *Listen, I am never going to give anybody that hears me on the air an opportunity to say, 'Oh, okay, you've got a bone to pick with Dan because he cut you.'* So I said he would always get a fair shake from me on the air."

Logan let bygones be bygones. "I went out of my way to really take the high road. I'd always speak to Dan and was cognizant of being fair to him on the air. Because I thought Dan was a good coach," Logan said. "We only had that one dustup."

Logan had a prior breakfast meeting scheduled with his boss, Lee Larsen, president and market manager for Clear Channel Radio, at 6:30 in the morning at Village Inn. Logan read an article in the newspaper that morning about how Reeves was really upset with "all these so-called experts," and he included Logan in that group.

"I was livid," Logan said. "I was really pissed, because I knew I'd never said anything even remotely critical of Dan at any point publicly. And for him to take a shot at me in print, honestly, to me was a huge slap in the face"

Logan headed for breakfast with his boss. As they finished up, Logan told Larsen of his intent. "I just want to tell you that as soon as I leave here, I'm heading to Dove Valley and I'm going to have a conversation with Reeves," Logan told Larsen.

"I would very much prefer you not do that," came Larsen's reply.

"I appreciate that," Logan said, "but I'm just telling you I'm going."

Logan got pulled over on his way to Broncos headquarters. "True story, I got a friggin' speeding ticket," he said, chuckling.

Unbeknownst to Logan, Larsen had called John Beake, the team's general manager, to warn him that Logan was headed there in a huff.

## Dave Logan's Log

Lee had called ahead, so when I got there, there were two security guards who met me in the parking lot. "How you doing, Dave?" I said, "Doing good, fellas." "Hey, uh, John Beake wants to see you for a minute." I said, "I'm not here to see John Beake." They said, "I know. But can we walk you to John's office?" We just stood there for a moment. So, I finally said yeah.

Now, I'd had a bit of a run-in with John years earlier—live on the radio. John said, "How are you doing, Dave?" I said, "Morning, John, not very good." I showed him a copy of the newspaper. John shook his head and said, "Oh, boy." Then, he said, "Dave, I understand why you're upset, but you've got to just let this go." I said, "John, I appreciate that, but you know I'm not going to do that." So we talked a while in his office, and I finally left. I walked out looking for Jim Saccomano—then the Broncos' vice president of public relations—saw him in the hall, showed him the article, and said, "Jim, here's the deal. I need to see Dan and have a conversation with him." Jim said, "Okay, Dave, no problem. He's in a meeting right now." I said, "That's okay, I'll wait."

So I waited. It got to be 11 o'clock, and there I was, still waiting, standing outside, and I saw Dan walk out with a plate of food to the patio to have lunch with a bunch of the coaches. I started walking right to him. Saccomano saw me and intercepted me about halfway to Dan and said, "Dave, Dave! Wait a minute." By that time I was mad that I'd been standing there for a couple of hours. So, I said to Jim, "Here's the deal. You need to tell him to come talk to me right now or I'm walking over in front of all the coaches." He said, "I'll go get him."

One of the positives of me waiting there most of the morning was I'd actually gotten a recording of the interview Dan had done. I'd had enough time to listen to it, and I heard what he said. Saccomano approached Dan and talked to him. Dan looked over at me, got up, and started to walk over.

"How you doing, Dave?" Dan asked as we shook hands. "Not worth a shit," I said. "So, what's the deal? Why is my name in this?" And I held up the paper. He said, "Yeah, Pam said this morning you were going to be pretty upset about that." Pam was his wife. Dan continued, "I was misquoted." At that point, I held up the tape recorder and I said, "No, you really weren't misquoted. I got what you said right here." So, we talked it out. He basically apologized. I at least got him to hear me out, and we both went on with our business. And that honestly was the only time we had a disagreement or words since my career was over. Years later, we went into the Colorado Sports Hall of Fame in the same year.

Looking back, I guess I've come to the conclusion that, for some reason, Reeves had lumped me in with media members he was angry with that particular day. He was pissed off at somebody who said something on national TV, and for whatever reason, he just threw my name into the mix. I had never said anything about him negatively because of him releasing me a few years before. I already said, "When I get up there, I'm not going to give anybody an opportunity to think that I had an ax to grind unfairly with Dan." I wasn't going to overlook strong opinions but I'm going to give him the benefit of the doubt when I'm on the air with respect to me criticizing him or his play-calling or whatever. Because I just didn't want to be portrayed as a guy who had a bone to pick and was just using his platform in order to harbor resentment.

As the color analyst for Broncos games, Logan didn't have any need to interact with Reeves again until his time as head coach ended after the Broncos went 8–8 in 1992.

Years later, Reeves again lumped in Logan with other members of the national media, but this time was different. "Dan said some really nice things about me. He was doing a Sirius Radio show. Somebody gave me a tape of it a few years ago, and when the host asked him about ex-players doing radio and play-by-play, Dan said, 'I'll tell you this, I think one of the best play-by-play guys in the entire league is Dave Logan. He is a former NFL player.' And he didn't have to say that. The question didn't lead him to that at all…he just said it," Logan said. "And I really appreciated that coming from Dan. I've had him on a handful of shows to interview him since then, and we're fine."

Then, there was the dustup with Broncos general manager John Beake.

"Oh, man," Logan said. "I'd almost forgotten that one."

# CHAPTER 6
## SO, AM I FIRED?

"**M**y dad raised me never to start a fight," Dave Logan said, "but never to run from one, either."

"Playing wide receiver in the NFL in the '70s and '80s, you couldn't be easily intimidated. You might catch a ball over the middle and get blown up, and the DB would say something like, 'Boy, don't come back in here. Next time, you might get hurt.' At that point, you have to make a decision: you're either going back in or you're not, and I lived my NFL career in the middle of the field. So, I felt that was my territory, not his."

That mind-set served Logan well throughout his career in sports and is something he carried with him after his playing days ended—and it's something then-Broncos general manager John Beake discovered in 1992. Logan and Larry Zimmer were hosting *Broncos Talk with John Beake* at Jackson's Hole, a Denver sports bar in 1992, when Keith Jackson's name came up.

Rare is the tight end who lights up the league coming out of college. Mike Ditka did it with the Chicago Bears in 1960, and Keith Jackson did it with the Eagles in 1988 when he caught 81 passes for 869 yards and six touchdowns and added seven catches for 142 yards in a playoff game against the Bears.

In his four seasons in Philly, Jackson had 20 touchdowns. Logan figured he'd be a terrific fit in Denver, where Shannon Sharpe wasn't yet the Shannon Sharpe who would win three Super Bowl rings, two in Denver and one in Baltimore, and earn a ticket to the Pro Football Hall of Fame. In fact, in his first two seasons, Sharpe had only played a combined 11 games and caught 29 passes for 429 yards and two touchdowns.

Jackson was about to move on from the Eagles and "I thought the Broncos could have really used a tight end," Logan said. "So did a lot of fans."

A caller suggested the Broncos bring in Jackson, and Beake "gave a very curt answer I thought was a tad dismissive," Logan recalled. "He just cut the guy off." A second call came in. Same thing. After a third caller brought up Jackson only to get shut down, Logan interjected.

"I'm sort of compelled here as host of the show to say something," Logan said, "and I thought I gave John the kind of question that he could easily answer."

"John, I think what the callers are really trying to say is Keith Jackson with his skill set and his ability to stretch the defense—"

Beake cut Logan off too. "He said, 'Dave, listen, Keith Jackson just doesn't fit our system, all right? Period,'" Logan recounted.

That didn't sit well with Logan, who quickly decided he wasn't going to let it go. "The easy thing to do here would be to change the topic, but I just couldn't do that. To me, that would have been bad radio."

Logan didn't start this scrape, but now he was fully engaged. "Well, respectfully, I've got to say if you're telling me that Keith Jackson's skill set does not fit the offensive system here, the offensive system stinks or you've got a real issue with it," Logan retorted.

Beake stared right at Logan. "I'll tell you what, Dave, you can say that on your show. You're not going to say it on *my* show!" Beake fumed.

"At that point, I was a young and rather inexperienced broadcaster trying to establish my credibility in the market, and what John said to me almost felt like that defensive back standing over me chirping," Logan said. "I had to make a split-second decision as to whether or not I was going to be intimidated out of the middle of the field—or, in this case, a confrontation with the team that I was a broadcaster for and its general manager—and I had to make that decision in about two seconds."

Logan was raised not to run from a fight. "Well, here's the deal," Logan countered. "It's not *your* show. This is *Broncos Talk with John Beake*, and I'm the host and I'll ask you whatever the hell I want to."

Beake's response was classic.

"You will, but you're going to be talking to yourself," Beake grumbled before ripping off his headphones, slamming them on the table, and storming out.

"I was stunned," Logan said. "I looked over at Larry, and his face said it all. So, I tried to gather myself and get to a commercial.

"Well, general manager John Beake has just walked off the show. We'll pause for a very brief moment, come back, and reboot," Logan told listeners.

An hour later, Logan was driving home and the first cell phone he'd ever owned rang in the passenger seat of his car. It was a call from the man who had hired him two years earlier: his boss at KOA, Lee Larsen. "So, am I fired?" Logan asked instead of answering with a hello.

"No, you're not fired," Larsen said. "But we've got to find a way to coexist. He is the GM of the team, Dave. We're the flagship station of the team. And this is something that people will be talking about."

Larsen was right. The interaction between Logan and Beake on KOA was written about the next day in articles in both the *Rocky Mountain News* and *Denver Post* sports sections.

Larsen had Logan and Beake talk it out and smooth things over later that week. "And he came in for the next week's show. I apologized to John, he apologized to me, and I've never had a cross word with him since," Logan said.

Jackson ultimately went to the Miami Dolphins and later won a championship with the Green Bay Packers, who beat the New England Patriots 35–20 in Super Bowl XXXI following the 1996 season when the AFC's top seed, the heavily favored Denver Broncos, was upset 30–27 at home by upstart Jacksonville in the divisional playoffs. Denver had gone 13–3 in the regular season and had earned a first-round bye.

The following season, the Broncos were on a mission. Finishing 12–4 in the regular season, they routed the Jaguars 42–17 in a rematch in Denver in the wild card round, then beat the top-seeded Chiefs on the road 14–10, then won the AFC championship with a 24–21 victory over the Steelers in Pittsburgh.

After the game, John Elway called his mother, Janet, as the Broncos flew home with another Lamar Hunt Trophy. "I said, 'Mom, guess what? We get to go back to the Super Bowl!'" Elway told her.

"Do we really have to go back?" she replied.

After so many Super Bowl letdowns—three losses by an average of 32 points—she wasn't sure watching her son face the two-touchdown-favorite Packers led by Brett Favre and Reggie White was such a good idea.

Something told Elway this one was going to be different.

# CHAPTER 7
## REVENGE TOUR

T he only thing missing from John Elway's remarkable career was a Super Bowl ring. Three times he'd made it to the Super Bowl, and three times his Broncos had been blown out by teams that were quite simply more talented.

After three ugly Super Bowl losses early in his career, not even his mother wanted him to go to a fourth Super Bowl.

But things were different. This time, Elway was bringing Terrell Davis. Or was it that Davis was bringing along Elway? Either way, the Broncos were once again heavy underdogs, this time against the powerful Green Bay Packers, the defending world champions led by three-time MVP quarterback Brett Favre, in his prime, and defensive end Reggie White, the "Minister of Defense." White's arrival in Wisconsin as the first superstar free agent to switch teams in the NFL heralded in the Packers' return to greatness after a quarter century of futility following the Vince Lombardi era.

Just getting to the Super Bowl had become tantamount to winning it all for the teams that won the George Halas Trophy as champions of the National Football Conference in those days. The NFC had won the previous 13 Super Bowls, and oddsmakers saw no reason this one would be any different. Ever since the 49ers beat Miami 38–16 in Super Bowl XIX on January 20, 1985—when Dave Logan got his first real taste of radio by previewing the Joe Montana–Dan Marino matchup on KRXY-AM 1600 in Denver—reaching the Super Bowl had become merely a coronation for the NFC's top teams. The Packers looked like the next NFC dynasty, too.

NFC teams dominated AFC teams ever since the Los Angeles Raiders' 38–9 win over Washington in Super Bowl XVIII on January 22, 1984. The San Francisco 49ers won four Super Bowls behind Joe Montana; the Dallas Cowboys won three Super Bowls behind Troy Aikman, Emmitt Smith, and Michael Irvin; and the New York Giants won a pair of Super Bowls.

San Francisco, New York, and Washington had all clobbered Elway's Broncos during the NFC's streak. The New England Patriots weren't yet the dynasty they would become under Tom Brady and Bill Belichick, and they were smothered by the Packers 35–21 a year earlier and 46–10 by the Chicago Bears in Super Bowl XX in 1986.

The Buffalo Bills had lost an unprecedented four consecutive Super Bowls and only the first of them was close, when Scott Norwood's missed 47-yard field goal with eight seconds remaining handed the Giants a 20–19 win.

The Broncos had lost their three Super Bowls by a combined 136–40, each one a bigger blowout than the one before. No wonder Janet Elway wasn't thrilled her son was going back to the Super Bowl stage.

Favre, who had just won his third straight Most Valuable Player award (this time sharing it with Detroit Lions running back Barry Sanders), remarked the week before the big game that if he were to lose the Super Bowl, "Who better to lose to than John Elway?"

"He may have said that, but I'm sure he was pretty confident and he was going to do everything he could to win that game," Elway would later say.

To a man, the Broncos thought they'd have played in the Super Bowl a year earlier, when Jacksonville stopped them in their tracks. Instead, the Packers faced off against the Patriots at the Louisiana Superdome, near Favre's hometown of Kiln, Mississippi. That devastating loss against the Jaguars served as their incentive the following season, when the Broncos went 12–4, finishing a game behind the Kansas City Chiefs in the AFC West and earning a wild-card berth in the playoffs.

That made the Broncos the fourth seed, and they exacted a measure of revenge on the Jaguars in the wild-card round on December 27, 1997, routing Jacksonville 42–17 at old Mile High Stadium behind two touchdown runs from Davis.

"When you're an old quarterback, your best friend is a running game and a running back, and that was T.D.," Elway later said.

Elway was an efficient 16 of 24 for 223 yards and a touchdown throw to Rod Smith from 43 yards out, but it was Denver's great ground game that led them to victory. Davis set franchise postseason single-game records for rushing attempts (31), rushing yards (184), and longest run from scrimmage (59) before leaving in the third quarter with bruised ribs.

Jacksonville safety Travis Davis pulled the Jaguars to 21–17 when he blocked a punt and returned it 29 yards for a touchdown in the third quarter. Derek Loville took over for the injured Davis and ran for 103 yards on 11 attempts, scoring twice in the fourth quarter, on runs of 25 and 8 yards, tying the club record already achieved that afternoon by Davis. Vaughn Hebron got into the act, too, scoring on a six-yard run with 1:11 remaining to finish off the rout.

Now it was time to take their revenge tour on the road, where they hadn't won a playoff game in 11 years.

Next up was a trip to Arrowhead Stadium in Kansas City, where the Broncos had lost to the Chiefs 24–22 on November 16, a heartbreaker that proved the difference in the AFC West title. Elway again put up modest passing numbers: 10 of 19 for 170 yards on a cold, overcast day on January 4, 1998. Davis again tied the franchise postseason record with a pair of one-yard touchdown runs, the first one giving Denver a 7–0 halftime lead in a defensive struggle in which the Chiefs gained just 58 yards of offense in the first half.

The Chiefs, who had earned a bye the week before, finally got on the board with Pete Stoyanovich's 20-yard field goal, and with 10 seconds left in the third quarter Kansas City took its first lead on Elvis Grbac's 12-yard touchdown throw to tight end Tony Gonzalez to make it 10–7.

Derek Loville again came up big for Denver, returning the ensuing kickoff 20 yards to the Denver 36, and an unnecessary roughness flag on Chiefs fullback Tony Richardson gave the Broncos the ball at the Chiefs' 49-yard line. On third-and-5, Elway hit Ed McCaffrey for 43 yards to give Denver a first-and-goal at the 1. After getting stuffed twice, Davis muscled his way in for his second touchdown of the day and his fifth in the playoffs, setting another franchise record.

Denver's defense took over from there, turning away the Chiefs on their last three drives. The Chiefs reached the Broncos 31, and on fourth-and-6 cornerback Darrien Gordon stopped punter Louie Aguiar three yards shy of a first down on a fake punt.

The teams exchanged punts before Kansas City got the ball back with four minutes left at its 17 and Grbac completed a 12-yard pass on fourth-and-9 at midfield to keep the drive going. But on fourth-and-2 from the Broncos 20-yard line, Grbac threw a pass to Lake Dawson that Gordon knocked down in the end zone, ending the Chiefs' hopes and propelling the Broncos to the AFC Championship Game.

On to Pittsburgh's Three Rivers Stadium, where the Steelers had beaten New England 7–6 the week before, and where they had handed the Broncos a 35–24 setback on December 7.

January 11 looked like it would be another dominant day by the Steelers when Levon Kirkland intercepted Elway on the game's second play. Although Norm Johnson's 38-yard field goal attempt sailed wide left, the Steelers jumped ahead 14–7 when quarterback Kordell Stewart answered Davis' eight-yard touchdown run with a 33-yard touchdown rumble around right end and Jerome Bettis powered his way into the end zone from a yard out in the second quarter.

When Elway trotted out the next time, Denver's dominance was about to begin. After the Broncos stalled at the Steelers 25-yard line, Jason Elam's 43-yard field goal made it 14–10. Then cornerback Ray Crockett made two huge plays before halftime, scooping up Darrien Gordon's muffed punt at the Denver 25-yard line and then intercepting Stewart's pass to Yancey Thigpen in the end zone. Elway then drove the Broncos 80 yards in just five plays, hitting Howard Griffith with a 15-yard touchdown pass and giving Denver its first lead at 17–14 with 1:47 left before halftime.

Denver wasn't done. The Steelers went three-and-out and Gordon's 19-yard return set up Elway & Co. at their own 46-yard line with 43 seconds left in the half. Elam began warming up on the sideline for his second field goal try of the day, but Rod Smith drew a 37-yard pass interference penalty on Steelers star cornerback Carnell Lake to give Denver a first down at the Pittsburgh 20. Davis' 10-yard run and Ed McCaffrey's nine-yard catch got the Broncos to the 1. Davis was stuffed on second-and-goal before Elway found McCaffrey in the end zone to put Denver ahead 24–14 at halftime.

Denver's defense would stamp the Broncos' trip to the Super Bowl with a dominant second half. Linebacker Allen Aldridge intercepted Stewart in the end zone and Neil Smith's strip sack of Stewart resulted in defensive tackle Mike Lodish's fumble recovery at the Broncos 32 to end the third quarter.

Stewart finally got the Steelers back on track with a 14-yard touchdown throw to Charles Johnson with 2:46 remaining to pull Pittsburgh to 24–21.

The Broncos had gone three-and-out on their previous two drives and the next one didn't start out that well, either, when Davis was knocked for a two-yard loss, bringing up third-and-6 at the Denver 15-yard line at the two minute warning.

Now Johnson was the kicker warming up on the sideline, anticipating a stop on the next play and good field position for Pittsburgh to at the very least get a shot at sending the AFC championship into overtime. But when play resumed, Elway hit tight end Shannon Sharpe for 18 yards on what many feel might have been the biggest play in Denver Broncos history, and Ed McCaffrey for 10 more before Davis' 19-yard run around left tackle allowed the Broncos to go into victory formation and Elway to take a knee, sending the Broncos to their fifth Super Bowl, and first since 1989.

The defending champion Packers were coming off their second straight 13–3 season and had won five consecutive playoff games, all by double digits. Just as they did the year before, when they beat New England 35–21 in Super Bowl XXXI, the Packers brought a streak of seven consecutive double-digit wins into the big game, including a 21–7 victory over the Tampa Bay Buccaneers in the NFC divisional round and a 23–10 thumping of the top-seeded 49ers in the NFC title game at muddy San Francisco.

So it seemed about right when the Las Vegas oddsmakers made the Packers 13½-point favorites over the upstart, wild-card Broncos. Denver's revenge tour wasn't over, however.

The Packers had used a similar stretch of double-digit victories to secure the Vince Lombardi Trophy for the first time since coach Vince Lombardi roamed their sideline in the 1960s and brought Green Bay five titles in a seven-year stretch, including the first two Super Bowls and before the championship trophy was renamed in his honor. Included in that run of routs was a 41–6 regular-season pounding of the Broncos, who brought a 12–1 record in Lambeau Field on that December 8 afternoon to face the 10–3 Packers but were missing Elway, who was sidelined by a torn hamstring, and star left tackle Gary Zimmerman, who had shoulder surgery the week before and missed a game for the first time in his 11-year career.

The shellacking was the Broncos' worst loss since a 42–0 shutout at New Orleans on November 20, 1988. "I'm sure other teams are playing and looking up at the scoreboard and they're saying, 'Good Lord, Green Bay just beat the you-know-what out of Denver. We don't want to go there and play them,'" Brett Favre said after throwing four touchdown passes, including three to Antonio Freeman. The victory established Green Bay as a legitimate threat to put the title back in Titletown, U.S.A.

Broncos coach Mike Shanahan had the luxury of resting Elway in that Packers game because the Broncos had already clinched home field advantage throughout the AFC playoffs, and six-year veteran Bill Musgrave made his first NFL start as the Broncos stagnated and saw their nine-game winning streak come to a halt behind just 93 rushing yards and 83 passing yards. Davis, the league's leading rusher, was held to 54 yards.

"Let's not take anything away from Green Bay. They're an excellent football team and they kept us off balance," Shanahan said. "But you take out two players and obviously the cohesiveness wasn't like we'd normally have."

Another future Hall of Famer, tight end Shannon Sharpe, said he didn't think the Packers were 35 points better than the Broncos, but, "all we can do now is look at what we did wrong, which is a lot, and look at what we did right, which is very little."

Sharpe also suggested the whooping wouldn't mean a thing if the teams were to meet again in Super Bowl XXXI at the Louisiana Superdome, as many expected. "How would I feel? I would feel good," Sharpe said. "We'd play a lot better, mainly because of what would be at stake." Of course, the Broncos wouldn't make it to the Super Bowl that season, losing to Jacksonville in the playoffs, while the Packers got to the big game and won it all.

The Broncos and Packers were meeting in the Super Bowl a year later, however, and Denver was seen as a heavy underdog by just about everyone outside of Denver—unless you take Mike Holmgren at his word. "Spreads don't mean much to me," Holmgren said about the lopsided betting line. "There is no team that should be favored by two touchdowns against any other team in this league. That is ludicrous."

Holmgren, who was 74–35 in his six seasons in Green Bay, noted, "Elway is still Elway" and Holmgren suggested the emergence of Davis as a bona fide superstar made Elway all the more dangerous. "What Denver has done, winning a game in Kansas City and winning a game in Pittsburgh—now that is huge," Holmgren said before the game. "That is not an easy thing to do. They can feel real good about that."

The Broncos also felt real good about exacting a measure of revenge on the Packers just like they'd done to the Jaguars, Chiefs, and Steelers.

# CHAPTER 8

## THIS...ONE'S... FOR...JOHN!

John Elway had built a reputation as a quarterback who could get his team to the big game, but once there, he couldn't quite will the franchise to its first title. All their warts were always exposed on Super Bowl Sunday.

This time, though, Elway brought a better supporting cast along. Looking back at the names in their starting lineup, it's hard to fathom how they were such a big underdog going in. There were Gary Zimmerman, Shannon Sharpe, Steve Atwater, and Terrell Davis, whose bronze busts would end in the Pro Football Hall of Fame in Canton, Ohio, alongside Elway's. And the Broncos also had Rod Smith, Mark Schlereth, Tom Nalen, Ed McCaffrey, Howard Griffith, Neil Smith, Alfred Williams, John Mobley, Bill Romanowski, Trevor Price, David Diaz-Infante, and Jason Elam.

"I thought that they had a puncher's chance in the game," Dave Logan said. "A 13½-point underdog. But again, I'm around the team a lot, so my perspective can be skewed or even biased because I want them to win, I want them to play well…. I thought it depended on their ability to run the ball, stay on the field and keep Brett Favre off the field."

Logan's faith only grew stronger when he sat down with John Elway to tape his pregame quarterback show, looked into his eyes, and saw a confidence that he'd never seen before in No. 7. Soon, he'd also sense daggers shooting out of those eyes when a technical glitch nearly ruined one of the best interviews he'd ever gotten.

"We were out there the week prior to the Super Bowl and I was doing the quarterback show, which is a six-minute interview, and a head coach's show, a six-minute interview," Logan explained. "So we did the quarterback show on Friday, and we were situated in the lobby of the Hyatt Hotel. And we got the curtains up so we could have some privacy while doing the interview. The players have their own little part of the hotel that is cordoned off where they're playing pinball and all that sort of stuff. So John came over and we knocked out the show. He was as confident during that pregame show as I'd ever heard him."

It wasn't bravado, false or otherwise, just a supreme peace about Mike Shanahan's game plan and the blueprint for beating the mighty Green and Gold. "It wasn't boastful at all but very, very confident—quietly confident," Logan recalled. "He said basically I think we've got an excellent chance to win. He talked about the running game and all the things to do. I just sensed that he was in a different place, and it was a great interview. It wasn't a Joe Namath moment where he said, 'I guarantee we're going to win.' But it was only a couple of rungs down from that on the guarantee ladder. He was really confident."

The six minutes elapsed, and Logan and Elway shook hands. Elway went back to the players' lounge, and Logan turned to his producer. "Wow, that was great," Logan told him. "This is going to be an unbelievable interview to play right before the game." And the producer was like, 'Yeah, that was awesome.'"

Logan looked over at the show's engineer, Kenny Dhainin, whom Logan had nicknamed "the Wizard." "Kenny has this blank look on his face and he's, like, pale," Logan said. "And he's looking at the control board in front of him, just sort of staring at it, touching something. He's silent for like 45 seconds. Finally, he blurts out, 'I don't think we got that.' I was packing up some study material, not paying much attention to him at that moment.

"We didn't get what?"

"He said, 'Dave, I don't think we got the interview...none of it.'"

Logan just sat there dumbfounded.

Don Martin, the coordinating producer, walked up and heard the bad news for himself. After a long silence, he said, "Well, there's no choice. We've got to get him to do it again."

"Good luck with that," came Logan's retort.

"Dave, the only guy who even has a shot at getting him to do it again is you," Martin told Logan.

"I said, 'I'm not going in there. I can't believe we screwed this up.'"

Martin fired back, "Well, then we don't have a quarterback interview for Super Bowl XXXII."

"Well, I guess then we don't have a quarterback interview," Logan replied.

As a former player, Logan never liked going into the locker room as a member of the media. But there he was, being begged to go behind the ropes at the team hotel at the Super Bowl and violate the players' inner sanctum. "I don't like intruding in their space, especially in a setting like the Super Bowl where it's players-only and they're relaxing, with all of their media obligations finished. They're playing pinball, they're playing pool, they're relaxing," Logan said. "I know how players view outsiders, and at that point, that's exactly what I was."

But it was Logan's job, and Martin, his boss, was ever so convincing. So, after a while he agreed to go see if Elway would come back for a do-over. "Honestly, I got looks from some of the guys like, 'What the hell are you doing in here?'" Logan recounted. Finally, he saw Elway playing pinball with three of his teammates.

"Hey, what's up?" Elway asked.

"Dude, here's the deal. We didn't get the interview you just did," Logan told him. "There was a technical problem. So, we've got nothing. Now, listen; you can say no, you don't have to do the interview again if you don't want to. But you'd be doing us a huge favor if you would."

"You didn't get any of that freakin' interview?" Elway fumed.

"I don't know what to tell you, man. But no, we screwed it up."

Elway blurted out some choice words, wincing as he hit the flippers on the pinball machine, sending the metal ball clacking hard off the glass. "So, I'm just standing there in a place I should not be standing, asking the quarterback who's about to play in the Super Bowl a question that I should not be asking," Logan said in recalling the most awkward moment of his career in radio. "And I never wanted to not be in a place more than that particular place in my entire life. Or at least not many times."

Elway crossed his arms and stared at Logan. "And if looks could have killed, I would have been dead many times over," Logan said. "And in about 15 seconds he barked, 'Let's do it again.'"

So, Logan and Elway walked back out to the lobby and put their headphones back on.

"Well, he wasn't very happy," Logan chuckled. "And at that point, I was thinking, *This is going to be a really bad interview.*

"After we got the headphones back on, I looked at Kenny and said, 'Are we good?'" Dhanin nodded. "Kenny, are we good to go this time or what?"

Logan got two thumbs up, and he began the interview again.

"I put my headphones on, do the interview," Logan said. "And to his credit, you know, if the first one was a 100, the second one was about a 98."

In radio, this never happens. If you have to do a do-over, you usually have to accept that it's impossible to recapture the beauty of the original, the off-the-cuff, honest, magical moment. "But Elway was up to the task. He was pretty damn good," Logan said. "He recreated the whole thing—which in our business is a very hard thing to do, especially in a spontaneous way where you can really feel the emotion of a particular comment. It's very difficult 20 minutes later to say, 'Hey, could you replicate exactly how you felt and how you said that?' But to John's credit, he made it work. When we finished and were walking out of the hotel, I remember thinking, *That was pretty good. That's not bad for a do-over.* But man, oh man, it was embarrassing at the time."

There are always going to be glitches, but this time the stage was the Super Bowl and John Elway had just given him gold—twice.

Forty-eight hours later, Elway helicoptered his way into NFL immortality in his fourth shot at a title, and Broncos owner Pat Bowlen thrust the Lombardi Trophy into the air following the Broncos' 31–24 win over Green Bay and yelled those four famous words: "This...one's...for...John!"

Elway would look back and call it the greatest moment of his career.

Green Bay general manager Ron Wolf had a simple measure for dynasties: back-to-back championships, like Lombardi's '60s Packers powerhouse, the Dolphins and Steelers in the '70s, the 49ers in the '80s, the Cowboys in the '90s.

Wolf had built his Packers by luring Holmgren from the 49ers, acquiring Favre from the Falcons, and luring Reggie White in free agency from the Eagles. Those Packers had both greatness and Davis in their grasp and let both slip away.

Favre later acknowledged that when the Packers marched down and scored on their opening drive, visions of Dallas' 52–17 rout of Buffalo in Super Bowl XXVII swirled in their heads, and that 41–6 whipping of the Broncos at Lambeau Field from the previous season also came to mind.

"I remember the fact that they got beaten badly," Logan said of the Broncos' loss in Green Bay. "I remember the fact that Green Bay was a hell of a team and that was the year that they beat the Patriots at the end. That was their Super Bowl championship year and I remember that John did not play. And I do think the Packers were really confident coming in because the NFC had just waxed the AFC in recent Super Bowls. And I think it's pretty telling that Eugene Robinson is miked up during that game and he's talking about how 'these guys aren't even any good. What are we doing?'"

Robinson added, "These are the Indianapolis Colts," a reference to Green Bay's stunning 41–38 loss to the hapless, pre–Peyton Manning Colts on November 16, 1997, the last time the Packers had lost a game.

"Players at moments like that will say really honest things. So I think Green Bay was completely shocked that the Broncos were able to do what they were able to do against the Packers defense," Logan said. "And I think the game plan was excellent. The game plan was we're going to run at these guys. We're going to run at Gilbert Brown and those big people inside, we're going to make them move and run and tackle and continue to do that and we'll see how a guy that's 350 pounds moves in the third and fourth quarter. And I think if you go back and look at that game, the Packers defense was completely worn out—physically worn out. To me, that's how the Broncos won the game."

While the Broncos celebrated, Wolf lamented the lost opportunity. "We're a one-year wonder," he seethed, "a fart in the windstorm."

The Broncos, on the other hand, weren't about to be one-and-done.

# CHAPTER 9
# LOOK WHAT WE DID

John Elway was right. He had an inkling Super Bowl XXXII wouldn't be like the Denver Broncos' four previous flops in the big game, three of which came on his watch when the fourth quarter was an excruciating exercise in waiting out the anguish of watching another team celebrate their overwhelming victory.

He had displayed that confidence in the pregame interview do-over with Dave Logan, and now instead of talking about another devastating defeat, Elway was at long last a champion, something he always figured he had to be if he was to go down as one of the NFL's elite quarterbacks.

Elway set the tone for victory by scrambling and diving into two defenders for a first down to set up a Denver touchdown late in the third quarter.

"You wonder if you're going to run out of years," Elway said shortly after Brett Favre's fourth-down pass to Mark Chmura was batted away by John Mobley with 28 seconds remaining, clinching the Broncos' 31–24 upset in what many immediately dubbed the greatest Super Bowl ever. The Broncos had taken down the powerful Packers and the mighty NFC.

In many ways, Elway's Broncos getting blown out in the Super Bowl had come to define the AFC's 13-year losing streak, at least as much as Jim Kelly's Buffalo Bills reaching four consecutive Super Bowls and losing each one. "I've been hearing it a long time, that AFC streak—13 years is a long, long time—and it's great that I'm not going to hear it anymore," Elway said. "I'd hear question after question if my career would be complete if I didn't win a Super Bowl. I no longer have to answer that one: it can be complete, and it's hard for me to believe I am saying that."

The Broncos had been installed as an early 13½-point underdog and the betting line was still 11½ points at kickoff. "No one gave us a chance, and look what we did," tight end Shannon Sharpe said. "We shocked the world. But we didn't shock the Denver Broncos."

Favre threw for 256 yards and three touchdowns, but a pair of turnovers gnawed at him. "I think I played okay, but not great," Favre said.

"We got three touchdowns and I thought going in that would be enough to win. But they got 10 points off turnovers and that was the difference."

Elway didn't do nearly as much to help—or hurt—his team this time. He completed just 12 of 22 passes for 123 yards, no touchdowns, and an interception. But a trio of takeaways by Denver's defense and a ground game that produced 179 yards made Elway's stat line a moot point.

The MVP of the game was Elway's wing man, running back Terrell Davis, who rushed for 157 yards and a Super Bowl–record three touchdowns despite missing most of the second quarter with a migraine. He was even used as a decoy on one play even though he couldn't see. Coach Mike Shanahan implored him to go in because otherwise the Packers would realize Elway was keeping the ball on third-and-goal from the 1.

Davis knew that whenever he had a migraine his vision would return with crystal clarity, and because halftime at the Super Bowl is an hour, he knew he'd be good by the third quarter. And he was, but on the first play of the second half, Packers cornerback Tyrone Williams punched the ball out of Davis' hands and smothered it at the Denver 26-yard line. Denver's defense held and Ryan Longwell's field goal tied the game at 17.

Davis' second one-yard touchdown run put the Broncos back on top 24–17 heading into the fourth quarter. Then Antonio Freeman tied it at 24 with a 13-yard touchdown catch, his second of the game (he also had an 81-yard touchdown catch in the prior year's Super Bowl to put Green Bay ahead for good).

Davis' third touchdown, again from a yard out, put Denver ahead 31–24 with 1:45 left. The Broncos' undersized O-line, which didn't have a single member over 300 pounds, had dominated the Packers' bigger defensive line that sported defensive end Reggie White and massive defensive tackle Gilbert Brown, whom his coach had once quipped was "as big as two men put together."

When Davis scored his third touchdown, Shanahan thought it was just another example of his undersized underdogs coming up big, but he soon realized Packers coach Mike Holmgren was simply playing the odds. "I thought we did a heck of a job blocking, but obviously they really let us score," Shanahan said. "I thought that was one of the bigger holes I've seen for a while. I thought our offensive line really knocked them off the ball. But after looking at the replay, I could see I was wrong."

Holmgren had decided just after the two-minute warning to let Denver score so that he could give Favre as much time as possible for a game-tying touchdown drive to send the game into overtime. The next day, Holmgren would acknowledge he mistakenly thought it was first-and-goal when Davis scored, instead of second-and-goal.

Maybe it didn't matter, but had Green Bay stopped Denver on the next two plays and used its two timeouts, it theoretically could have forced a field goal and gotten the ball back with about 90 seconds remaining. The Packers would reach the Denver 31 before Favre's fourth-down pass was batted down. Had they only trailed by three, it would have been an easy field goal try for Ryan Longwell to send the game into overtime.

"Second-and-goal from the 1?" Holmgren said. "If that was the case, then we made a mistake. I thought what would happen if they used their timeouts, kick the field goal, we would have had about 25 seconds. But at any rate, we made the decision. I wanted the ball back."

No matter the down, Packers safety Eugene Robinson said he thought it made perfect sense to concede the touchdown and not burn any timeouts, giving Favre and the rest of Green Bay's star-studded offense as much time as possible to go tie it up.

"At least we made it interesting," Holmgren said. "It was a strategy I felt was our only chance to win."

Robinson said linebacker Bernardo Harris brought in the play from the sideline right after Davis reeled off a 17-yard run on first-and-goal from the 18 following a Denver penalty.

"He said, 'We got to let them score.' And I said, 'Let them score?' And I looked at the clock and I said, 'Okay, this is right,'" Robinson

His efforts leading the Broncos over the Green Bay Packers in Super Bowl XXXII earned Terrell Davis MVP honors.

recalled. "I wasn't surprised at all. I thought it was pretty smart. The real estate was this much to get," Robinson added, holding his hands a foot apart. And when Elway threw his arms up and celebrated T.D.'s third touchdown, Robinson walked past him and said, "Yeah, we're trying to get the ball back."

No matter. Elway had a seven-point lead and the Broncos were 1:45 away from the franchise's first Super Bowl triumph.

Robinson said he doubted the Packers could have held Denver to a field goal anyway "because the ball was on the one-foot line and the way they were running the ball, they would have scored."

On the ensuing drive, Favre threw four consecutive passes to running back Dorsey Levens for 39 yards, giving Green Bay the ball at the Denver 31-yard line with 42 seconds remaining. But a short gain and three consecutive incompletions knocked Green Bay from its throne and crowned Elway. Favre's pass to Chmura on fourth-and-6 was batted away by Mobley, sending Denver's sideline into delirium.

"I was very confident," Favre said afterward. "We moved the ball down again, but we didn't make the plays when we had the chance."

What ate at Favre was Green Bay's three turnovers, which led to 10 points by the Broncos. Safety Steve Atwater's blitz led to an interception of Favre and a subsequent touchdown by Denver, and later in the first half, he hit Favre so hard he fumbled the ball and Denver recovered at the Green Bay 33, leading to Jason Elam's 51-yard field goal and an early 17–7 lead.

Favre responded with a brilliant 17-play, 95-yard drive to pull the Packers to 17–14 at halftime—and that was the kind of drive they needed again after intentionally allowing Davis to score his final touchdown with 1:45 remaining.

"After T.D. scored, we went to a commercial break. Scott Hasting, the color commentator, had already left the booth to head down to the field for postgame interviews," Logan recalled. "And it hit me: if they can hold on for 1:45, they're going to win a Super Bowl! I thought about all those years in the '60s when the Broncos were so bad. But as a kid, I would watch them every Sunday. I thought about the fans from all those years who had lived and died with this franchise, and now…they're one defensive stop from wiping out all those bad memories."

Before Favre's final pass hit the grass, Logan momentarily turned off his mic to compose himself. "I got so emotionally wrapped up in the moment that it almost got the better of me," he said. "I did something that normally I would never do: without realizing, I was openly rooting for the team on the air."

After Favre's final pass hit the grass, Elway trotted out and took a knee as the seconds ticked away for the first Super Bowl victory in franchise history. His teammates spilled out onto the field and carried him off like the conquering champion at long last he was.

On the postgame stage, team owner Pat Bowlen jubilantly proclaimed, "This…one's…for…John!"

Elway, the only member of the vaunted Class of '83 quarterbacks to win a Super Bowl after nine losses, relished in the moment. "I know that I've been labeled as the guy who's never been on the winning Super Bowl team," Elway said. "Boy, am I glad to get rid of that."

Elway was peppered with questions about retirement now that he'd finally won a Super Bowl after three ugly losses in the big game. This wouldn't be a bad way to go out, really, but Elway needed time to ponder his future. "I am going to really enjoy this, because I worked 15 years in the NFL and through college for it," Elway said. "They made this game for quarterbacks and you've got to win this game to be up there with the elite." His legacy secure, his future in doubt, Elway walked off to celebrate the championship that had eluded him for so long.

"Like I said all week, if we were unfortunate enough to lose this ball game, I'd be happy for John, and I am," Favre said. "He's played a long time for this and I know the feeling he's going through right now, because it's a wonderful feeling to win this game. I know he's worked very hard."

Favre said if Elway did retire, what better way to go out than on the shoulders of your teammates?

As for himself, Favre said he was confident he'd get another shot or two. "I'm 28," he said. "I think I'll be back to several Super Bowls." He wouldn't, of course.

Shanahan said he figured Elway would put off retirement for at least another year, but he cringed when asked about another R-word: repeat. "You always worry about having the same work ethic, about remembering what kind of dedication it took to get to this point," Shanahan said. "But how about giving me a chance to enjoy this one before we start talking about a repeat?"

Not far away, Sharpe wasn't holding back like Elway and Shanahan were. He talked freely about defending the title Denver had just won. "We can do this again," Sharpe said. "We were a wild card. We had to go to Pittsburgh and win, we had to go to Kansas City and win, then we had to play Green Bay in a neutral site. We'd already been to hell and back. This was the easy part."

# CHAPTER 10
## NOT SO EASY

Instead of joining the likes of Bart Starr, Terry Bradshaw, Joe Montana, and Troy Aikman as winners of consecutive Super Bowls, Brett Favre's failure to finish the final drive allowed John Elway and Denver to finally taste Super Bowl success. And after giving it some thought, Elway announced he was coming back to try to do what Favre couldn't and defend the Vince Lombardi Trophy now glistening in the lobby at team headquarters.

Shannon Sharpe hadn't waited for Elway's announcement to start talking about a repeat, suggesting winning it all as an underdog was the hard part. Despite Favre's example, staying on top of the peak, he suggested, wasn't nearly as hard as scaling the mountaintop.

Packers safety Eugene Robinson also was looking ahead to Super Bowl XXXIII at Pro Player Stadium in Miami in the aftermath of Denver's 31–24 triumph in Super Bowl XXXII in San Diego. "When you lose a game like this," Robinson said, "you're thinking about only one thing: *How do I get back here and win it next time?*"

Robinson would indeed return to the Super Bowl the following year, not with the Green Bay Packers but with the Atlanta Falcons, whom he joined in the off-season.

The Falcons went 14–2 in 1998, edging San Francisco 20–18 in the NFC divisional round before traveling to Minnesota, where a remarkable rookie named Randy Moss had led the Vikings to a 15–1 regular season record and a 41–21 rout of the Arizona Cardinals in the playoffs. The Falcons stunned the heavily favored Vikings 30–27 in overtime of the NFC Championship Game, setting up a Super Bowl showdown with the defending champion Broncos, who went 14–2 to earn the AFC's top seed before bouncing out the Miami Dolphins and New York Jets to return to defend their title.

"They were such a dominant team the entire year," Dave Logan recounted. "Terrell Davis had a sensational year and there were games— it never happens in the NFL this way—they were taking starters out midway through the third period. Just stuff that you just rarely see in the NFL."

It wasn't a cakewalk the whole time. After winning their first 13 games, the Broncos suffered back-to-back road losses in December to the New York Giants (20–16) and Miami Dolphins (31–21). Elway missed several games with injuries but backup Bubby Brister went 4–0 in his place, leading the Broncos to victories over the Washington Redskins, Philadelphia Eagles, San Diego Chargers, and Kansas City Chiefs to keep Denver's title defense alive. Elway was healthy again for the playoffs, and once again his supreme supporting staff shined in the postseason.

The revenge theme that had burned so brightly a year earlier worked once more as the Broncos earned a first-round bye and Miami beat Buffalo in the wild card round to earn a trip to Mile High Stadium. Three weeks after their 10-point loss in Miami, the Broncos routed the Dolphins 38–3 in the AFC divisional playoffs behind a defense that limited the Dolphins to just 14 rushing yards on 13 carries.

The 35-point margin of victory was the largest ever by a Broncos team in the playoffs and the three points were the fewest they'd ever allowed in a playoff game. Davis scored twice—from a yard out and from the 20, when he juked two defenders—highlighting a 199-yard rushing performance that carried Denver to its second straight AFC Championship Game appearance.

Denver's defense kept the Broncos in the game while the offense sputtered early on January 17, 1999, when the Jets jumped out to a 10–0 lead in the AFC Championship Game in Denver. John Hall's 32-yard field goal marked the only scoring in the first half and Curtis Martin powered his way in for the score after a blocked punt early in the third quarter gave the Jets possession at the Broncos' 1-yard line.

Elway responded with a 47-yard completion to Ed McCaffrey to the Jets 17 that woke up both Denver's sleepy offense and the unusually quiet crowd at Mile High Stadium. Davis caught a six-yard pass and Elway found fullback Howard Griffith from 11 yards out to pull Denver to 10–7.

James Farrior fumbled the ensuing kickoff and Broncos special teams ace Keith Burns recovered, leading to Jason Elam's 44-yard field goal to tie it. The Jets went three-and-out, and Elam's 48-yarder put Denver ahead for the first time all afternoon.

Again the Jets went three-and-out and Darrien Gordon returned the punt 36 yards to the Jets 38-yard line. Two plays later, Davis burst around the left end 31 yards for a touchdown that gave Denver a 20–10 lead heading into the fourth quarter. Elam added the finishing touch with his third field goal and Denver's defense finished with a half-dozen takeaways, four fumbles, and Gordon's two interceptions.

The Broncos were back in the Super Bowl, only this time they were the hunted.

Two years earlier, their 30–27 loss to Jacksonville in an opening playoff game at home, when the Broncos were the gold standard of the AFC, was both crushing and a catalyst, sending Denver on a mission that ended with the third-biggest upset in Super Bowl history over the heavily-favored Green Bay Packers 31–24.

"It ate at us throughout the off-season," coach Mike Shanahan said. "And it ate at me personally. Any time you go through an experience like that, when you have an opportunity to do something very special and you don't get the job done, it just eats at you."

Unlike in Super Bowl XXXII, however, this time the Broncos were the ones wearing the target, and they'd survived a difficult December that included their only two losses and close calls against Kansas City and Seattle. It had been expected the Broncos would meet Randy Moss and the Minnesota Vikings in Super Bowl XXXIII. Instead, the Atlanta Falcons had upset the Vikings in overtime of the NFC Championship Game.

For the first time, Elway and the Broncos would learn what it felt like to put away an opponent early in the Super Bowl and enjoy the final minutes without having to sweat it out.

# CHAPTER 11

# THIS...ONE'S... FOR...YOU!

While the Denver Broncos were going 14–2 in 1998, the Minnesota Vikings, behind dynamic rookie receiver Randy Moss, were doing one better, going 15–1. Most people watching the NFL were expecting the two teams would meet in Super Bowl XXXIII in Atlanta.

"Everybody was really excited about the prospect," Dave Logan said. "I think from a national perspective there were people that felt like the Vikings were unbeatable with the offense. I mean, they scored over 500 points in the regular season. They were good on both sides of the ball. But I'll tell you this, I think the Broncos would have found a way to win the game. They could control the game running the ball and they were good enough that they could throw the ball as well.

"And that was a really balanced Denver Broncos team. They were more balanced through the playoffs I think in that year than the preceding year. They were run-heavy in '97, certainly in the Super Bowl. I mean, John threw for 123 yards. They won that game because they could run the ball on the Packers. They just wore them down."

John Elway may have been showing the effects of 16 seasons in the NFL, but he still had some big moments left in that rocket right arm of his. In Super Bowl XXXIII, the Broncos were on top of their formidable game.

"They could run it, they could throw it," said Logan, "they ran boots, and they did on offense pretty much whatever they wanted to do."

Only it wasn't against mighty Minnesota. An old friend—or was it foe?—had taken care of the Vikings before they could get to the Super Bowl to face Elway and the balanced Broncos. Dan Reeves was coach of the Broncos in 1983 when he arranged the trade to get Elway, who'd been drafted by the Baltimore Colts out of Stanford. The following year, he added Mike Shanahan to his staff. Three times the three of them went to the Super Bowl and three times they lost. Now they were at the center of a feud that was still reverberating as the Broncos prepared to face Reeves' Atlanta Falcons in Super Bowl XXXIII.

Stung by criticism from Elway and suspecting that Shanahan was plotting with the quarterback behind his back, Reeves fired his most trusted assistant after the 1991 season. A year later, Reeves himself was dismissed by the Broncos, replaced by Wade Phillips, who in turn would give way after two seasons to Shanahan in 1995.

"There's still a lot of hurt that won't ever go away," Reeves said in the days leading up to the Super Bowl. "You never forget those things."

The feud may have faded but it wasn't forgotten. "First of all, I'm a Mike guy, so I come at this from probably a biased perspective," Logan said, "but I think both of them had come at this from a public standpoint that they had buried the hatchet. They said nice things about each other. But let's be honest about this. There was no love lost between Mike and Dan. I mean, there just wasn't. There were hard feelings.

"Dan thought that Mike was going behind the scenes and scripting his own plays with John. Mike had a good relationship with John from an offensive coordinator standpoint, and I think that probably didn't sit all that well with Dan. And there's a competitive spirit amongst coaches at every level of football, certainly in the NFL. If somebody fires you and then you get the opportunity, you're going to want to go put it on 'em. But again, I thought both guys handled it professionally and with a lot of class leading up to the game—because honestly, nobody wants to hear about dirty laundry, about what you think about this guy or that guy from 10 or 15 years ago. Fans don't care. But it was there. There's no question about it."

And not just with Shanahan but with Elway, too. "Listen, if you said to John, 'You can win the Super Bowl and that will be your last game, you'll be the MVP, you'll throw for over 300 yards, and you'll run a quarterback draw late in the game and score—all of that and you get to pick whatever coach you want to be on the other sideline,' I'm pretty damn sure John would have picked Dan. That doesn't mean that there's not a respect level there, because as you get older you get farther away from the emotion. I mean, you mellow, time goes on, and it changes your perspective," Logan said. "There are other things that become more important to you. But there wasn't any love lost in that relationship either."

Going into the matchup, Reeves was the winningest active coach in the NFL, with a 162–117–1 record. What he lacked was a Super Bowl win, something Elway finally achieved with Shanahan a year earlier when the Broncos beat the Packers in San Diego. The Broncos were an even better team this year, but Reeves had a talented team himself, one he thought was perfectly capable of upsetting Denver, even though his roster was filled with players who had never played in such a big game. Denver was installed as 8-point favorites over the Falcons.

"I remember I was doing Mike Shanahan's TV show with Ron Zapollo in Miami on the Friday night before the game, and we talked with Mike about the game and the key matchups and all the things you would expect in a 30-minute live TV show," Logan said. "And after the show Ron and I were kidding each other because we both felt pretty strong about the Broncos and their chances of winning: 'You know, we ought to just hop on a flight and go to Vegas right now and put some money down on the Broncos.'" The two shared a laugh.

Shanahan, while leaving the set, overheard them. "What's the spread in this game?" he asked.

"And I said, 'Denver's an 8-point favorite.'"

Shanahan turned around and as he started to walk away, he muttered just loud enough for everyone to hear: "If we play well, they've got no chance."

This time, it was the Broncos who had an air of confidence, but they also remembered how the Packers puffed out their chests a year earlier, and they were determined not to repeat Green Bay's mistake.

Still, they conducted themselves with the utmost confidence all of Super Bowl week. "The Broncos were so certain that if they played well, just because of the matchup, that it was going to work in their favor," Logan said.

They didn't fall into the trap that had snared the favored Packers a year earlier. "First of all, I thought there was a pretty significant gap in talent between the Broncos and Falcons," Logan said. "I think when you look at Super Bowl XXXII, those two teams were fairly even talent-wise. I think you look at Super Bowl XXXIII and the fact that the Falcons upset the Vikings, the Broncos were just the better team. Denver was an 8½-point favorite, and going into the game I didn't think the Falcons matched up well, particularly on the back end of their defense.

"At 14–2 that year, the Broncos were as good as any team in football. They could run it, they could throw it. They could stress your defense in so many different ways. Plus, I think Mike was very comfortable going against Dan. It's not like those two guys didn't know each other and it's not like they hadn't worked together for a long time. I think Mike had a comfort level that from a schematic standpoint, he felt the Broncos would have an edge. They were just a better team, and they didn't lose their focus going into that game, and it's a credit to the players and to the staff."

One of the handful of Falcons who knew what to expect from the Super Bowl was Pro Bowl safety Eugene Robinson, who had started in the previous two Super Bowls for the Green Bay Packers and who was the NFL's career leader among active players with 53 interceptions, including four in his first season in Atlanta in 1998. On the day before the biggest game of the year, Robinson, a deeply religious man known as "the Prophet," was honored with the Bart Starr Award by the religious group Athletes in Action for his "high moral character."

Only a few hours later, police arrested Robinson on Biscayne Boulevard, a major street frequented by sex workers and drug dealers. He was driving alone in a rented car at about 9:00 P.M. when he offered an undercover officer $40 for oral sex, said police spokesman Angel Calzadilla. He was released from Miami police headquarters two hours later to Falcons general manager Harold Richardson.

"I was as shocked as anybody," Logan said. "I just couldn't believe it. I didn't know Eugene personally. I knew he was a hell of a player. But you know, in that case, I was like anybody else in the public. I knew what I knew of Eugene through the media and he seemed like a stand-up guy,

In Super Bowl XXXIII against the Atlanta Falcons, the Broncos' second win in as many trips, it was John Elway who got to partake in MVP honors.

great character guy, but obviously he made a huge mistake. And he made it at a really bad time. You've got to have your focus on one thing. The best teams are teams that can compartmentalize and focus in on the task at hand and leave everything else outside until after the most important thing is done."

Reeves allowed Robinson to start the Super Bowl even though Robinson acknowledged that he didn't sleep at all the night before the biggest game of the year. He was consoled privately in his hotel room by a group of teammates including Cornelius Bennett, Ray Buchanan, and William White.

"It was a little distracting, but I don't think it was a major factor," Reeves said. "My major concern was whether he was going to be ready to play, and he said he was. I thought he did a good job."

Robinson broke up Elway's first pass but was beaten by Rod Smith down the middle of the field on the game's biggest play, an 80-yard touchdown pass from Elway that put Denver in command 17–3 late in the first half. In the third quarter, Robinson broke his left pinkie trying to tackle Terrell Davis. Robinson was limited the rest of the game and lingered in the training room for almost an hour afterward, getting treatment on his injured finger.

When he finally met a horde of media, he was focused on healing the wounds his family had suffered.

"I was extremely focused on the game today," Robinson said afterward. "It didn't affect my play because it was pretty much therapeutic."

"I truly love my wife. I truly love my kids," he continued. "I'm sorry that I had to drag them through that type of deal."

Meanwhile, the Broncos were still on the field basking in their second consecutive Super Bowl triumph, this one coming much easier than the last one as they built a 31–6 lead on their way to a 34–19 triumph.

Davis set an NFL record with his seventh consecutive 100-yard playoff game, Darrien Gordon had a pair of interceptions just like he had in the AFC Championship, Denver's defense collected four takeaways altogether, and Elway completed 18 of 29 passes for 336 yards and that 80-yard touchdown to Smith. He also rushed for a three-yard touchdown after Gordon's second interception, giving the Broncos a 25-point cushion with 11:20 remaining.

The Falcons only did their crazy "Dirty Bird" dance after two essentially meaningless touchdowns in the fourth quarter.

"I hate that dance," said Gordon, who set a Super Bowl record with 108 interception return yards. "We just wanted to make sure they didn't have any chance to do the 'Dirty Bird.' They can't do it if they can't score touchdowns and they didn't do that until we were way ahead."

Elway had finally tasted victory in the Super Bowl a year earlier when Davis scored three touchdowns to win Super Bowl MVP honors. This time, the Falcons focused on Davis and dared an aging Elway to beat them—and he did, completing 18 of 29 passes for 336 yards and a touchdown in a more personally satisfying performance, one that garnered him a Super Bowl MVP nod.

"I remember broadcasting the game, when Mike took him out and Elway took his helmet off with his right hand, extended his left hand with his fist clenched," Logan said. "And I said on the air, 'Well, this might not be John Elway's last game, but it sure looks like it.' You could just almost feel it from the way he celebrated that game, coming out of the game before it ended."

Broncos 34, Falcons 19.

Back-to-back Super Bowl triumphs.

Greatness guaranteed.

A year after dedicating the franchise's first Super Bowl win to Elway, team owner Pat Bowlen took the Vince Lombardi Trophy and again held it high.

"This...one's...for...you!" he hollered, dedicating this one to the fans.

By the time the Broncos would win their third title in 2016, Bowlen was homebound, having been forced by Alzheimer's to step down from his daily duties running the team two years earlier.

Elway, who had returned to his beloved Broncos in 2011 as the team's general manager and vice president of football operations, grabbed the trophy and jabbed it into the night sky at Levi's Stadium in California, hollering the four words he so longed to say: "This...one's...for...Pat!"

"That was my goal when I took the job," said Elway, adding that considers himself "the luckiest guy in the world to get an opportunity to play for him and also get an opportunity to come back and work for him."

# CHAPTER 12

## THE GREATEST AMBASSADOR

The 1983 NFL draft is known as the "Year of the Quarterback," for the six signal-callers selected in the first round: Hall of Famers John Elway, Jim Kelly, and Dan Marino, plus Ken O'Brien, Todd Blackledge, and Tony Eason.

In the 84-year history of the National Football League draft, there have never been more quarterbacks taken in the first round. What's more, the subsequent two years didn't feature *any* QBs selected in the first round. Boomer Esiason was the first quarterback taken in 1984, going 38th overall in the second round to the Cincinnati Bengals, and in 1985 Randall Cunningham was the first quarterback selected, going to the Philadelphia Eagles with the 37th overall pick.

In 1983, the Baltimore Colts drafted Elway following his stellar career at Stanford and a brief stint in minor league baseball with the New York Yankees organization. Elway didn't want to play in Baltimore, and the Colts ended up trading him to the Denver Broncos.

Penn State's Blackledge was the next quarterback selected, at No. 7 by the Kansas City Chiefs, followed by the Miami Hurricanes' Kelly, who went to the Buffalo Bills at No. 14. Illinois' Eason went to the New England Patriots one pick later; UC Davis' O'Brien came off the board 24th to the New York Jets and the University of Pittsburgh's Marino went to the Miami Dolphins at No. 27.

This group would come to be regarded as the greatest quarterback draft class ever, and after their rookie seasons in 1983, nine of the next 10 Super Bowls featured a member of the '83 QB class.

Unfortunately, they had a devil of a time once there, going 0–9 and losing by an average score of 40–15.

Marino went 0–1, losing to Joe Montana and the San Francisco 49ers 38–16 in Super Bowl XIX. Eason made it the next year, but his Patriots were blown out by Jim McMahon's Chicago Bears 46–10. Elway reached three of the next four, but the Broncos were blown out 39–20 by Phil Simms and the New York Giants, then 42–10 by Doug Williams and the Washington Redskins and 55–10 by Montana and the 49ers.

Kelly then led the Bills to an unprecedented four consecutive AFC championships, but Buffalo lost all four Super Bowls: to Jeff Hostetler's Giants 20–19, Mark Rypien's Redskins 37–24, and twice to Troy Aikman and the Dallas Cowboys, 52–17 and 30–13, respectively. Elway finally gave the Class of '83 its first Lombardi Trophy when the Broncos broke through against Brett Favre and the Green Bay Packers 31–24 in Super Bowl XXXII on January 25, 1998, and he successfully defended the Broncos' title on January 31, 1999, when he led the Broncos to a 31–19 win over Chris Chandler and the Atlanta Falcons in Super Bowl XXXIII.

The backup for the Falcons that day was Steve DeBerg, a 45-year-old who served as a mentor and occasional play-caller. Elway was a rookie when he first met DeBerg, the man he would soon replace as Denver's starting quarterback.

"He was what, six or seven years in the league? I thought he was ancient," Elway said on the eve of his successful Super Bowl title defense. "Now I feel ancient." A record 555 sacks will do that.

DeBerg was most famous for having been displaced by famous quarterbacks—Elway in Denver, Montana in San Francisco and Kansas City, and Steve Young and Vinny Testaverde in Tampa. In 1998, he became the oldest quarterback to start an NFL game when he replaced the injured Chandler against the New York Jets, losing 28–3. But there he was in the Super Bowl, on the opposite sideline from Elway.

DeBerg had been retired for four seasons before making his comeback in 1998, two of them spent as quarterbacks coach for the Giants under Dan Reeves. He didn't follow Reeves to Atlanta but decided while playing in a coed touch football league that he still had the arm to play in the NFL as a backup quarterback. He landed in Atlanta when Rypien, whom the Falcons had signed as Chandler's backup, decided to take the year off to tend to his ill wife and son.

On Super Bowl Sunday, DeBerg would not only relay the play calls from the sideline to Chandler but he'd call a few of his own, a role he had taken over during the three weeks while Reeves was away to undergo quadruple heart bypass surgery.

"Steve's been around long enough to see things some of the coaches don't see," Reeves said.

DeBerg would walk away from the NFL after the Super Bowl.

And so would Elway. After winning his first Super Bowl title in 1998 following three ugly losses in the championship game, Elway spent four months pondering his future, finally deciding to come back for what he said would be his final season.

After winning his second title, Elway admitted the chance to three-peat had thrown a "kink" into his thinking. But he had nothing left to prove, having capped his career with the only achievements that had eluded him, and the clock finally ran out on Denver's superstar quarterback.

"To John Elway, football was the greatest game in the world," Commissioner Paul Tagliabue said. "And to the game of football, John Elway was the greatest ambassador imaginable. He combined talent and character to become an incomparable performer and champion on the field."

Elway delayed his official retirement announcement first because team owner Pat Bowlen was out of town, and then further out of respect to the grieving families and community following the Columbine High School shooting.

When he finally took the podium at a suburban hotel to announce he was calling it a career, he did so through sobs. "It was emotional. If you were in that room, you could tell how hard it was for him to walk away," Dave Logan recalled. "And, I got it. It's hard for all of us. But for John, it probably just felt like the right time, and I'll never forget the line he said while fighting back tears: 'I just can't do it anymore physically.' And I think that was the deciding factor.

"You know you love the competition, you love the locker room, you love having a common goal and it changes every single week because of the opponent. But this game takes its toll on you physically, and I think that was maybe the hardest thing for him to come to grips with. And when he said, 'I can't do it anymore physically,' I really felt for him. Because I know that had to be really, really tough to walk away."

The third transcendent superstar to retire that year, joining NBA great Michael Jordan and NHL great Wayne Gretzky, Elway announced his retirement at a packed news conference where he was at first jovial, flashing that famous toothy smile, cracking jokes, and regaling his audience with tales from his 16 seasons with the Denver Broncos.

Then he turned to his retirement, and that's when it hit him, like one of those 250-pound linebackers who had been chasing him his whole career. "It's hard to walk away. I can't explain in words how much everyone has meant to me." As tears kept chasing tears down his cheeks, Elway cracked, "The over-under in the locker room yesterday was how many times I'd cry. I took the under." After crying some more, he added, "I lost the bet."

While he was eager for the next chapter in his life, Elway acknowledged, "I'll never be able to fill the void of playing a football game." Like most NFL players, he said he'd miss the huddle and the camaraderie of the locker room.

And he'd really miss telling talkative tight end Shannon Sharpe "to be quiet," he added. "I know you're open, I know you're open, I know you're open," Elway said about Sharpe, drawing loud laughs from the audience where Sharpe was among his teammates in attendance.

Joining him onstage was coach Mike Shanahan and team owner Pat Bowlen, who said, "I truly believe John was the very best to ever play."

Elway, who set the standard for improvisational skills before Brett Favre and Patrick Mahomes followed suit, remembered the good moments, and there were many, as well as the bad, and there were plenty of those too.

There was "the Drive" in Cleveland in the 1986 AFC Championship game, that 98-yard march that sent Elway to the first of his five Super Bowls. "That one put me on the map," Elway said.

There was his first pro game, on September 4, 1983, at Pittsburgh, when he completed just two of eight passes—and one of them was an interception by the Steelers. "I didn't think I was going to last a year," Elway said. "Jack Lambert was snarling at me with no teeth."

For 14 years, a Super Bowl title was the only thing missing from Elway's impressive résumé, and he took care of that by winning two straight to end his career. He capped it with Super Bowl MVP honors in his final game, a 34–19 win over the Atlanta Falcons.

"I'm glad to see him retire a champion," Marino said. "I'm sure it was a tough decision, knowing how much John enjoys competing on the football field."

Elway became the only starting quarterback ever to retire after winning a Super Bowl. (He'd be joined by Peyton Manning 17 years later, after Elway returned to his beloved Broncos as general manager.)

Elway was hit more than any quarterback in NFL history, absorbing 555 sacks in 256 games, including the playoffs, but he missed only 15 starts because of injury or illness. So while Marino has better numbers and Montana and Terry Bradshaw have twice as many rings, Elway has a legacy all his own.

"He's got to be the most durable quarterback ever," former Broncos coach Wade Phillips said. "He's the Lou Gehrig of that position."

Although he posted a career-best passer rating of 93.0 in his final season, hamstring, back, and rib injuries caused him to miss parts or all of six games, and his arthritic left knee also gave him problems. Still, that didn't diminish a career defined by his toughness and productivity: when he retired he was the NFL's winningest and most durable quarterback. The NFL has since changed the rules, making the game safer for quarterbacks, allowing them to last longer and pile up bigger numbers.

When Elway retired, he had guided his team to more victories (148) than any other quarterback and he had thrown for 51,475 yards and accounted for 54,882 total yards, second only to Marino.

## Dave Logan's Log

The game has changed for the better and they're trying their best to protect players. I've done this a long time. I played a long time. When I see games now—and I'm all for players getting what they can get—I applaud the way that it is played in terms of the hits, the head hits and all the stuff that went on with wide receivers in the middle of the field, and I think to myself, *Golly, I wish I could have been born 25 years later*, right? Good for wide receivers, you're taking care of them.

It's the same way with quarterbacks. John played at a time where you could take a quarterback down to the ground any way you wanted to. And when you got to the quarterback, you tried to inflict as much damage as you possibly could. And same for wide receivers: catching the ball in the middle of the field, there was a price to pay. So it's not that way nowadays, and I think it's certainly better for the players. John was a very physical player. He was a really good athlete for a long time. He wasn't necessarily a running quarterback but he was a quarterback who could run.

He was a heck of an athlete, so there was always a threat with him that if things broke down, he'd tuck it and run and he'd pick up the first down. He looked to do that. With his skill set, he was one of the greatest throwers this league had ever seen, but he also could run. And John was not a small-framed guy. He was a barrel-chested, big, athletic dude when he played.

Elway could also finish games like no one else, with 47 game-winning or game-tying drives in the fourth quarter or overtime, and he was selected to nine Pro Bowls and won the NFL's MVP Award in 1987.

"They talk about 47 comebacks," Shanahan said. "The thing that was so impressive was the concentration level and poise and thriving on pressure."

Elway was the first quarterback to start in five Super Bowls, and his 5–1 record in AFC championship games was the best in league history.

Elway had an economics degree from Stanford and would venture into the business world after his playing career was done. He'd already been part-owner of auto dealerships in Denver that he and his partners sold for $82.5 million two years earlier (although Elway's name remained on some of the businesses).

"I don't look at it as a retirement," Elway said. "I look on it as graduation. You graduate from high school and you graduate from college. I'm graduating from pro football." He would return, in that case, to earn his doctorate degree in pro football after a little more than a decade away honing his management skills.

# CHAPTER 13
## THE MASTERMIND

**M**ike Shanahan and John Elway had a heck of a run together. After going 8–8 in 1995 the first season they were paired as head coach and quarterback, the Broncos went 46–10 in the next three seasons, including 7–1 in the playoffs, and won back-to-back Super Bowls, the first in franchise history. Elway retired after the second one, the only starting quarterback at that time to go out on top, much less as a two-time defending champion.

After seasons of 13–3, 12–4, and 14–2, Denver dived in 1999 when Elway retired and Terrell Davis and Shannon Sharpe suffered season-ending injuries. The Broncos tumbled to a six-win season that year, beginning a decade-long run in which the Broncos would go 92–73— still a respectable .558 winning percentage—but win just one of five playoff games in that decade following Elway.

That off-season, Shanahan invited Dave Logan out to lunch, and they met at a golf course restaurant near Broncos headquarters.

"I want you to coach my wide receivers," Shanahan told Logan.

They talked for 20 minutes about the three-year offer, the schedule and all of its demands. "And then he closed his pitch by saying, 'Dave, I really believe you'll be an NFL head coach within five years if you take this deal,'" Logan recounted.

"I was very flattered and honestly, every fiber in my body wanted to accept the offer. But it just wasn't the right timing for me and my family," Logan said. "I called him the next day, told him how much I appreciated him and the offer, but said I had to decline."

With Gus Frerotte at quarterback, the Broncos' 2000 season ended with a 21–3 loss at Baltimore in the wild card round, when Denver managed just 177 yards, the club's third-lowest output in 28 playoff games.

Jake Plummer threw for 181 yards, a touchdown, and two interceptions in Denver's 41–10 loss to Peyton Manning and the Indianapolis Colts in the AFC wild card round that ended the Broncos' 2003 season.

Plummer did much better the following season, throwing for 284 yards with two touchdowns and one interception at the RCA Dome in

Indianapolis, but the result was similar: Manning piled up 458 yards and four touchdowns in a 49–24 wild-card win over the Broncos.

Plummer's breakthrough came after the 2005 season, when he helped Denver hand Tom Brady his first loss in 11 playoff games with a 27–13 win over the New England Patriots in an AFC divisional playoff game in Denver. Plummer didn't even top 200 yards passing, while Brady had 341 yards. But Brady was intercepted twice, including one that star cornerback Champ Bailey returned 100 yards in a highlight of his Hall of Fame career.

The Broncos were 14–3 and thrilled when the Pittsburgh Steelers upset Manning and the top-seeded Colts in Indianapolis 21–18. That set up an AFC championship in Denver between the sixth-seeded Steelers and the second-seeded Broncos.

An interception in his grasp. The end zone in his sights. Bailey was so close to another game-turning interception on January 22, 2006, a week after his spectacular 100-yard return. Steelers wide receiver Hines Ward was falling and the fluttering football hung in the air, along with the fortunes of two of the National Football League's most storied franchises. Somehow, Ward came down with the deflected pass and held tight through a jaw-jarring hit from safety John Lynch.

"It appeared right when Ben [Roethlisberger] threw it that Champ was going to the house," Lynch remembered. "Hines Ward made a great play to get his hands on the ball. The ball was hanging up there in slow motion, and I knew what a competitor and tough player Hines was, but I was sure I was going to knock the ball out. And I put a lick on him like all licks. He got up smiling at me, first down. He also stuck his knee right up my quad, so I was gimpy the rest of the game. I could barely run."

Ward smiled.

Lynch grimaced.

Bailey pounded the ground with his right fist.

Roethlisberger whooped.

The Broncos would never grab the lead, and three hours later they trudged off the field hanging their heads while the Steelers celebrated their 34–17 victory and their return to dominance like they'd enjoyed in the 1970s. They would reach three Super Bowls in a six-year span and win two of them, including Super Bowl XL two weeks later, 21–10 over the Seattle Seahawks.

"It was a tough game, because, gosh we had a great opportunity and I believe to this day that if we get through that game, we go beat Seattle and go win the Super Bowl," Lynch said.

In the aftermath of that devastation in Denver, Gary Kubiak, Elway's former backup, QB coach, and offensive coordinator, left for the Houston Texans' head coaching job, and Shanahan's go-between with his players was gone. Lynch has said losing Kubiak was as big a deal as losing that AFC Championship Game to Pittsburgh.

"First of all, there was that relationship with Jake Plummer that kind of fell apart after that," Lynch said. "I think probably more than that, Gary's a tremendous offensive mind and Mike had a lot of trust in him, and when he left I don't think we were the same team. I really don't." Shanahan never returned to the playoffs, going 9–7, 7–9, and 8–8 in his final three seasons in Denver—where team owner Pat Bowlen had previously dubbed him his "coach for life," something Shanahan believed right up to the point he was summoned to Bowlen's office on December 30, 2008.

"Lunch," Shanahan said when asked what he thought the meeting was about. But the Broncos, who had missed the playoffs for a third consecutive season by losing their last three games, including a 52–21 embarrassment at San Diego in the finale that allowed the Chargers to win the middling AFC West with an 8–8 record, had decided Shanahan was no longer the man to lead them.

Although he didn't do much in the playoffs once Elway retired, Shanahan went 146–91 in 14 seasons in Denver, including the playoffs, and he won five of the eight games against Bill Belichick's New England Patriots.

"I don't know Coach Belichick personally, but I do know Mike and have called a lot of games in which those two guys went after it, and to me they're very similar," Logan said. "I think Mike understood that when he played Bill, there was a pretty good chance that what he saw in preparing his team for the game, what he saw from the Patriots the

Mike Shanahan and John Elway had a heck of a run together in Denver. Overall, Shanahan went 146–91 in 14 seasons in Denver, including the playoffs.

previous three, four, five games, was not going to be what he saw to start the game. And then you almost had to be prepared to have a second game plan, because what Bill would give you to start a game defensively, at some point, the second quarter or sometimes second half, he would completely change.

"Mike was similar in that fashion. I thought he was a brilliant strategist, a great play caller. He was a numbers guy but he was a gut instinct guy," Logan said. "When they were rolling, I would put Mike Shanahan in the top five play designers and callers the league has ever seen. He'd have his first 15 scripted and you go back and look at the success they had, especially '96, '97, and '98: they're blowing out people early in games. They would get on top of you and just strangle you. But it was always a great matchup with Mike and Bill, two of the great coaches in NFL history. It was fun to see the strategy involved and the game of chess, because that's exactly what it was."

While Belichick had Tom Brady for two decades with the Patriots, Shanahan only had his Hall of Fame quarterback with him for his first four seasons as Denver's head coach. Of course, Shanahan didn't find the same measure of success with subsequent quarterbacks that he had with Elway, one of the greatest of all time.

"People talk a lot about the record Belichick has, and it's true. If you go back and look when he was head coach of the Browns, it was a different story. Although, he was close to getting that thing turned around," Logan said.

Belichick was 36–44 in Cleveland between 1991 and 1995, including 11–5 in 1994 when the Browns went 1–1 in the playoffs, their only trip to the postseason during his tenure.

"It boils down to the guy you have at quarterback. Unless you have a guy that you can hang your hat on, it's really tough over a sustained period of time to be considered a great coach," Logan said. "It's hard enough to win in the league, period. But unless you have one of 'those guys' at quarterback, it's almost impossible to win consistently. And that's been proven to be true throughout the history of the league.

Maybe Vince Lombardi's considered the greatest coach ever, he had Bart Starr. Chuck Noll won four Super Bowls, he had Terry Bradshaw. I mean, Hall of Fame coaches normally have Hall of Fame quarterbacks. Bill Walsh and George Siefert had Joe Montana and Steve Young. Don Shula had Bob Griese and Dan Marino, both in the Hall of Fame. That's one thing that has not really changed much in the NFL."

In fact, the only Hall of Fame coaches who didn't have Hall of Fame cohorts at quarterback were Joe Gibbs, whose Washington Redskins won Super Bowl titles with Joe Theismann, Doug Williams, and Mark Rypien at quarterback, and Belichick's mentor, Bill Parcells, who won Super Bowls with Phil Simms and Jeff Hostetler.

"That's a position you've got to be settled on," Logan said. "It's got to be *The* Guy; it can't just be any guy. You look at Baltimore now and the success they have. Well, it's largely due to Lamar Jackson and John Harbaugh completely altering his offensive system to fit the skill set of his young quarterback. Now, we'll see what happens in the next three, four, five years, but it's sure a lot of fun to watch now. Look at Drew Brees and Sean Payton. How many seasons have those guys been together? Historically in the NFL when you start talking about a Hall of Fame–worthy coach, you can usually go back and find that guy worked with a Hall of Fame quarterback for a long time.

"And you can look at it from the other perspective, too. You can say Hall of Fame quarterbacks usually have worked for great coaches. So it takes one to have the other, in a lot of cases."

Logan always enjoyed doing his weekly shows with Shanahan, talking strategy and football with the man who came to be known as "the Mastermind," the king of finding and exploiting the mismatch.

"Mike was great with me," Logan said. "He wasn't going to give you much of the game plan in terms of the pregame show, but he still would make it entertaining."

Shanahan was calculating in what he would say on the air. "I think Mike was a brilliant strategist and technician and understood the game as well as anybody I've ever been around," Logan said. "But he also understood the media game. He didn't have much time for guys who didn't really work at their craft. That wasn't his thing. You had to earn his respect from a football knowledge standpoint. We had some great conversations on and off the record."

Shanahan was always acutely aware of who was saying what and who was writing what about him and his team. "Mike always has been a very intense guy, and he was keenly aware of everything that was said during the week about him or his team. If you said something that he disagreed with, he might call you to talk about it. And then he might try to persuade you that you were looking at it the wrong way," Logan said. "But if he thought you were taking a cheap shot or being mean-spirited or just didn't know what you were talking about, he'd call you out on it every time. It was war."

Players and coaches often like to feign indifference to what is said and written about them on the airwaves and in the news media, even if they're tuned in to social media posts, but Shanahan was keenly aware of all the news coverage of his team. Just as he had staff produce reports on the upcoming opponent, he pored over the daily newspaper clippings when he arrived at work at the team's Dove Valley training complex before dawn each day, and whenever he had the chance he'd watch the city's television stations and listen to the sports talk shows on the radio.

Shanahan gained more and more power over personnel decisions the longer he was with the Broncos and by the final few years, Mike Shanahan the vice president of football operations wasn't doing Mike Shanahan the head coach many favors.

Shanahan's one-cut, zone blocking scheme had helped him overcome Terrell Davis' retirement as the Broncos churned out successful running backs in Olandis Gary, Reuben Droughns, and Tatum Bell, all unheralded tailbacks who ran for 1,000-plus-yard seasons in Denver, leading to the notion that anyone could gain yardage in Shanahan's system. But Shanahan also burned through three starting quarterbacks, five defensive coordinators, and many millions of dollars trying to get the Broncos back to the Super Bowl in the decade after No. 7 retired.

The last straw for both Shanahan the personnel man and Shanahan the sideline strategist came with a 52–21 loss at San Diego on December 28, 2008, when the Broncos became the first team since divisional play started way back in 1967 to blow a three-game lead with three games left to play. The brunt of the blame was a dreadful defense—one built by Shanahan.

But nobody really saw the end coming. Bowlen had always been fiercely loyal to his head coach, who constantly modernized his schemes to keep ahead of the curve in an ever-changing league. Shanahan was opening a steakhouse in Denver and building a 35,000-square foot house in Denver, and he had three years and $20 million left on his contract.

So, it was a shock when the Broncos emailed out a press release quoting Bowlen: "After giving this careful consideration, I have concluded that a change in our football operations is in the best interests of the Denver Broncos." The simplest of reasons for the most difficult of decisions.

"This is as tough as it gets," Bowlen said he next day, his eyes moist as he explained his decision to fire the coach who had finally brought not one but two Super bowl trophies to Denver.

Shanahan, too, choked back tears. "These are tough decisions," Shanahan said, "but that's what leaders do."

By reflex, Shanahan often used the word "we" when discussing the team who had just handed him divorce papers. "This is the best I've felt about the team in the last five, six years," Shanahan said regretfully. "They're young, they're character guys, the direction we're going."

The Broncos had several young rising offensive stars, guys like Jay Cutler, Brandon Marshall, and rookie Ryan Clady, but the defense needed lots of help. Still, Shanahan figured Denver was just one solid draft and a few good free-agent signings away from shoring that up.

"Pat Bowlen and I will be best friends forever," Shanahan insisted. "He stood by me when I had to make tough decisions. I know this was tougher on him than it was on me."

Bowlen acknowledged that he had often called Shanahan his coach for life. "I guess nothing's forever," Bowlen said with a sigh.

With tears in their eyes, Pat Bowlen and Mike Shanahan said their sad farewell after more than 20 years together in Denver. "I may end up regretting this decision," Bowlen admitted.

# CHAPTER 14
## THE WUNDERKIND

After becoming the first NFL owner ever to fire a coach who had led his team to consecutive Super Bowl triumphs, Denver Broncos owner Pat Bowlen hired Josh McDaniels, the 32-year-old wunderkind from the New England Patriots, to replace the mastermind, Mike Shanahan, whom he'd just tearfully removed from the organization, if not the payroll.

The Broncos' new head coach was 25 years younger than Shanahan, but like his predecessor, who won two Super Bowl rings in Denver and one in San Francisco, McDaniels owned three Super Bowl rings himself having worked with Tom Brady and Bill Belichick in New England. He aimed to bring more both to himself and to Denver.

"Josh McDaniels is one of the finest people and brightest, most talented coaches I have ever worked with," Belichick said upon McDaniels' hiring in Denver. "Since joining us eight years ago, Josh performed a variety of roles and excelled in every one of them."

In his first season in Denver McDaniels would win his first six games, including a 20–17 victory over his mentor in overtime in 2008, when his hiring began to look like a stroke of genius by Bowlen. Shanahan had won just a single playoff game in the decade since John Elway's retirement—although it was against the Patriots after the 2005 season, when McDaniels was Brady's position coach. The Patriots were on the cusp of the go-ahead score in an AFC divisional playoff game at Denver when cornerback Champ Bailey, whom Shanahan had acquired from Washington in a blockbuster trade for running back Clinton Portis, swiped Brady's hurried pass in the end zone and returned it 100 yards. That sparked Denver's 27–13 victory over New England, saddling Brady with his first loss in the playoffs after 10 victories and three Super Bowl trophies in a four-year span.

It was after that season that Belichick officially promoted McDaniels to offensive coordinator. He also kept his title as quarterbacks coach and two years later, McDaniels designed the offensive plays when the powerful Patriots set NFL records by scoring an astonishing 75 touchdowns and scoring 589 points—and landing within a whisker of becoming the first NFL team to go 19–0 in a season.

Trailing 14–10 in Super Bowl XLII at University of Phoenix Stadium in Glendale, Arizona, New York Giants quarterback Eli Manning somehow escaped the grasp of three New England defenders and lofted a 32-yard pass to David Tyree, who famously pinned the ball against his helmet and held on as he fell backward at the Patriots 24-yard line with 59 seconds left. That set up Manning's 13-yard fade pass to Plaxico Burress with 35 seconds remaining for the winning touchdown that denied the Patriots perfection.

Shortly after that heartbreaking loss, Belichick gave McDaniels a five-page typed report on what it takes to be an effective head coach and run a winning organization. McDaniels called this golden blueprint his football bible, and he religiously followed the readings from the Letter of Belichick to McDaniels to prepare for his crack at becoming a head coach in the NFL.

Seven months later, Brady suffered a season-ending knee injury in the 2008 season opener, leading to predictions of doom and gloom and projections of a losing season for the team that had come so tantalizingly close to perfection the year before. McDaniels, however, only burnished his credentials, padding his résumé by directing the New England offense under backup quarterback Matt Cassell to another double-digit win season. The Patriots ultimately finished 11–5 in 2008 but missed the playoffs. (Miami and Baltimore also went 11–5 that season and both teams had better conference records that New England. So, the Dolphins won the AFC East crown and the Ravens earned the second wild-card spot.)

Bowlen felt the Patriots' pain. Since the NFL adopted its 16-game regular-season schedule in 1978, only one other 11–5 team missed out on the playoffs: the Denver Broncos in 1995. The Broncos finished a game behind the Los Angeles Raiders in the AFC West in '95 and lost out on the wild-card tiebreakers to the New York Jets and the Patriots. The Jets earned the first wild-card spot by virtue of their better conference record among the three 11–5 teams, and the Patriots' superior record against common opponents trumped the Broncos for the second wild-card spot. Adding insult to injury, the Broncos stayed home and the Cleveland Browns advanced, winning the AFC Central with an 8–8 record.

The Broncos' late collapse that led to Mike Shanahan's firing allowed the San Diego Chargers to win the middling AFC West with an 8–8 record. But one good thing came out of this scenario for both the Broncos and Josh McDaniels: because the Patriots weren't busy marching toward another Super Bowl, the Patriots assistant was free to interview right away with Denver about its sudden and surprising head coaching vacancy.

Also interviewing for the coveted job in Denver were several candidates with deep defensive roots: Steve Spagnuolo of the Giants, Raheem Morris of the Tampa Bay Buccaneers, and Leslie Frazier of the Minnesota Vikings.

Even though the Broncos were coming off a season in which they gave up more points and collected fewer takeaways than any team in the NFL, Bowlen zeroed in on the man who had guided a New England offense that led the Patriots to 18 consecutive victories and had come within 38 seconds of perfection in the previous year's Super Bowl.

"What I was trying to do was pick the best guy," Bowlen explained. "It didn't matter really that much whether it was an offensive or defensive guy; he's going to be the head coach. I think Josh has the ability to go out and find a very good defensive coordinator."

The man behind the Patriots' scoring machine inherited an offense in Denver that seemingly needed only a tweak here and there but a defense in need of a major overhaul. Much like Shanahan, McDaniels came to Denver with a reputation for constantly coming up with creative formations, turning the usual Xs and Os into *Xs* and *Os* as he stayed fresh and innovative in the ever-evolving NFL.

Bowlen, who still owed Shanahan $21 million over the next three seasons, signed off on a four-year, $8 million deal to bring McDaniels to Denver.

Meanwhile, Shanahan set up shop in a nearby strip mall, renting out space to watch game film and plot his coaching comeback, which would come a year later with the Washington Redskins, relieving Bowlen of some of the millions he still owed his former coach.

Dave Logan was sad to see Shanahan go. They had known each other since 1984, when Logan was still an NFL wide receiver and had just been traded to his hometown Broncos. The man who picked him up at the airport was Shanahan, who had just gotten his first NFL job when Dan Reeves hired him off the University of Florida's football staff to coach Denver's wide receivers.

While Shanahan would end up as the Broncos' head coach after a short stint with the division rival Oakland Raiders, Logan worked his way up through various radio and television gigs in his post-playing career to become the play-by-play voice of the Broncos.

Logan would soon realize that he'd have a good working relationship with the fuzzy-faced whiz kid, too. "Josh was great. He would pretty much answer anything," Logan recounted. "If I asked him about how he viewed the Chiefs secondary—knowing that they'd had some issues the previous two or three games—he might say, 'Oh yeah, here today we ought to have some success in the middle of the field, depending on personnel groupings and formations. We feel like we can work on both of their safeties." And he would say stuff like that where nobody else would go that far—I mean, pretty much he just told me, *Their safeties suck.* It was really insightful stuff coming from a head coach, where normally most coaches I'd dealt with were reticent to ever say anything like that in our pregame show. Now, it wasn't like the Chiefs were listening to the pregame show, and I really don't know whether it was Josh just being completely forthright and entertaining, or it was just a young coach not completely understanding that those were things that normally weren't said. But he was terrific to interview."

The Broncos' 24–24 record over Shanahan's final three seasons in Denver was unacceptable to Bowlen. (Although that was a level of play the Broncos faithful would gladly have taken during their three consecutive losing seasons from 2017 to 2019 during the franchise's ever-turning coaching carousel and perpetual musical chairs game at quarterback.) Bowlen reached out to a man half his age to resurrect his once-proud but now floundering franchise.

McDaniels insisted that being so young had never been a negative factor in New England and he was determined to make sure it wasn't going to be an issue in Denver. McDaniels had been around football fields since he was a boy hanging out at the high school in Canton, Ohio, where his father coached in the shadow of the Pro Football Hall of Fame.

The engineer of the Patriots' powerful offense inherited another high-octane bunch in Denver that featured strong-armed quarterback Jay Cutler, wide receivers Eddie Royal and Brandon Marshall, tight end Tony Scheffler, and tackles Ryan Harris and Ryan Clady. That group just hadn't been able to make up for a dreadful defense that yielded a league-high 448 points in 2008 and pried away an NFL-low 13 take-aways. He hired former 49ers head coach Mike Nolan as his defensive coordinator to turn things around.

McDaniels said his coaching philosophies were shaped by Bill Belichick, Charlie Weis, and Nick Saban, who had given him his first job as a graduate assistant at Michigan State in 1999. Along with three Super Bowl rings from his time in New England, McDaniels said he would bring the trio's influences with him to Denver—along with a little something that Belichick, Weis, and Saban weren't really known for.

"I think you'll certainly see me bring a little bit of a different vibe," McDaniels promised, revealing that he would wear a hoodie on the sideline just like his mentor Belichick. The scowl? He'd leave that in Foxborough.

"I'm going to have a lot of energy," McDaniels said. "I can smile." Indeed, he had every reason to beam. The baby-faced up-and-comer who never had been a head coach in high school or college was now calling the shots at age 32 for one of the league's most iconic franchises.

Cutler wasn't happy about Shanahan's firing, and he was upset when his position coach, Jeremy Bates, bolted for USC after McDaniels declared he'd be the one calling plays in Denver now.

When he hired McDaniels, Bowlen proclaimed that Cutler "is the man around here now." Not for long he wasn't.

When Bowlen fired Shanahan, he said he'd decided not to give his replacement as much power and would search for a general manager after finding his new coach. Once he hired McDaniels, however, Bowlen decided instead to promote assistant GM Brian Xanders to general manager. But it was McDaniels who in many ways would end up calling the shots as he built his roster, and he'd even wheel and deal on his own. Before McDaniels would even coach his first game, he'd add another job to his title that he'd never had: de facto general manager.

A similar setup of dual duties is exactly what ultimately buried Shanahan. "I think it's really tough to be a great head coach and the guy to oversee every single personnel decision," Logan said. With the way things are done today with the draft, free agency, and all those personnel moves, it's tough on anybody to wear both of those hats.

"I thought Mike was a brilliant football coach," Logan continued. "I've always thought that. One of the all-time greats in that regard. But I think the job was too big, too all-consuming, to be able to do everything that you have to do and basically run the football operation and also be the head coach."

That's no knock on Shanahan. "I can understand the want to do it, right? Because guys want to have a say and they want to be in charge of who they take in the draft and who they sign in free agency. I understand that. It reminds me of the famous Bill Parcells line, 'If you're going to make me cook the dinner, then I want to be in charge of buying the groceries.'

"Looking back, I think Mike had a tremendous run. And when you talk about coaching in the NFL and staying somewhere that long—14 years—it just doesn't happen that many times."

McDaniels would soon learn that same painful lesson.

# CHAPTER 15

## HECTIC HONEYMOON

Pat Bowlen figured Jay Cutler and Josh McDaniels would make the perfect pair, just like John Elway and Mike Shanahan had been so good together a decade earlier when Denver was celebrating back-to-back Super Bowl victories. But a rocky relationship would quickly develop between his cranky 25-year-old rocket-armed but thin-skinned quarterback and the novice 32-year-old first-time head coach, whose stint shadowing Bill Belichick for several seasons equipped him with the National Football League's equivalent of an Ivy League education. It would end in an ugly divorce before McDaniels ever had a chance to call a play for Cutler.

Cutler was finally starting to get over Shanahan's firing and the subsequent departure of his position coach, Jeremy Bates. He told McDaniels in February he was eager to learn the Broncos' new offense. Cutler even told people at team headquarters he and McDaniels were going to light up the league. But that all changed on February 28, when Cutler and his agent learned that McDaniels had talked about trading him to the Tampa Bay Buccaneers in a three-way deal that would have brought McDaniels' protégé, Matt Cassel, from New England to Denver.

When Tom Brady blew out a knee in the 2008 regular season opener, Cassel, who hadn't started since high school, stepped in and led the Patriots to an 11–5 record, sending McDaniels' stock soaring as a head coaching candidate that next hiring cycle.

By the time McDaniels landed in Denver, Brady was on the mend and Cassel was on the move. The deal didn't get done in Denver— Belichick ended up sending Cassel to the Broncos' AFC West division rival Kansas City Chiefs instead—but the damage in Denver between coach and quarterback was already done.

Having just returned from his first Pro Bowl, Cutler was incredulous to learn that McDaniels, after assuring him he was his guy, had talked to other teams about trading him. Cutler and his agent, Bus Cook, complained that McDaniels hadn't been upfront with them about his trade talks, and the feud festered for weeks.

Fans took sides. Some lined up behind Cutler—he wouldn't really force his way out of town just to end up on a bad team, would he? Others got behind McDaniels—he wouldn't really want to let go of his best player and locker room leader, would he?

One player McDaniels did get to bring with him to Denver was free-agent wide receiver Jabar Gaffney, who said during the off-season training program that year that McDaniels was just like Belichick, both on the football field and in player personnel decision-making. "Just how he handles business, the way he goes about treating everybody the same. Not showing favoritism to any one player who is supposed to be I guess a 'star,'" Gaffney said. "They don't care. They want a team. A team to go out there and win—because the individuals won't win."

Gaffney saw those philosophies firsthand when McDaniels was New England's offensive coordinator during the previous three seasons, when even Brady caught plenty of guff from McDaniels. "Yeah, I think Tom got [criticized] just about as much as everybody else did," Gaffney said with a chuckle. "So that's great. Once you see your quarterback get talked to, then you know Coach is showing no favoritism. Everybody has to show up and play."

Which is exactly what the Broncos wanted Cutler, the face of their franchise, to do. Two meetings designed to clear the air only raised Cutler's level of distrust. But McDaniels remained resolute, insisting they would work things out. He declared at the NFL's owners meetings in the last week of March that he would do everything he could to repair their fractured relationship.

But when Cutler refused to return the Broncos' phone calls, Bowlen had heard enough. He gave his new brain trust of McDaniels and Brian Xanders the go-ahead to shop around the quarterback who had made the Pro Bowl in his second season as a starter. On April 2, 2009, Cutler got his wish when the Broncos traded their disgruntled Pro Bowl passer to the Chicago Bears for veteran quarterback Kyle Orton, two first-round draft picks, and a third-rounder.

In his 37-game career in Denver, Cutler was 17–20 but an impressive 13–1 when Denver held opponents to 21 points or less. Now he would get to play for the Bears, the team he rooted for while growing up in tiny Santa Claus, Indiana. But he sure would miss Denver's offensive line, anchored by left tackle Ryan Clady.

After chasing away his best player, McDaniels jettisoned the father-son duo that had been building the team's draft board. Upon Xanders' promotion to GM, the Broncos fired fellow assistant general manager Jeff Goodman and his father, Jim, who was the Broncos' vice president of football operations. What followed was one of the worst drafts in franchise history as McDaniels frittered away some of the capital he had acquired from Chicago in the Cutler trade.

Denver had two first-round picks in 2009 and selected running back Knowshon Moreno at No. 12 and defensive end Robert Ayers at No. 18. Those were solid picks, but neither player turned into a star befitting his high draft status. A trio of second-rounders, cornerback Alfonso Smith, safety Darcel McBath, and tight end Richard Quinn—who admitted on a conference call moments after getting drafted that he wasn't even expecting to get picked in the seventh round, much less as the 62$^{nd}$ overall pick in the second round—all flamed out. Of Denver's 10 picks that year, only safety David Bruton Jr. turned into a longtime contributor, mostly on special teams.

Still, McDaniels won his first six games as head coach, including the overtime win against Belichick, but then came a 2–8 freefall that rendered the Broncos just the third team since the 1970 AFL-NFL merger to squander a 6–0 start and miss the playoffs altogether.

McDaniels began his tenure by chasing off Cutler and ended his first season with star receiver Brandon Marshall and tight end Tony Scheffler in his doghouse over behavioral issues. He accused Marshall of exaggerating a hamstring injury, but never gave a reason for deactivating Scheffler in the crucial season finale that the Broncos lost to Kansas City. The next day, Marshall and Scheffler embraced on their way out of Dove Valley for the last time. They joined a long list of holdovers from the Shanahan era who punched their ticket out of town in the aftermath of Shanahan's firing.

Guard Ben Hamilton was benched in favor of Russ Hochstein, one of several players McDaniels brought with him from New England. Wide receiver Eddie Royal went from 91 receptions to 37, from five touchdowns to zero. Slot receiver Brandon Stokley's catches dipped from 49 to 19. Right tackle Ryan Harris was pressured to return to action despite a broken toe and ended up on injured reserve. Peyton Hillis went from starting tailback to forgotten fullback.

"Any locker room's going to have its issues with a new coach and 60 percent new guys and 40 percent holdovers from the old regime, the old system," Scheffler said. "There's obviously going to be issues, and I think Coach is working on taking those issues away. If that means moving players out of here and kind of getting his own deal going, then that's the NFL. That's something you've got to deal with. That's why there's 32 teams."

McDaniels didn't set out to make Shanahan's players less involved in 2009, but switching systems takes its toll on players who were brought in to do different things. "Maybe it's harder, maybe it's easier. Some maybe embrace it and some may not. But each system brings with it different challenges for players," McDaniels said. "I think that the first year of a new system is not totally different than a rookie having to learn a new offense himself because that's what some of these guys had to do.

"Same thing on defense. And some guys may end up having more production because of it. Elvis [Dumervil, who had 17 sacks] is an example of a guy who flourished defensively, and Brandon had a very similar year to what he had before. I think it's a case-by-case basis. Again, we weren't working with the same philosophy I know they had worked with previously."

Two other holdovers, punter Brett Kern—who's still in the league in 2020—and defensive back Jack Williams, were waived during the season and were quickly signed by other teams. All this didn't go unnoticed in the locker room.

"I do understand how this league works and new coaches love to have their guys," superstar cornerback Champ Bailey said. "That's been a staple in this league for a long time. I mean, whether it's bringing in coaches that you want or bringing in players that you want, that's just the way it is. And if you fit into what the new coach wants, then more than likely you'll stay around. But obviously when a coach brings you in, you're his guy. I am one of the holdovers, so who's to say whether I fit into their future plans or not?" McDaniels said he did, but in 2010 he would stall contract talks for an extension with Bailey.

A powerful coach making decisions on the sideline and the front office. An 8–8 record after a late-season pratfall. Sounds a lot like the last coach.

"It was interesting that what they didn't like about Mike in terms of having complete control and the ultimate power they pretty much gave to Josh right off the bat," Logan said. "I'll say this about Josh: I think he's a very, very bright football coach. But I think, if you look at the history of Bill Belichick's history of assistant coaches and you look at their success...you can count the really successful ones on one hand and have a lot of fingers leftover.

"I think Bill is a master of identifying the strengths of a coach and then putting him in the position to where he can really be useful and have success in that position but he might not—and more than likely doesn't—know everything about the organization and how the organization is run," Logan said. "And I've had people tell me that about how New England runs their organization with Belichick. I mean, look at the assistants that have come out of there: almost universally they just, when they first get that opportunity, don't have success. Then again, even Belichick was fired from his first job, as the Cleveland Browns head coach. But look at him now."

A week after McDaniels' first season in Denver ended, the NFL announced that the Broncos and the 49ers would play in London on Halloween 2010. Nobody knew it at the time, but this would mark the beginning of the end of McDaniels' short stint in Denver.

McDaniels was big on catchphrases. As he settled into his new job, he put his stamp on the organization by having various motivational messages painted on the walls throughout team headquarters such as Iron Sharpens Iron and The Eye in the Sky Doesn't Lie.

In some ways McDaniels was better in his second season as head coach of the Broncos. He followed his dismal first draft with an outstanding 2010 class featuring first-rounders Demaryius Thomas, who had a long stint as Denver's best receiver, and Tim Tebow, who burned bright before flaming out. Other members of that year's rookie class were Zane Beadles, Eric Decker, and J.D. Walton.

But McDaniels didn't start off with a bang like he had a year earlier. After finishing his first season with a 2–6 slide, the Broncos began 2010 by dropping six of their first eight games. A year earlier, the fiery McDaniels was chewing out players on the sideline. Now, he was chewing his fingernails.

He'd only make it through 12 games that year before getting fired with a 3–9 record amid a series of embarrassments, including Denver's own version of "Spygate," a sequel to the original video flap in New England in which the Patriots were caught videotaping an opponents' signals on the sideline. A member of the Broncos' video crew, Steve Scarnecchia, had followed McDaniels from Foxborough to Denver. The son of longtime Patriots offensive line coach Dante Scarnecchia, he illegally filmed the 49ers' practice ahead of the game in London, and McDaniels failed to report the rules infraction as required.

Spygate, as Boston-based Associated Press sports writer Jimmy Golen noted when the Patriots found themselves dealing with another videotape infraction in 2019, "helped fuel a widespread distrust of the Patriots that reverberated a decade later when the Patriots were accused of illegally deflating footballs used in the 2015 AFC Championship Game." Brady was suspended four games, and the team was fined $1 million and docked a first-round draft pick.

"I think Josh will eventually get another shot at being a head coach," Logan said. "I think the Indianapolis thing [when McDaniels reneged on his agreement to coach the Colts after the Patriots lost Super Bowl LII to the Philadelphia Eagles] did not help him in terms of how the league views him. But I do think Josh will get another chance to be a head coach. And you know what? I think he'll learn from some of the things that he did in Denver. And it wouldn't surprise me if he has some real success."

McDaniels never did win over the holdovers from the Shanahan era. "You have to be careful how you choose to interact with NFL players," Logan said. "It's real simple for players. They look at a new coach and say, *Do you know what you're talking about? Can you help me get better? Because if you can help me get better, we're going to games and I'm eventually going to make more money.* But you've got to be careful when you first walk in the building. You don't walk in with any street cred just because you've been a very successful assistant coach on a Super Bowl championship team. That's not how NFL locker rooms work. Players have got to get a feel for you and your style. And you've got to be deliberate and careful with every interaction initially.

"I knew of some of the interaction that was happening on the sideline and how it really bugged Broncos players, because I had a couple of veterans tell me that. There was a Jets game in Denver, a game in which the Broncos played pretty well but didn't win—and I had players tell me that the next week, Josh went absolutely crazy on them in practice," added Logan. Players were getting their asses chewed. Coaches weren't spared, either.

"There's a way NFL guys get used to practicing," Logan continued. "And you're not going to be able to reinvent the wheel and change that very much based on how your team played the weekend before. Josh had them in full pads that week and really went after them. It was probably too quick for him to use that tactic, and honestly, it sounds strange, but he probably didn't have enough credibility with that team to go after them like that.

"And you know what happened? The next game in Denver, they came out, played the Raiders, and lost 59–14. They just completely stopped playing. It was a game that I remember calling on the radio and saying, 'This is one of the worst showings that I can remember from a Broncos team.' It was embarrassing. And when that happens, you can't fire two handfuls of players. Ultimately, it's going to cost the coach his job. It was bad—real bad."

It was about to get a whole lot worse the following week in London, where the Broncos lost to the 49ers 24–16, hitting the midway point of the 2010 season at 2–6.

Unlike Shanahan, McDaniels didn't like talking to local media members one-on-one off to the side of the podium after news conferences. So even sensitive questions had to be tossed out for the TV stations all to replay on their newscasts. After one particularly harsh grilling, McDaniels stepped off the podium and told a member of the team's public relations staff that he thought he had lost the media room; nobody was defending him, everyone seemed out for blood. The thing was, he never had the media room to lose. He never fostered relationships outside of the football operations. And now he was paying the price as his team was spiraling out of control.

"You'd better get used to finding some sort of common ground with those who buy their ink by the barrel," Logan said. "If you think you're going to walk in and say, 'Listen, I'm going to tell you how this shit's going to work this week,' then you'd better win a lot of games. If you win a lot of games, you can tell all of us how this shit's going to work."

But when McDaniels did nothing to foster relationships with members of the media, he had nowhere to turn when things spiraled out of control. "Nobody came to his rescue," Logan said. "It was a learning process for him. My hope for him moving forward is that he learns a few lessons from that experience—and I think he will.… If I were making a suggestion to Josh as he gets his second chance to be a head coach in the league, I'd tell him this: you should get to know every single person in the media who covers your team. Get to know them by name and use their names a lot when you talk to them. Get to know who you can trust and get to know the big hitters in the market, the people the audience listens to or reads. Those are the ones who sway opinion, and you're better off acknowledging that and trying to find common ground. And then I would suggest he also identifies the sort of shitheads and give them one chance to change how they cover the team. And if they don't, I'd let them know that they're going to have to learn how to answer questions on their own."

Take McDaniels' spat with San Diego Chargers outside linebacker Shaun Phillips in McDaniels' first year in Denver. Before a home game in late November, the Broncos' brash young coach exchanged taunts with a group of Chargers linebackers during warm-ups, at one point telling them, "We own you!" Then, he watched those same players lead a 32–3 rout of his free-falling team that knocked the Broncos out of first place in the AFC West and sent them tumbling to their fourth straight loss.

McDaniels brushed aside questions about his heated pregame exchange and the wisdom of jawing at an opponent before a game. His main target was Phillips, whose strip sack of Chris Simms on his first dropback set the tone for San Diego's statement victory.

"As a coach, I hope he has that mind-set, but to say you own us? You beat us one time," said Phillips, who is just five years younger than McDaniels. "How much has he really done in this league? He had a team 6–0 and now he's looking up at us in second place."

While McDaniels refused to address the exchange, his trash talk became the talk of the league.

Denver safety David Bruton Jr. said he didn't see anything wrong with his coach jawing with the opponent: "It shows that he cares and is fighting for his team. Our coach is an emotional coach, he is a very fiery coach. He has a lot of passion for the game and for the Broncos. What he did wasn't Woody Hayes. Hayes would reach up and hit you on the side of the head."

Which is what Pittsburgh Steelers safety Ryan Clark suggested players should be allowed to do when coaches taunt players from the other team: "Honestly, my thought on that is, I would like to petition

Mr. [Roger] Goodell and say, if a coach can talk to me like that, I should be able to fight him. I don't know where he's from, but where I'm from, when somebody talks to you like that, they've got a problem with you. And we should be able to fight."

By November 2010, McDaniels found himself fighting for his job after a series of embarrassing episodes, a yearlong slide and the videotape scandal in London, after which McDaniels and the Broncos each were fined $50,000 and Scarnecchia was fired. The Broncos pledged to restore a sullied reputation as they tried to sway skeptics. They had convinced the NFL that Scarnecchia acted alone in filming San Francisco's practice in London and that nobody ordered him to do it or even viewed the incriminating tape.

The NFL called Scarnecchia a repeat offender, and the Broncos' embittered fan base wondered why McDaniels was allowed to hire a buddy who had already run afoul of the league and why he didn't do anything about it when Scarnecchia brought him an illicit six-minute snippet of the 49ers practice on the eve of Denver's game against San Francisco.

This was not the first time Bowlen had found his team at the center of controversy. The Broncos were penalized for violating salary cap rules back in the 1990s when they were winning Super Bowls under Mike Shanahan. Now, they were breaking rules *and* losing games, a toxic combination.

Days later, more bad news surfaced for the staggering franchise. Almost three months after injured Broncos wide receiver Kenny McKinley killed himself at his home not far from the team's training facilities, the Associated Press obtained an investigative report by the Arapahoe County Sheriff's Department that revealed McKinley had a gambling problem and was deep in debt when he died.

The report also noted he shot himself with a gun he'd bought from teammate Jabar Gaffney and that the Broncos were aware of McKinley's dire financial straits because ex-Broncos backup quarterback Tom Brandstater had lent him $65,000 and the team's player development director, Harold Chatman, had been asked by Brandstater's representative to hold onto a copy of a contract Brandstater had with McKinley, stating McKinley would repay the $65,000 loan.

Because he was on injured reserve after suffering a season-ending knee injury during training camp, McKinley would receive $240,000 that year instead of $395,000. He told friends he was worried about how he would support his toddler son after his football career was over. A few weeks after undergoing his knee operation, McKinley retrieved the gun he'd bought off Gaffney, put the barrel to his left temple at his rental home near the Broncos' practice facility, and pulled the trigger.

"Kenny told me he wanted a gun for his personal protection and being that I have a couple of legally owned firearms, I sold him one of mine that I didn't want anymore," Gaffney said in a statement to deputies.

After falling to 3–9 with a 10–6 loss to Kansas City in a Sunday night game, the Broncos returned to Denver. It was after 1:00 AM on that freezing morning. Logan had guided his high school team to another state championship that weekend. "Most of the Broncos coaches and players were already on their buses to head from the airport back to Dove Valley," Logan recounted. "I had just grabbed my bag and was walking across the tarmac to my car when Josh got off Bus 1 and ran about 20 yards to stop me. He extended his hand and said, 'Hey Dave, congratulations on the win yesterday. That's a pretty cool thing.' I really appreciated that gesture from a guy who was in the midst of a really tough season and had just lost a big game about three hours earlier." Later that morning, McDaniels insisted at his Monday news conference he had no reason to suspect his job was in jeopardy. Two hours later, he was summoned to Bowlen's office and let go.

While they kicked him to the curb, the Broncos didn't throw McDaniels under the bus. After determining that two-time Super Bowl winner Shanahan had amassed too much power, the Broncos pledged they wouldn't give McDaniels the same amount of responsibility when they hired him as Shanahan's replacement in January 2009. Yet they did exactly that.

Speaking on behalf of Bowlen, then–chief operating officer Joe Ellis said the organization accepted the blame for giving McDaniels too much power too soon and with so little experience. "I think the responsibilities that he was burdened with, it's fair to say that we probably burdened him with too much of that and we were unfair to him in that respect," Ellis said. He added that the next coach probably wouldn't have as much say in personnel matters.

McDaniels, who was 32 when he was hired, had no head coaching experience at any level and had never made personnel decisions when he was handed the keys to the franchise. What cost McDaniels wasn't running off Cutler or Marshall, his best two offensive players, or inexplicably scuttling contract negations with Bailey, his best player on defense. Ultimately, it was his hiring of Scarnecchia, whose secret tape of the 49ers' practice in London would weigh heavily in McDaniels' dismissal five weeks later.

Ellis said he told McDaniels upon his firing that he still believed in him. "I said, 'I'm disappointed that it didn't work out for you but you're going to be a good coach. Unfortunately, it's going to be somewhere else,'" Ellis recounted. "I think he'll grow from this and learn from it and you know his intellectual mind when it comes to football is...superior, it's terrific."

McDaniels was the fourth disciple of Belichick to get fired from his first head coaching job, joining Romeo Crennel in Cleveland, Eric Mangini with the Jets, and Charlie Weis with the University of Notre Dame.

McDaniels drove off into the night in his silver Range Rover with a honk and a wave, but not a comment to reporters gathered outside the parking gate.

"I was disappointed to see that for Josh. Unfortunately, I know what it feels like," said Belichick, who was fired from his first job in Cleveland.

McDaniels would spend a year as the St. Louis Rams' offensive coordinator under head coach Steve Spagnuolo, who had been the Giants' defensive coordinator in Super Bowl XLII while McDaniels was coordinating the Patriots' offense. Spagnuolo was fired after the 2011 season and McDaniels was allowed to leave even though he was under contract for the 2012 season. The Patriots rehired McDaniels as an offensive assistant coach during their 2011 playoff run and he resumed his role as offensive coordinator and Brady's position coach when Bill O'Brien left to coach Penn State following the playoffs. O'Brien maintained play calling duties through Super Bowl XLVI.

In his second stint with Brady, McDaniels would win another three Super Bowl rings. He was hired as the Colts' head coach after the 2017 season but after New England's loss to the Eagles in Super Bowl LII, McDaniels changed his mind and decided to stay with Brady, Belichick, and team owner Robert Kraft in New England. His longtime agent, Bob LaMonte, terminated his representation of McDaniels.

"I think he clearly made a mistake in accepting the job if he wasn't completely certain he was going to take it," Logan said. "What I was told is that both Belichick and Kraft convinced him late in the process that it was not a great move. But it's still his name, and it wasn't a good look for Josh even if some understood it. Honestly, I would not be surprised if he's the next coach of New England. I could see that happening."

Belichick wasn't Belichick until he took his second job in New England after a nondescript run in Cleveland, and Logan said he feels McDaniels will be much better in his second gig, too, because he'll have a better feel for everything involved in being a head coach.

Belichick can be gruff but he also circles back from chewing out a guy to building him back up, a trait that doesn't seem to extend to the branches of Belichick's coaching tree, Logan said. "The most successful coaches are guys who can relate individually to their players and then collectively as a team. Even if a guy's making millions of dollars, he has to have a certain amount of, *Hey I really want to play for this guy,* and as a coach if you can't bring that out of your players, and I'm talking about the majority of your team, it's going to be hard to be successful. Winning games covers for just about anything, but invariably you know you're going to hit a pothole. And when a team doesn't have that sort of commitment to the coach, things can splinter very quickly."

On that cold winter day in Denver in 2011, McDaniels was no longer the Broncos' problem, save for the few millions of dollars they owed him.

The Broncos were left trying to restore the franchise's battered image. "We've got a long way to go," Ellis said. "We've got a *long* way to go."

One way the organization could start winning back the fans was to expand Elway's consulting role, perhaps by making him the team's top football executive.

"The conversations that we've had with John clearly indicate one thing, and that is he loves the Broncos and he loves Denver and he wants to help if he can," Ellis said. "I don't know where that's going to go, if anywhere."

# CHAPTER 16
## ELWAY'S COMEBACK

F orty-seven times in his NFL career, John Elway brought the Denver Broncos back from fourth-quarter deficits to win games, and the floundering franchise needed its favorite son for one more colossal comeback.

Josh McDaniels' 22-month misadventure left the Broncos shamed and defamed. Given too much power at too young an age, McDaniels had veered the Broncos into the ditch. He lost 17 of his last 22 games, chased off his two best players in quarterback Jay Cutler and wide receiver Brandon Marshall, and threw Champ Bailey's status into question by calling off talks on a contract extension, leading the star cornerback to put his Denver home on the market.

Worst of all, McDaniels embarrassed the Broncos with the Spygate II videotape scandal in London that cast them as cheaters much like the original Spygate had stained the Patriots. This wasn't exactly what Broncos owner Pat Bowlen had in mind when he hired Bill Belichick's protégé to bring some of New England's famously fastidious culture to Denver.

McDaniels was gathering his things following his late-afternoon ouster on December 6, 2010, when Eric Studesville's phone rang. The first-year running backs coach saw it was Mr. Bowlen, who asked Studesville to come see him right away.

As he hurried to see Mr. Bowlen, Studesville's mind raced. Surely, he was the next one to get fired. Bowlen asked him to have a seat and then told him he needed Studesville to do him a huge favor: Would he coach the Broncos in the final four games as the team's interim head coach? Consider it a four-week job audition.

Studesville's head was spinning. He gladly accepted the owner's offer and went right to work, calling a meeting with the rest of the coaches and cobbling together a game plan while learning all the duties that the head coach handles, including news conferences with the local media, conference calls with the opponent's media, broadcast production meetings, the coach's weekly radio and television shows. Not to mention running practices, reviewing the film, and collaborating with coordinators on that week's game blueprints and script of the first 15 to 20 plays, the ones that the team executes the best in practice and is most comfortable going with.

Six days later, the Broncos played at Arizona in a game that was hardly a résumé builder. Kyle Orton was awful, completing 19 of 41 passes for just 166 yards and three interceptions in a 43–13 thrashing at the hands of the Cardinals.

It was time for a bold move, and Studesville made a big decision three days later, announcing that Tim Tebow, the two-time Heisman Trophy winner from the University of Florida whom McDaniels had drafted in the first round of the 2010 NFL draft, would start for the remainder of that 2010 season, beginning with a game at Oakland on December 13.

The unconventional quarterback provided a tantalizing taste of both his boundless energy and his physical limitations when he completed just half of his 16 pass attempts for 133 yards and a touchdown and ran eight times for 78 yards, including a 40-yard barrel up the middle on a broken play. But the Broncos' 39–13 loss at Oakland meant the Raiders had piled up a whopping 98 points on the Broncos that season, when Denver's league-worst defense gave up an NFL-high 471 points.

The Broncos' final two games were at home. On the day after Christmas, the Broncos faced the Houston Texans, who were coached by Gary Kubiak, John Elway's longtime backup quarterback and onetime Broncos offensive coordinator whose departure from Denver following the 2005 AFC championship loss to the Pittsburgh Steelers robbed the Broncos of their buffer between Mike Shanahan and the roster.

Trailing 23–10 early in the fourth quarter, Tebow threw a 23-yard touchdown pass to running back Cory Buckhalter that made it a six-point game. On his next drive, Tebow kept the ball on a six-yard run around the left tackle with 3:02 remaining and fill-in kicker Steven Hauschka's extra point gave Denver its first lead at 24–23. It also left the Texans plenty of time to get into range for a Matt Turk field goal. Tight end Joel Dreessen's 15-yard catch put the Texans on the Denver

40-yard line. Two plays later, Matt Schaub's throw to tight end Owen Daniels was intercepted by cornerback Syd'Quan Thompson at the 27. Tebow took two knees to close out both his and Studesville's first career NFL victory.

The next week, Tebow threw for 205 yards and two touchdowns and ran for 94 yards and a score in a 33–28 loss to the San Diego Chargers that closed out the Broncos' worst season in a non-strike year since 1967.

At 4–12, the Broncos owned the second overall pick in the 2011 NFL draft, behind only the Carolina Panthers, who had gone 2–14 and fired longtime coach John Fox, who was 71–57 in his first eight seasons and had reached the Super Bowl after the 2003 season, losing a 32–29 heartbreaker to Tom Brady and the Patriots.

The Broncos not only needed a new coach, they had to restore the team's tarnished image and bring back its winning culture. Bowlen turned to Elway, the beloved Hall of Fame quarterback who led Denver to five Super Bowl appearances and back-to-back championships before retiring in 1999.

"Why am I here? I love the Broncos," Elway said when Bowlen introduced him as the team's new chief football executive on January 5, 2011. "I understand what the Broncos are all about. They are about the integrity, about the winning, and about the things you do and how you handle yourself."

Bowlen, whose team was coming off just its fifth losing season in his 27 years as owner, said, "I think John will return this team to a very high level of competitiveness. I think we'll win some more Super Bowls."

At 50, Elway felt like a rookie again. But he insisted he'd get up to speed quickly, tapping his experience growing up as the son of a football coach, playing for 16 seasons in the NFL, and running an arena league team for six seasons (he had led the Colorado Crush to a championship in 2005 as its co-owner and chief executive officer).

"I know what I don't know," declared Elway, who added that he'd already sought the advice of former NFL executive Ernie Accorsi, who drafted him in Baltimore—and traded him to Denver—and who was Cleveland's general manager when Elway engineered "the Drive" in the 1987 AFC championship game to beat the Browns. "So, thank God there was no animosity and he took my call," Elway said.

Inducted into the Pro Football Hall of Fame in 2004, Elway said he wasn't worried that he'd tarnish his legacy by returning as the team's top football executive. Sure, fans would inevitably disagree with his decisions, draft picks, hires, fires, signings, and releases. But he could handle the heat. Nor was he concerned that so few great players make successful transitions to the front office, the most recent examples in the NFL being Dan Marino and Matt Millen.

"No, because I'm not them," said Elway. Additionally, chief operating officer Joe Ellis became team president and Brian Xanders, who was basically relegated to consultant status under McDaniels, went from general manager in name only to one who was empowered in the new organizational chart.

"The question wasn't whether John would be smart enough, whether he understood football or whether he loved the franchise. It was whether he was willing to dedicate the amount of time necessary to make it work," Dave Logan said.

"John's been very successful with many other things in his life. He certainly doesn't need money. But people outside the organization wanted to know, *Why would he want to do that now? Why would he want to come back and spend all the necessary hours?*"

Because he's John Elway, a man who had taken his fierce competitive streak from the football field to the business world, from the huddle to the executive suites. Now he was bringing it back to the Broncos front office, and it was something that a year later would help him land the biggest free agent in NFL history, Peyton Manning.

"He answered all those questions early on when he returned to the team," Logan said. "Signing Peyton was obviously a huge move...just look at the result. And that's something that will forever be a part of John Elway's legacy here in Denver."

Elway's first task in his new job was finding a new head coach, and one of the biggest questions the franchise faced was whether Tebow, who had supplanted Orton for the final three games, was their quarterback going forward. "Tim Tebow is a darn good football player," Elway said on the day he returned to work at Broncos headquarters. "What we have to make him is a darn good quarterback, and that is what we have to figure out."

Elway would leave it to the next head coach to determine if Tebow was his starting quarterback. But he added something that would shape his field of candidates, saying, "I don't believe that anyone is going to come over and say, 'I don't want Tim Tebow.' If they do, then maybe they are not the right guy for the job."

# CHAPTER 17
## FOX THE FIXER

To rescue the floundering franchise, Denver Broncos new chief football executive John Elway chose a man who had done it before when he selected former Carolina Panthers head coach John Fox over four other candidates to replace Josh McDaniels.

Although Eric Studesville, Perry Fewell, and Dirk Koetter all had interim head coaching experience and Rick Dennison had been with the Broncos for almost a quarter century as a player and an assistant coach, none of them had the coaching chops of the 55-year-old Fox, whose Carolina teams posted three 11-win seasons, won two NFC South titles, went 5–3 in the playoffs, appeared in two conference championship games, and reached one Super Bowl, losing to New England in 2004.

Despite never having consecutive winning seasons in Charlotte, Fox touted a top of the-pile résumé that featured a road map for leading the Broncos back to respectability after a five-year playoff drought. "It's not my first rodeo, so to speak," Fox said. "So, I think I do have a blueprint to do it."

The Panthers were coming off a 1–15 season and owned the league's worst defense when Fox arrived in 2002 and led them to a 7–9 mark, and the defense rose all the way to No. 2 in the league, the biggest turnaround since the 1970 AFL-NFL merger. He guided them to the Super Bowl in his second season, when Carolina lost to New England.

The Broncos were in a similar state of disrepair upon Fox's arrival in Denver. Coming off a franchise-worst 4–12 season, they owned the second overall pick in the upcoming NFL draft and were looking at a major defensive overhaul.

In keeping with the organization's new emphasis on transparency as it tried to reconnect with a disenchanted fan base, Elway broke the news of his head coaching choice on Twitter. And in keeping with the time-honored tradition of getting the story, a few reporters ignored admonitions not to show up at team headquarters until the introductory news conference the following day. Elway rewarded their perseverance when he rolled down his window on the way out of the parking lot.

"For what this building needed, John Fox was the perfect fit for us," Elway said. "The one thing I saw in John, he had great football wisdom, and I think that comes with the experience that he has. But not only does he have it on the defensive side, but overall his football wisdom is what won us over." Then the window rolled up and off into the night zipped Elway in his Bentley.

Fox had gone 78–74 in nine seasons with the Panthers, who didn't renew his contract following a league-worst 2–14 season in 2010 (they were the only team to finish worse than the Broncos).

"I'm very competitive," Fox said as he left the team's Dove Valley headquarters that same night. "Last year was obviously a very disappointing and very hard season, but that's all the more reason to jump back in and get things turned around here."

One of Elway's criteria when he went looking for his first head coach was a willingness to work with quirky quarterback Tim Tebow, who had started the final three games of the season, going 1–2 with a win over the Texans. Fox said he was a big believer in the former Florida star.

"Welcome to Denver Coach Fox!" Tebow tweeted later that night. "Can't wait to get to work with you!!!"

"I'm real excited. It seems like the stars have aligned," Fox told 1,200 business leaders gathered at the Pepsi Center a few weeks later for the annual breakfast to benefit the Boy Scouts of America, his first public appearance in Denver since his hiring. Fox listed the parallels to his previous gig in Carolina, where he took the Panthers to the Super Bowl two years after his arrival in Charlotte, having selected Julius Peppers with the second overall draft pick in his first draft.

"In Carolina when I first went in 2002, they were 1–15.... That team was in disarray. We had the second pick in the draft, much like we do here in Denver." He grabbed Peppers from the University of North Carolina and the Panthers were on their way back to respectability.

"That's our goal, to repeat and [get] a player like him in this draft," Fox said. "I think we're set up very well to have some success."

Coming off the worst season in their 51-year history, the Broncos' top priority was fixing a defense that surrendered a whopping 471 points in 2010. Elway's overall mission was fixing all the problems left by McDaniels' 22-month reign of error, including inexplicably taking an extension offer to star cornerback Champ Bailey off the table. Those two aims converged.

"From everything I had read, he wanted to come back," Elway said. "So all the talk was that the deal had been pulled off the table and I wasn't there when it got pulled. So I said, 'Let's put it back on the table and see what the reaction is.' And then once we got back on the table, it was just a matter of negotiating the deal and getting him back here, because we knew we wanted him back."

Elway had spent his whole career studying defenses, and he said his Fox-Bailey 1-2 punch was the best way to rectify a slide that marked Bowlen's lowest point as team owner. Fox had the best defensive pedigree of any of the head coaching candidates, and Bailey was the defensive anchor the Broncos needed to hold onto as they began a resurgence.

"The thought I had going into the hiring process was the fact that we'd struggled so much on defense and had five different coordinators, with Dennis Allen being the sixth coordinator in six seasons on the defensive side," Elway said. "So I thought the best place for us to start was on the defensive side of the ball, get some continuity on the defensive side of the ball, and that would allow us to get better faster.

"And so that's really why the mind-set was to get a defensive-minded head coach, and that's why John was perfect," Elway continued. "We knew he'd provide that stability on the defensive side because that's his discipline. So, to me we could get better faster if we got better on that side of the ball and then built from there."

Some fans were surprised that Elway, being an ex-quarterback, didn't just try to load up on offense to outscore opponents. "Well, I think that you have to have a special guy to outscore everybody, and if you look at where we were with Kyle, we didn't have the Tom Bradys or the Peyton Mannings or the Drew Breeses—those are the guys that outscore everybody, and there's three or four of those guys in the league and they're very difficult to find," Elway said.

"And where we were with Kyle and then even with Tim, to be able to find out where Kyle was and to have Tim develop…the best way for him to develop was to be good on the defensive side and take our time with him on the offensive side and that wouldn't dump all the pressure on him and say, 'Here you go. In your second year you need to go out and score 35 points a game.'"

Elway said what gave the Broncos of his day such a good home-field advantage was a stingy defense, which held opponents in check and allowed him to figure things out by the fourth quarter and lead Denver to victory. "That crowd noise helps the defense," Elway said. "And when you're not really good on defense, it's hard to have the home field be a benefit for you when you can't stop people and you can't get off the field. So I think all of those factors weighed in and then John, coming out of where he came out of in Carolina, you like getting competitors with a chip on their shoulder. And I think that's where John was. He really wanted to prove his last couple of years there with what happened wasn't him."

With Bailey back in the fold, the Broncos turned their attention to the draft, where they hit the jackpot by selecting Texas A&M outside linebacker Von Miller one pick after the Panthers chose quarterback Cam Newton at No. 1. The two would square off five years later in Super Bowl 50.

For now, the Broncos would pair the premier pass-rusher in the draft with 2009 NFL sacks leader Elvis Dumervil, who missed the 2010 season with a torn chest muscle a year after leading the league with 17 sacks.

Miller's coach at College Station, Texas, was Mike Sherman, who had coached the Green Bay Packers from 2000 to 2005, and he said the Broncos were getting "a freakish athlete. I've never seen a guy like

The Broncos made the playoffs all four years John Fox was at the helm as head coach. He's just the second coach in NFL history to win four straight division titles with a new team.

him. I mean, he could have been our tailback. He could have been an All-American tight end. He could return punts and kickoffs. He's just a phenomenal athlete.

"We didn't ask him to drop much in coverage because we wanted him affecting the quarterback's rhythm and timing, but that doesn't mean he can't do it," Sherman said. "He'd line up and play corner in practice against our receivers just messing around and he was able to hold his own."

When Elway was hired as the Broncos' front-office football chief earlier that year, he speculated that Tebow would be hurt more than anyone on the roster by a long lockout, and he was right. Tebow was buff when he showed up at training camp expecting to be the starter, but he hadn't spent the off-season working with the new coaching staff. So when trade talks with the Miami Dolphins for Orton fizzled, Tebow was ill-prepared to beat him out for the starting job.

Orton was way more polished. He had put up the best passing numbers of his career in Denver after McDaniels acquired him from the Chicago Bears in the highly unpopular Jay Cutler trade. He'd thrown for 7,455 yards and 41 touchdowns in his two seasons with the Broncos but he had won just 11 of his 29 starts.

Tebow had started the final three games in 2010—going 1–2— after Orton got hurt and the organization decided to see what it had in Tebow. Tebow completed 41 of 82 passes for 654 yards, five touchdowns, and three interceptions, and rushed for 227 yards and six scores his rookie year.

Heading into year two, his messy mechanics, faulty footwork, and pocket impatience were still major concerns. But his popularity trumped his polish as his legion of fans excused his poor practices because he was a gamer and dismissed his mechanical flaws because he was a winner.

If it were up to the fans decked out in No. 15 jerseys, Tebow would be the starter when the Broncos broke training camp that summer. "Thank God the people don't make the decisions," Orton proclaimed after one practice when the whole Tebowmania thing got under his skin.

No, the choice belonged to Fox, and as the season opener against the Oakland Raiders approached, Fox proclaimed Orton his starting quarterback. "It's simple," Fox said. "There was a competition, and Kyle won."

Tebow wasn't ready, and his rabid fan base wasn't happy, taking to the airwaves and social media to proclaim he should be starting. Some began to suggest it wasn't Tebow's play that his coaches had a problem with as much as it was his frankness about his faith or his personality.

Yet it was really this simple: in the NFL jobs are earned, not earmarked, and nobody was questioning Tebow's character or work ethic, just his readiness. Remember, even Josh McDaniels, his biggest supporter in the NFL, didn't turn to Tebow when his own job was on the line the year before. It wasn't until Orton got hurt and McDaniels got fired that Tebow got his chance. He ran with it, just not far enough to keep it.

But as Elway would suggest a couple of months later, maybe Orton caved in to Tebowmania.

Miller made a splashy NFL debut in the 2011 season opener. On his first snap as a pro, the second overall pick in the NFL draft speared the football out of wide receiver Jacoby Ford's arms and strong safety Rahim Moore, a fellow rookie, scooped up the loose football at the Oakland 15-yard line.

Unfortunately, everything else about the game was ugly. The Broncos couldn't punch it in from there and settled for Matt Prater's field goal and a 3–0 lead that would be their only advantage in a 23–20 loss to their archrivals in Hue Jackson's coaching debut. After a first half filled with fouls, fists, and frustration, the Raiders took a 16–3 lead into the locker room in wild celebration as Sebastian Janikowski's record-tying 63-yard field goal fluttered over the crossbar as time expired. That tied the mark set by Tom Dempsey in 1970 and matched by Denver's Jason Elam in 1998 at the old Mile High Stadium.

Not only did Fox lose his debut as Denver's coach, but he lost two playmakers in the process. In his first game in 21 months, pass-rusher Elvis Dumervil jammed a shoulder in the first quarter and was used only sparingly afterward, and star cornerback Champ Bailey pulled his left hamstring making a touchdown-saving tackle of Darren McFadden, who ran for 150 yards on 22 carries.

Without his top target Brandon Lloyd (groin) and best running back Knowshon Moreno (hamstring), Orton had a tough night, completing 24 of 46 passes for 304 yards with an interception and a fumble. The Broncos kept faltering deep in Oakland territory, none more painful than when they reached the Raiders 24 early in the fourth quarter and Orton had tight end Daniel Fells open going into the end zone. Only the ball slipped out of his hand and defensive end Lamarr Houston pounced on it. Not only did Houston recover the fumble, he was credited with a sack and forced fumble on the play.

"I just feel sick about the ball slipping out of my hands like that," Orton said after the game. "It's just one of those deals that's sickening to have happen to you. It never really happened to me before." As he left the field, fans were chanting, "Tebow! Tebow!"

A week after the football slipped from his hands with the game on the line, Orton seemed to strengthen his grip on the Broncos' starting quarterback job by leading Denver to a 24–22 win over the Cincinnati Bengals despite an ever-worsening injury epidemic.

Fans pining for Tebow got their wish. Well, sort of. With the Broncos' rash of injuries hitting epic proportions, the popular-but-polarizing backup quarterback lined up for several plays as a slot receiver. "We have that next-man-up mentality and everybody's here for a reason," wide receiver Eric Decker said. "Everybody can play. And it's what you make of your opportunities."

Next man up? How about last man standing? The Broncos entered the day with five starters sidelined, including Pro Bowl wide receiver Brandon Lloyd. By halftime, they'd also lost rookie tight end Julius

Thomas to a sprained ankle and wide receiver Eddie Royal to a pulled groin, forcing Tebow into action as a receiver.

"I'm going to do whatever I can to help the team," Tebow said.

Orton said he wouldn't hesitate to throw it to Tebow, "but we were never in one of those situations."

Orton only completed 15 of 25 passes for 195 yards, but Decker caught nine of those passes for 113 yards and two touchdowns in his first career start.

All eyes, though, were on Tebow. "I will say this: he's a very competitive guy; a very mentally tough guy," Fox said. "He's got excellent football character, so he can probably line up a lot of different places."

*How about under center?*

*Not yet.*

The Broncos lost 17–14 at Tennessee in Week 3 when the Titans intercepted Orton twice and stopped Willis McGahee on fourth-and-goal at the 1 early in the fourth quarter.

Denver had a 14–10 lead and seemingly all the momentum after Miller sacked Matt Hasselbeck with a minute left in the third quarter, knocking the ball loose, and defensive end Derrick Harvey smothered it at the Titans 13.

Hasselbeck rallied the Titans despite the loss of receiver Kenny Britt to a knee injury. His four-yard touchdown pass to tight end Daniel Graham with four and a half minutes remaining gave Tennessee the lead.

The Titans defense did the rest. The Broncos drove to the Titans 38 before Will Witherspoon sacked Orton. Two plays later, Jason Jones batted Orson's pass into the air and Witherspoon picked it off with 1:39 left. Even fans in Nashville were chanting, "Tebow! Tebow!" as the Broncos retreated to the locker room.

On October 2, Charles Woodson plucked Kyle Orton's pass to Eric Decker out of the air and sprinted 30 yards for a touchdown that set the tone for the Green Bay Packers' 49–23 rout of the stumbling Broncos, who fell to 1–3. Woodson's big play was the worst part of an up-and-down day for Orton, who threw three interceptions to go with three touchdowns, two of them to Decker.

Despite a pair of sacks from Miller, Denver's defense couldn't keep up with Aaron Rodgers, who threw for 408 yards and four touchdowns and rushed for two more scores. Backup Tebow came in for a brief appearance at quarterback early in the first quarter, losing a yard on a run, but Fox chose not to give Tebow more work when the game was out of hand in the fourth quarter.

"I thought our offense was very impressive, other than the turnovers," Fox said.

Tebow Time finally arrived in Denver on October 9, 2011.

Or did it?

John Fox wouldn't say who his starting quarterback was following Denver's 29–24 loss at home to San Diego that dropped the Broncos to 1–4, three games behind the Chargers at 4–1 in the AFC West.

Fox benched Orton at halftime and Tebow nearly rallied the Broncos from a 16-point fourth-quarter deficit. Ready or not, Tebow was thrust into action after Orton completed just 6 of 13 passes for 34 yards and an interception in the first half. With Tebow in the wings, it was Orton who was putting up ugly numbers.

Despite fumbling three snaps, a rusty Tebow ran for a touchdown and threw for another and he had one final shot for the win before his Hail Mary pass to wide receiver Matt Willis from the San Diego 29 fell incomplete in the end zone.

"He makes plays, you can't deny that," Chargers linebacker Takeo Spikes said of Tebow. "People can talk about the way he throws the ball, people can talk about his release. But at the end of the day, this league is about what have you done for me lately? And if you can come in and make the plays that another guy can't, then you'll play a long time."

With the loss, Orton fell to 6–21 since winning his first six starts in Denver.

Tebow's fans, who had been chanting his name ever since his awful training camp, were eager to know if he was Denver's starter now. But Fox wasn't ready to say, suggesting he had to watch the film, huddle with Elway and staff, and think things over some more.

"We're looking to have long-term success with somebody, and who that somebody is yet, I'm not sure," Fox explained.

The Broncos punted on their first three drives with Tebow under center before he scored on a 12-yard run. Willis McGahee's 2-point conversion cut San Diego's led to 26–18. After a fumble by Philip Rivers, running back Knowshon Moreno turned a short screen pass into a 28-yard touchdown. But Brandon Lloyd couldn't come down with the 2-point conversion pass that would have tied it.

After the Chargers tacked on a field goal with 24 seconds left, Tebow hit Lloyd for 20 yards and tight end Daniel Fells for 31. He hustled downfield and clocked the ball at the Chargers 29 with one second left.

Taking the final snap, Tebow spun away from a defender, scrambled around, and lofted a pass that fell incomplete in the end zone.

"It just shows the kid is a fighter; we always knew that," Dumervil said. "Some things just don't change from the collegiate level. Give him credit. He came in and gave us a spark."

As the Broncos trudged off the field, the stadium rocked with a thunderous roar:

"Te-Bow! Te-Bow! Te-Bow!"

The Broncos were headed into their bye week, so there was time either for Orton to shake off his bad performances and use his benching as a wake-up call or for the coaching staff to prepare Tebow to take over the offense.

Either choice would provide some intrigue going into their next game, at Miami on October 23. The Dolphins had pursued Orton in the off-season but trade talks crumbled, presumably over his desire for a long-term contract. Coincidentally, the Dolphins were planning to honor the 2008 national champion Florida Gators football team, the one led by Tebow.

\* \* \*

Kyle Orton was like his predecessor Jay Cutler in that he tolerated his media duties as the Broncos starting quarterback. He didn't enjoy that aspect of his job.

"I liked Kyle," Dave Logan said. "But he was a bit challenging to get to know and to do a pregame show with."

He wasn't as outwardly dismissive of questions as Cutler could be, but he made no secret of his disdain for reporters, especially as his play started to sour in Denver.

"NFL players have to have a certain level of comfort in dealing with the press. But when they try to sort of strong-arm the press or become just difficult to deal with, and just basically refuse to do even the easiest of requests, it makes no sense," Logan said. "It just doesn't. It doesn't make any sense in the short term, and it sure doesn't make any sense in the long term.

"Listen, get it. I was a player, and yes, there are some questions you're asked as a player where you're thinking to yourself, *What kind of dumb-ass question is this?* But there's a way to handle it. You've got to determine whether it was done intentionally to try to elicit some sort of flash response, or rather, is it just a reporter struggling to find a question of pertinence?" Logan said.

"The press is the conduit between the public and the players—now, not as much as it used to be because now the players have social media and their own ability to get their narrative out to the public—but, still, I just think guys don't do themselves any favors by making it really difficult and just acting like an asshole to the press. Fortunately, not many guys are like that."

One day, as the locker room access period was wrapping up and members of the Broncos public relations staff began to usher reporters out, Orton sat at his locker doing a very bad, out of tune imitation of Ray Charles.

"Hit the road Jack, and you don't come back no more, no more, no more," he belted, butchering the tune. "Hit the road Jack and you don't come back."

Don't quit your day job, somebody told him.

It turns out he couldn't hold onto any job in Denver.

Tebowmania was on its way.

\* \* \*

Elway told The Associated Press in an interview on December 19, 2011, that he felt Tebowmania got to Orton.

"Yeah, I do. No question. No question. I will say this, not only that, but it's the way that the Raider game went, the opener, he had a chance and it's wet but he has a chance at the tight end, fumbles the ball," Elway said. "And it's kind of the same atmosphere that came from last year and what happened to the Raiders and how we lost it. And so that kind of sent it south in a hurry. And all of a sudden, we come back and beat Cincinnati the next week and then we lose a tough one in Tennessee, but that was tipping that way."

Elway said he called Orton to tell him he was granting him his release and that he told him, "I'm not sure anybody could have survived what was going on here and everybody wanting Tim to play. And even if you had been great, they still would have wanted Tebow because everybody was curious about Tebow."

Fans who forgave Tebow his multiple flaws didn't cut Orton any similar slack.

"Every little thing. And you get tired of that, and you're the starting quarterback and you go out there and it's all No. 15 jerseys and he runs out there and everyone's cheering," Elway said. "I think it's human nature. Totally, no question. That's why it was good for him to get a new start and he played good" in leading Kansas City to a 19–14 win over previously unbeaten Green Bay on December 18, 2011, when he threw for 299 yards.

The Chiefs would play Oakland in Week 16 and end the season in Denver on New Year's Day.

"We knew we may have to face him down the line," Elway said, "and we kind of took that risk."

# CHAPTER 18
## TEBOWMANIA

It wasn't so much that Tim Tebow won the Denver Broncos' starting quarterback job as Kyle Orton simply lost it, just like he had the wet football in the opener.

"Well, I think 1–4 has a lot to do with it," first-year coach John Fox said in announcing on October 11 that Tebow would start against the Miami Dolphins when the Broncos returned from their bye week.

Despite being an All-America quarterback, two-time national champion, and Heisman Trophy winner, Tebow never came close to beating out Orton as a rookie in 2010 or again in 2011, when Tebow proved ill-prepared for a quarterback competition at camp when efforts to trade Orton failed. Tebow showed no progress in becoming the pocket passer that John Elway had repeatedly said he must become to make it long-term in the NFL.

Six weeks into the season, Tebow's footwork was still flawed, his throws were still off-target, and he even had trouble with the most basic of football plays: the center-quarterback exchange, after spending most of his college career playing out of the shotgun.

But Orton suddenly turned ordinary when the season began and now he'd be on the sideline when the Broncos played at Miami. Three months earlier, he figured he'd be barking out plays for the Dolphins before he ended up staying in Denver and cutting through the cacophony to outshine Tebow in every way except popularity, youthful exuberance and pure hustle.

Beginning in the opener when a wet football slipped from his hands when he had a tight end open for the touchdown, things hadn't gone well for Orton or the Broncos, who found themselves in 2011 navigating a rash of injuries and another season quickly going south.

Orton turned the ball over nine times in 20 quarters, losing the organization's confidence and turning up the heat on a franchise that had been mired in mediocrity since its last winning season in 2005.

After breaking down the game film of the latest loss and thinking things over, Fox went all-in on Tebow, his 24-year-old unconventional southpaw who didn't fit the mold of a prototypical pro passer but who had undeniable charisma and a track record of rallying his teams to great heights.

"He's just a baller, an all-out baller," Denver linebacker Joe Mays said. "Some people may call him unorthodox, but at the end of the day, he gets the job done."

Mixed in with that twinge of excitement in the locker room was a feeling from Orton's teammates that they'd let him down and he was serving as the fall guy for their many troubles. They ranked 25th in both offense and defense.

The Broncos had to adjust their offense for Tebow but Fox downplayed the difficulty, snapping, "Well, it's not like we signed him off the street."

Now that he was the starter and his snaps at practice were all about preparing him for the next week's opponents, the Broncos had to decide if they were going to let up on their efforts to fix flaws in Tebow's mechanics and motion or ditch their insistence that he show patience in the pocket and meet him halfway by sprinkling in the shotgun, the read-option and the designed runs, all the things that made him such a great college quarterback.

Tebow said he would do whatever was asked of him but he made it clear that he was very good at doing things his way, too, because he was convinced a running quarterback could succeed in the NFL despite so many opinions to the contrary.

"Honestly, I've heard that a lot, heard that my whole life and I see a lot of good quarterbacks running the ball really effectively from Steve Young all the way down," Tebow said as he prepared for his first start in 2011. "So, I'm going to try to do whatever they ask me to do and if that's hand the ball off, if that's drop back, if that's run around, I'll do whatever I can do to help this team win football games."

So far in the NFL, Tebow had completed just 49 percent of his passes, but he'd thrown for six touchdowns to go with three interceptions, rushed for seven scores, and had a 5.3-yard average per carry, some of the reasons he had a Heisman Trophy at his house and two national championship rings to wear if he ever wanted.

There was one thing that would hinder Tebow and the Broncos: the new collective bargaining agreement that had just been signed a few months earlier required that teams give players four consecutive days off during the bye week. Only injured players were allowed to come in during the four-day break, and then only to get treatment. And the new rules also forbade players from participating in club-supervised workouts or practices and from meeting with their coaches to study film or go over the playbook during the bye week.

"Well, I don't think there's any rules against like watching film or throwing on my own or continuing to work on things," Tebow said with a wink and a smile. "So, I'll probably try to do that."

Wide receiver Eric Decker offered to give up his vacation to help Tebow work out the kinks in this game.

## Faith and Football

Tim Tebow was as polarizing as he was popular, and some of that had to do with his Christian faith that he freely shared with the public. He dutifully listened to the first question at any news conference, whether during the week or after the game, and before answering, he would typically start out by saying, "First, I want to thank my Lord and Savior, Jesus Christ." He ended every interview, either at the podium or the locker room with, "Thank you, God bless you."

Dave Logan said he quickly learned Tebow was genuine in his convictions.

"I looked at it on two distinctly different levels. Because I did his show every week when he was the starting quarterback and I got to know him a little bit and I really, really liked him as a person," Logan said. "I admired him. He was everything that I thought he would be. You saw him on TV and you read things about him and you heard things about him and you sort of wondered if all that stuff was a little too good to be true. And the reality, my reality in dealing with Tim, was that he was exactly who I thought he was and even more. Just a great young guy whose heart was in the right place.

"I know there were some people that thought the dude wasn't genuine. But that's not the Tebow that I got to know. I really enjoyed getting to know the guy."

## Dave Logan's Log

I would do a weekly pregame show with Tim. Team spokesman Patrick Smyth must have told him I was a high school coach. So one day, Tim started talking about that and reminiscing about his high school days. "Hey, I'd like to come out to a game sometime if you wouldn't mind." And I said, "Okay, I'll give you my number and you just let me know when it might work out." As he walked out of the interview room, I was thinking to myself, *There's no way he's going to be able to come out to a game.* But I appreciated the gesture.

One morning about 6:15 Smyth called me at home. "Hey, Dave, Tim wants to come out to your game tonight. How can we facilitate this?" And I said, "Well, first of all, the game is about 45 minutes outside the metro area, so depending on when you leave, it would be close to an hour's drive or more."

"Okay, okay, let me get back to you," Smyth said. About an hour later, he called me back and said, "Nope, he wants to come out." I said, "Okay, well, would he like to talk to my team?" He said, "Yep, he wants to talk to the team."

A friend of mine from Channel 9—I work for Channel 9 also—approached me during warm-ups on the field. "Hey, is Tim Tebow coming to the game?" I said he was and he said, "Is he talking to your team?" And I said he was. So, he said, "Well, can we film him in the locker room before the game?" And I said, "Fellas, he asked to talk to my team. I just want this to be a moment for the kids with him."

Tim was on the sideline prior to the game. I went over and shook his hand. His brother Robbie was there, as well, and I'm pretty sure so were his mom and dad. I said to him, "Hey man, I just appreciate you showing up. You don't have to talk to the kids before the game if you don't want to." And he quickly said, "No, Coach, I'd love to come in and talk to your guys."

Normally, I don't say much in the locker room before the game because I've talked to my team the night before. So, I just said, "Hey fellas, give me your attention. We've got the starting quarterback of the Denver Broncos, Tim Tebow. He wants to share a message with you guys. Give him your attention."

I walk to the back of the locker room and Tim walks up to the front and he starts talking to the team—and frankly, he's in a monotone and in a really uninspired way. And I'm thinking, *Wow. I was sort of hoping for more.*

Well, about a minute into this, he started getting revved up and started talking about his high school experience and how much it meant to him and how he stays in touch with his teammates and his coaches and how that was the best football experience of his lifetime and how he'd made lifelong friends.

I'm standing next to one of the managers in the back of the locker room and I said, "Do me a favor. Open that door and just stand away from it, but get the locker room door opened." By that time, Tim was at an incredible level, just a fever pitch of emotion: "You play for your school! You play for your teammates! Your coaches! And, most importantly, you play for yourself! Whatever you do tonight, go out and have no regrets, lay everything on the line." My guys went absolutely out of their minds and burst out of the locker room onto the field. It was a really cool moment for my kids.

# CHAPTER 19
## MIAMI MIRACLE

Finishing strong is something Tim Tebow did plenty of times at Florida. He wrote about it in his best-selling autobiography, *Through My Eyes*:

> You have to finish in football; you have to learn how to finish in the weight room, through the line, finishing a sprint; everything gets hard. Finish. Eventually some people are going to start going slower, but the people who can finish and finish at the same pace or stronger than when they started, those are the ones who are going to succeed; those are the ones who are going to be great.

Linebacker Wesley Woodyard said Denver's defenders came to realize that season that that if they could keep the game within reach, Tebow would pull out some of his last-minute magic. "It does have an effect on us," he said—whether Tebow looks pretty doing it or not.

"I'm sure he's still going to have some haters," linebacker Von Miller said. "But he's been leading our team consistently. You don't have to throw for 400 yards. All you have to do is manage the game right."

Tebow's first start of 2011 came at Miami's Sun Life Stadium, where he had experienced two of the biggest thrills of his life: winning a state high school football championship in 2005 and winning the 2008 national title with the Florida Gators.

Yet even the return of Tebow and a halftime celebration of that Gators team didn't ensure a sellout for the game between the Broncos (1–4) and Dolphins (0–5). Still, there were plenty of No. 15 jerseys in the stands, and Tebow drew a big roar when he trotted onto the field for his first series.

Midway through the third quarter, Denver had netted two yards on 10 pass plays, an average of seven inches per play. By the fourth quarter, Tebow's fans were quiet, replaced by fans chanting Tebow's name in derision, hooting and hollering with every open receiver he missed, every blitzer he couldn't avoid. The Broncos appeared beaten when they trailed 15–0 with 5:23 left and took over at their 20.

"I remember thinking, *They're dead in the water. Game's over, 15–0 and they haven't shown one iota of offensive firepower,*" Dave Logan recounted. "They couldn't move the ball. They couldn't get anything going. No sustained drives. They couldn't run it, they couldn't even complete a pass. And then how that game ended was as magical as any game that I've ever called in my career.

"You play a lot of football, you call games on the radio for three decades. So, I've seen a lot of NFL football either as a player or a play-by-play guy, and there are just some days when it's not your day and nothing works. And that's what I was feeling about the Miami game. Honestly, in the fourth quarter, I was thinking about the four-hour plane ride home."

All of a sudden, things changed. "I mean, everything the Broncos had to have go right went right, and it was like a light switch that got flipped on and the Dolphins couldn't do anything right," Logan said.

When Tebow went back out with 5:23 left, the Broncos had punted on all five of their second-half drives after their first-half possessions ended with three punts, two missed field goals, and a fumble. Tebow had been sacked six times. He'd completed four passes for 40 yards. And he hadn't converted a single third down. This came as little surprise to his detractors who said he wasn't a bona fide NFL quarterback, and it was no surprise to his legion of faithful fans who said forget style points, all he does in win games.

Now it was crunch time, or Tebow Time, as his fans liked to say, and suddenly Tebow looked like, well, John Elway. With the Broncos on the verge of being shut out for the first time since 1992, Tebow led an eight-play drive that got them back into the game.

A 42-yard strike to wide receiver Matt Willis got the Broncos going and Demaryius Thomas hauled in Tebow's five-yard touchdown throw with 2:44 remaining. Matt Prater's extra point made it 15–7. The Broncos then lined up for the onside kick.

Consider this: John Fox had been a coach for a long, long time, starting out as an assistant at his alma mater, San Diego State, in 1978 after an NFL playing career consisting of time spent on the Tampa Bay Buccaneers' practice squad. He also had coaching stints at U.S. International, Boise State, Long Beach State, Utah, Kansas, Iowa State, and Pittsburgh. His first job in pro football came in 1985, coaching defensive backs for the Los Angeles Express of the USFL. He made it to the NFL in 1989 as secondary coach for the Pittsburgh Steelers and would take the same job with the San Diego Chargers before a year as a personnel consultant for the St. Louis Rams in between gigs as defensive coordinator for the Los Angeles Raiders and the New York Giants. He'd been head coach of the Carolina Panthers from 2002 to 2010 before coming to Denver in January 2011.

And not once in Fox's 33 years in college or professional football had any one of his programs ever successfully executed on onside kick. Not. One. Single. Time. That was about to change.

Miami receiver Marlon Moore leaped to catch the ball but bobbled it, and the Broncos' Virgil Green recovered at the Denver 44 with 2:31 left.

*So you're saying there's a chance...*

As the clock ticked below one minute, Tebow's strike to a diving Daniel Fells gained 28 yards to the Miami 3. Two plays later, Tebow fooled the Dolphins by rolling left and firing back to Fells, who swooped across the goal line for the touchdown with 17 seconds remaining.

Denver still needed a two-point conversion to stay alive, and Tebow blasted his way in to tie it at 15.

Miami won the overtime coin toss but both teams went three-and-out on their first drives. The Dolphins had first down at their 43 on their next possession when Matt Moore took the snap and Broncos linebacker D.J. Williams took things into his own hands. He sacked Moore, stripped the football from his grasp, and recovered it at the Miami 36. Tebow handed off three times to Lance Ball, then retreated to the sideline to watch Matt Prater, who had missed field goal attempts of 49 and 43 yards in regulation, line up for a 52-yarder. He split the uprights with 7:24 left in overtime.

"It's tough to say, but man, Timmy did a great job," said Dolphins center Mike Pouncey, who played with Tebow at the University of Florida. "Hopefully the critics will get off him about what he can't do and talk about the things that he can do—and that's figure out a way to win the game, no matter what."

Far from polished were his mechanics. Far from perfect were his passes. But the unorthodox quarterback scrutinized by skeptics since former coach Josh McDaniels drafted him with the 25th pick in 2010 had somehow rallied the Broncos from 15 points down for the improbable win. Since the 1970 merger between the AFL and the NFL no team had ever overcome that big of a deficit in the final three minutes of a game.

"One thing you can say about this team is that we have a lot of heart. We have a lot of courage. We're going to fight until the end and continue to believe," Tebow said. "It's my fault that we were in that position in the first place. I just have to play better in the first three quarters so we don't have to make that comeback in the fourth."

The Broncos were just 2–4, but Tebow was the talk of football, and beyond.

"Congrats to @TimTebow for that comeback win today. Impressive! He's just a winner," tweeted LeBron James.

Fox stepped up to the postgame podium with a smile as wide as a football. "It was never in doubt," he cracked.

All these years later, Logan still shakes his head thinking about that Miracle in Miami. "I still don't know how they won the game," Logan said. "But there were so many moments that were like that in the second half of that season. Some people felt like it was divine intervention. Well, it was definitely something. I'm not smart enough to figure out what it was. I just know that I witnessed all of it."

Tebow's first start, save for his late-game heroics, wasn't as bad as first portrayed. The NFL made an official scoring change after reviewing the game, giving the Dolphins credit for six sacks on Tebow instead of seven. The league determined a second-quarter play originally ruled a sack was a designed run by Tebow, who took a shotgun snap with 41 seconds left in the first half and ran a draw play. He was tackled for a loss by Kendall Langford and fumbled. The stats crew at the stadium ruled it a sack because it was viewed as a pass play.

Tebow would get no such reprieve when he followed the Miracle in Miami with the Dud in Denver, a 45–10 dismantling by the Detroit Lions, who sacked him seven times and turned his two turnovers into touchdowns. Chris Houston had a 100-yard interception return for a touchdown and Cliff Avril had a strip sack and scoop that he turned into a 24-yard score, part of the Lions' biggest road onslaught since scoring 45 points at San Francisco on October 29, 1967.

Lions linebacker Stephen Tulloch celebrated his sack of Tebow by joining the "Tebowing" craze, striking a prayerful pose near the prone second-year quarterback after the takedown. Tebow had started the phenomenon the week before by dropping to a knee after his dazzling comeback against the Dolphins.

In the locker room afterward, several Lions questioned Tebow's ability to succeed in the NFL. "It's too early to say. I haven't even taken a shower yet, let alone look at the tape," Fox said when asked who would be his quarterback the following week at Oakland. "But we'll look at it and make changes where we see are needed. We've definitely got to get better."

What he had in mind wasn't another switch at quarterback but tweaks to an offense that would help out his unconventional quarterback.

After their dismantling by Detroit, the Broncos went all in on Tebow as their quarterback. No longer were they going to try to fit him into the pro-style offense and pretend he could be a prototypical passer. Instead, they would pull a page from his college playbook, where he relied on his legs much more than his left arm.

Over and over that afternoon in Oakland, Tebow took the snap, put the football in running back Willis McGahee's belly, and read the unblocked edge rusher to decide whether to hand off or pull the ball back for his own run. The read option. It was Tebow's bread-and-butter play in college. But it was a completely foreign concept to McGahee, who learned the offense in a crash course that week in practice.

"As long as it worked, that's all I care about," McGahee said. "Tim did a great job as far as reading the ends on what he had to do as far as keeping it or giving it. When I got the ball it was my job just to get some yards."

Tebow befuddled the defense, throwing for two touchdowns and running for 177 yards, and McGahee added 163 yards rushing and two more scores and the Broncos overcame a 17–7 halftime deficit, rolling to a 38–24 win over the Raiders. The only other Broncos quarterback to have rushed for at least 100 yards in a game was Norris Weese, with 120 in 1976.

And after getting sacked 13 times in his first two starts, Tebow only was sacked once. Gaining 298 yards on the ground, their highest total since 2000, the Broncos (3–5) pulled within a game of the Raiders (4–4) for the AFC West lead.

Then it was on to Kansas City. The Broncos rattled off their third win in four starts for Tim Tebow as Denver's run-first, option-style offense gave Kansas City fits. Tebow threw only eight passes and completed two. But one of them was a sweet 56-yard touchdown toss to Eric Decker in the fourth quarter which helped the resurgent Broncos to a 17–10 victory over the Chiefs.

"I'm a football player first, before quarterback," Tebow said. "Whatever we can do to win games."

The Broncos had enough on the ground to churn out a critical victory even after losing McGahee and Knowshon Moreno to injuries in the first quarter. While Tebow threw for just 69 yards, he ran for a touchdown and patiently led an offense that churned out 244 yards on the ground with Lance Ball carrying 30 times for 96 yards.

Denver built a 10–0 halftime lead despite Tebow missing all four of his throws in the first half. That made the Broncos the first team to lead at the break without a completion in more than a decade.

Tebow hit Decker with the long touchdown pass with 6:44 left in the fourth quarter for a 17–7 lead, and here's the thing: it was as sweet a throw as you'd ever seen from the likes of Brett Favre or Tom Brady or Peyton Manning.

"That's what I mean about you'd see him sometimes in practice or in a game like that and you'd be like, 'Where's that been?' But he couldn't replicate it, couldn't duplicate it on a consistent basis," Logan said. "But we talked about that in the postgame. I was like 'I don't know how many times the Broncos have ever won a game completing only two passes, and for that matter, how many times has anyone ever won an NFL game like that? It's just unnatural.'"

Ryan Succop kicked a field goal with seven seconds left for Kansas City to bring the Chiefs within a score, but Denver's Mario Haggan recovered the onside kick and Tebow took a knee in victory formation as the clock wound down, and another in prayer after the game was over.

*This was getting borderline ridiculous*, Logan thought. "They just won a game at Arrowhead and completed two passes the entire day. I never thought I'd see an NFL road team win completing two passes the entire game. But it happened."

In Week 11 against the New York Jets, Tim Tebow's 20-yard touchdown run with 58 seconds left capped a 95-yard drive and sent the Broncos to a 17–13 victory over the stunned Jets for Denver's second win in four days, evening their record at 5–5.

"I like winning," Tebow said after his third comeback victory in a month, "but I wish it wasn't this stressful."

The debate raging across the NFL was whether the read option was sustainable. After all, when John Elway joined the team's front office earlier that year, he firmly declared that Tebow had to become a pocket passer to make it in this league. But with each game, the Broncos were molding their offense more and more to fit Tebow's unique skill set that made him the most successful combination college quarterback in NCAA history, just as former Florida coach Urban Meyer once suggested an NFL team would have to do. And they kept watching him run roughshod over defenders who were bigger, faster, and stronger than they had been in the Southeastern Conference.

"He did it to us in college and he's doing it here," said teammate Robert Ayers, who went to Tennessee. "It doesn't have to be pretty, it doesn't have to be Aaron Rodgers–like. As long as we get it done, that's all that matters."

Four days after completing just two passes in a win at Kansas City, Tebow was held to 104 yards on 9 of 20 passing on a Thursday night thriller, and the Jets' disciplined play on the edge limited Tebow to two runs for 11 yards until Denver's final drive. At that point, the Broncos were 1-for-11 on third downs.

Then, in a performance reminiscent of the Miracle in Miami— when he was ineffective for 55 minutes before leading the Broncos to a stunning victory in overtime—Tebow took over and flipped the switch, running seven times for 58 yards, prompting Jets star cornerback Darrelle Revis to lament how the Jets had Tebow right where they wanted him...until they didn't.

"We played them well through the whole game, until that last play," Revis said. "Tim Tebow's legs took them to victory."

The Broncos had punted on their previous eight possessions when they got the ball back with less than six minutes and 95 yards to go. Tebow calmly drove Denver down the field against a Jets defense that had throttled him all night. Facing third-and-4 from the Jets 20-yard line with 1:06 remaining, the Broncos got some extra time to think about the play call when a fan ran onto the field and was corralled by security. During the break, the Jets dialed up their first all-out blitz of the night, and Tebow took the snap from shotgun, read the blitz, and outflanked safety Eric Smith around the left edge, then cut back and bulled his way past other Jets on his way into the end zone.

Jets coach Rex Ryan said he knew Tebow would keep the ball on the blitz; he just didn't think he'd get very far. "Hindsight being 20/20, obviously, we would've done something, anything but that," Ryan said of the decision to blitz. "I even told the defense before [the play], 'This kid is not going to take the ball out of his hand. He is going to keep it in his hand,' and that's exactly what he did. He ended up just making a great play. None of us saw it coming."

Tebow's latest comeback was one that could have been quashed on the first play of his final drive. The Broncos' anything-but-conventional quarterback threw an ill-advised pass to Eddie Royal in the right flat, but because he was so deep, the ball reached his receiver at the goal line, and Jets safety Jim Leonhard grabbed Royal in the end zone, but just as he was about to go down for a safety, Royal broke free for an eight-yard gain. It was a bad omen for a defense that had played well up until that point but appeared gassed as Tebow started running around the field.

Tim Tebow's 4–1 record was the opposite the 1–4 record that got Kyle Orton benched, and on November 22 the Broncos released the veteran quarterback they had tried to trade after the NFL lockout ended in July. Elway said he had decided against keeping Orton on the roster for the remainder of the season. This, he said, would be good for Orton, who now had "an opportunity to play somewhere else, and we wish him the best of luck."

The move was not without risk, as Orton could well face the Broncos in the coming weeks. Intriguing possible landing spots for Orton included Chicago and Kansas City. Jay Cutler had broken the thumb on his throwing hand that previous weekend and the Bears were set to visit Denver on December 11. And Chiefs quarterback Matt Cassel hurt his throwing hand in the Chiefs' 17–10 loss to the Broncos and underwent season-ending surgery the next day. His replacement, Tyler Palko, threw three interceptions in a 34–3 loss at New England.

Orton decisively outplayed Tebow in training camp for a second straight season but he turned ordinary when the season rolled around. When he was benched, Orton pledged to be a good teammate and stay ready in case his number was called again, but Tebow had won four of his five starts with the Broncos tailoring their offense to his unique skill set and reintroducing the old-school option to the NFL.

Although several teammates insisted Orton hadn't caused any problems, it was clear he was just biding his time until he would hit free agency after the season. And his demotion created some awkward moments. He retained his captainship after losing his starting job and would help lead the team in warm-ups before stepping aside to watch the less accurate but more mobile Tebow go to work.

A day before releasing Orton, Elway said on his weekly radio show that he wasn't sold on Tebow as the long-term answer at quarterback, suggesting the second-year signal-caller had to improve on his accuracy and third-down conversion rate.

The Chiefs claimed Orton off waivers a day after Elway granted him his release from the Broncos.

"Good for him," Tebow said. "Congratulations to him. That will be fun to play him the last game of the year."

Some people had a problem with Tebow wearing his religion on his sleeve, but he had been a savior for the Broncos since becoming the starter in the wake of his solid performance in a close loss to the Chargers in Denver. The Broncos were facing another close loss in the rematch on November 27 when San Diego kicker Nick Novak lined up for a 53-yarder in overtime.

Tebow didn't watch. He was on one knee in prayer. Did he ask for a miss?

"I might have said that. Or maybe a block. Maybe all of it," Tebow said with a laugh.

After Novak missed wide right, Tebow moved the Broncos into position for Prater's 37-yard field goal with 29 seconds left in overtime for a 16–13 win, giving Tebow a 5–1 record and pushing the Broncos above .500 for the first time since December 6, 2009.

Tebow, the talk of the NFL because he ran the read option and often struggled while passing, carried 22 times for 67 yards—the most carries by a quarterback in a game since at 1950, according to STATS LLC. He had a 12-yard gain on the last drive and McGahee ran 24 yards to set up Prater's winning kick.

A week later, Tebow figured the Broncos were heading for another overtime at Minnesota—at least he was praying for one when the Vikings got the ball at their 20-yard line with 93 seconds left after Prater's 46-yard field goal tied it at 32. Tebow completed 10 of 15 passes, his best percentage as an NFL starter, for 202 yards and two touchdowns and he posted a career-high passer rating of 149.3. But Christian Ponder countered with his best game as a pro, too, setting a team rookie record with 381 yards passing and a pair of long touchdowns to Percy Harvin.

Andre Goodman, however, stepped in front of Ponder's sideline throw on first down and returned the interception to the 15-yard line with 1:25 left. Lance Ball's first-down run for 11 yards made it first-and-goal at the 4 with 1:12 remaining. The Vikings decided against letting the Broncos score right away and took their chances with a shank or a block instead.

Prater's 23-yarder as time expired raised Denver's record to 6–1 with Tebow as the starter. Demaryius Thomas caught four passes for 144 yards and both touchdowns for the Broncos as Tebow finally looked like a pocket passer, running only four times all afternoon.

Tim Tebow was now dubbed the "Mile High Messiah," so another sellout crowd hardly flinched with the Broncos facing the possibility of their first home shutout in team's 52-year history after they failed to score on their first dozen drives and trailed the Chicago Bears 10–0 with under five minutes remaining.

It was Tebow Time.

Tebow threw a 10-yard touchdown strike to Thomas with 2:08 remaining and got the ball back with 53 seconds left after Marion Barber saved the Broncos precious time by inexplicably going out of bounds when the Bears were trying to run out the clock. Denver was out of timeouts after Thomas' touchdown and had to try an onside kick, which the Broncos couldn't recover. But on second down after the two-minute warning, Barber cut outside and was pushed out, stopping the clock.

"That's usually something that never happens with a veteran running back," Broncos linebacker Wesley Woodyard said. "It's just like things go our way."

The Bears would have to punt, and Tebow got the ball back at his 20 and went to work, not needing to go far with Prater's strong leg in the thin air. He drove the Broncos 39 yards for Prater's 59-yard kick, which he rocketed through the uprights to tie it at 10 with 3 seconds left in regulation.

Chicago won the toss and Caleb Hanie completed three quick passes to put the Bears in field goal range. Then, Barber, filling in for Matt Forte, burst through the line for a first down. Just then, Woodyard reached out in desperation and tugged on Barber's right arm, popping the ball loose. Elvis Dumervil recovered for Denver at the Broncos 34.

Tebow drove the Broncos downfield and Prater booted a 51–yarder to give Denver an improbable 13–10 win.

"If you believe," Tebow said, "then unbelievable things can sometimes be possible."

Prater's third straight walk-off field goal gave the Broncos their sixth consecutive win and moved them into sole possession of first place in the AFC West at 8–5, a game ahead of Oakland. Tebow improved to 7–1 since taking over as the starter in Denver, and six of those wins involved second-half comebacks, five of them necessitating fourth-quarter rallies, three of which went to overtime. No other quarterback in NFL history has produced six fourth-quarter comebacks in his first 11 NFL starts.

For Logan, this one was right up there with the Miracle in Miami. "Well, let's take a look at the Bears game in Denver. The Bears are in great position to win the game. They've got the lead and were basically killing the clock. Then, for whatever reason, Marion Barber runs out of bounds and stops the clock," Logan said. "If he stays inbounds, the game's pretty much over. And I made a point during the broadcast: 'I cannot believe he just ran out of bounds.'" And sure enough,

Denver came back and won that game, too. "I give a lot of credit to Mike McCoy and John Fox during that season, because it's exceedingly difficult to do what they did," Logan said.

It was like that old Tower of Power song, "Don't Change Horses (in the Middle of a Stream)." "And that's exactly what they did, and all of a sudden you put the zone read in during the course of the week and they made it work. And that's hard to do, man. Credit to the players and credit to the coaches for saying, 'This gives us our best chance to win.'"

By now even *Saturday Night Live* got caught up in Tebowmania, doing a skit about the Broncos and their miraculous turnaround under Tebow.

Against Tom Brady and the New England Patriots in Week 15, there would be no last-minute magic from Tebow, who had guided the Broncos to four consecutive fourth-quarter comebacks and six straight wins. Instead of another slow start followed by a fantastic finish, the Broncos started fast and fizzled. They jumped out to a 16–7 lead by outgaining the Patriots 167 yards to 4 on the ground in the first quarter.

Tebow threw for 194 yards and ran for 93 yards and a pair of touchdowns but he was sacked four times and fumbled, after which he watched Brady take it in himself from a yard out, then roar like a lion after a masterful spike in celebration of his first touchdown run of the year.

Take that, Tim Tebow.

"Sometimes setbacks are setups for bigger things to come," Coach Fox said.

In Week 16, Tebow ran out of fourth-quarter comebacks at Buffalo, where the Broncos quarterback belly-flopped, sealing a 40–14 loss to the Bills in the most dreadful performance of his two-year career with four second-half interceptions.

Two of them were returned for touchdowns 18 seconds apart.

At 8–7, Denver fell into a tie with Oakland atop the AFC West, but the Broncos owned the tiebreaker edge over the Raiders heading into their regular season finale against the Chiefs and former teammate Kyle Orton.

"Everything is still on the table," said Tebow, who threw for 185 yards and a touchdown and added 34 yards rushing with a score. That wasn't nearly good enough for his sixth fourth-quarter comeback. It was starting to look like the shine was off Tebowmania.

Tebow couldn't beat out Orton in training camp and he couldn't beat him in the regular season finale, either, as the Broncos lost 7–3 to the Chiefs to finish 8–8. Never in franchise history had the Broncos held an opponent to seven points and lost the game.

Although Orton got his revenge on the team that benched him and then cut him after he'd beaten out Tebow, he would be sitting out the playoffs while Tebow and the Broncos would be hosting a wild-card game in their first trip to the playoffs in six seasons the following week in the wild-card round of the playoffs.

"It's obviously a little bittersweet," Tebow said after completing just 6 of 22 passes for 60 yards and running six times for 16 yards.

"Well, we're AFC West champs," Fox said. "It doesn't matter how you do it. Once you get into the dance, they can't kick you out."

No, but they can knock you out and send you home early. And that's exactly what many fans were expecting with the powerful Pittsburgh Steelers (12–4) visiting Denver the following week.

The Broncos had revamped their offense to fit Tebow's unconventional skill set and captured their division title. They had also released Orton in the midst of a 7–1 run that included a series of fourth-quarter comebacks that captivated the football world. Never before in the four-plus decades since the AFL-NFL merger has a starting quarterback returned to start a game in the same season against his former team, but neither quarterback had a great day. The game's only touchdown came on Dexter McCluster's 21-yard scamper in the first quarter, so this game was as much about the Colquitt brothers, punters Dustin and Britton, the First Family of Fourth Downs, as it was about Orton vs. Tebow.

The Broncos saved $2.6 million by releasing Orton just before Thanksgiving but Orton nearly made them pay an even heftier price for that decision. Had Denver not backed into the playoffs, Elway's dangerous decision to release Orton at midseason would have gone down as one of the biggest blunders in Broncos history. And Fox would have been second-guessed for passing up on a 57-yard field goal attempt in the first half even though his kicker is the best in the business from long distance and points were at a premium.

None of that mattered now. Despite three straight losses, the Broncos were going back to the playoffs.

"Not the way you want to go in," Champ Bailey said. "But, hey, we've got another shot."

# CHAPTER 20
## PITTSBURGH PRAYER

**B**eep. Beep. Beep. Beep.

The Broncos were backing into the playoffs off a three-game skid in which they had been outscored 88–40 by the powerful New England Patriots as well as the lowly Buffalo Bills and Kansas City Chiefs, two teams that weren't even heading to the postseason party.

Over the course of a whipsawing 2010 season, Tim Tebow went from bust to pretty decent to occasionally spectacular—some would say miraculous—then back to being a bust as he alternately provided fodder for his die-hard fans, who chanted his name in adoration bordering on worship, and for his haters, who chanted his name in derision.

All the critics who kept insisting Tebow couldn't keep winning in the NFL playing quarterback as if he were still in college had been quieted by six straight wins. Now they were emboldened by Tebow's nosedive, and they were ready for the defending–AFC champion Pittsburgh Steelers to provide the final piece of evidence when they brought the league's top-rated defense into Denver for an AFC wild-card playoff game.

The book on beating Tebow was provided by Patriots coach Bill Belichick three weeks earlier, and it read like this: stack defenders close to the line of scrimmage to throttle the run, send a linebacker to shadow the unorthodox quarterback, and move D-backs around just before the snap to disguise the thin pass coverage and dare the erratic Tebow to put the ball in the air.

Ever since Belichick unsheathed the blueprint a week before Christmas, Tebow had completed just 41 percent of his throws (30 for 73) and averaged a measly 113 yards passing per game. In those three losses, Tebow had just one touchdown pass, four interceptions, 10 sacks, and four fumbles, two of which he lost. He ran for three touchdowns but only averaged 48 yards a game on the ground and had lost another fumble on a keeper.

Everybody around him may have figured the Broncos were in deep trouble, but Tebow wasn't rankled. Why should he be? He always played his best when the heat was on and he'd navigated this season of

Tebowmania with a low heart rate, unaffected by those who idolized him and unfazed by those who insulted him.

Television sets in the Broncos locker room and other parts of their headquarters were perpetually turned to ESPN and sportscasters were usually debating Tebow's tenacity, talents, and troubles, dissecting every part of his game and his personality. Yet Tebow never seemed to be affected by it. In fact, he actually seemed entirely oblivious to it.

"He obviously was very comfortable because he'd had a lot of practice at it," Dave Logan said. "Guys who have been in the spotlight develop an ability to deal with it. Whereas some other guys come into the league and it's a real eye-opening experience for them. They quickly realize everything they do winds up in somebody's social media post. Everything you say and do is documented one way or the other. But for a guy like Tim, he was used to that, and I really thought he dealt with it extremely well."

And even in uneven performances, Tebow's energy and enthusiasm, like his deep Christian faith, never wavered. Like great cornerbacks, Tebow had a knack of erasing any ugly play or poor performance from his mind in order to deliver in the clutch. Time and again he did it to overcome impossibly long odds with fourth-quarter comebacks and overtime triumphs.

Could he do it again? The Broncos prepared for their first trip to the postseason party in six years, when they were stopped cold in the AFC Championship Game at home by…the Pittsburgh Steelers.

That watershed afternoon of January 22, 2006, featured two proud franchises going in divergent directions. The Steelers won two Super Bowls and narrowly missed out on a third title with a 31–25 loss to the Green Bay Packers in Super Bowl XLV, and they had gone 69–35 since that fateful playoff victory in Denver. Meanwhile, the Broncos had won just 44 of 96 games with just one winning season. Worse, they'd cycled through three coaches, four quarterbacks, and six defensive coordinators.

"You can look at the direction[s] we both headed after that. They went up, we went down," cornerback Champ Bailey said in the lead-up to the wild-card weekend. "We haven't been back; they've won two since then. It's funny how it played out. But that was then, this is now. We have a chance to turn things around here and that's what we expect to do this weekend."

Bailey and linebacker D.J. Williams were the only Broncos still on the roster from the '05 conference championship team, whereas the Steelers brought back 16 players for the rematch.

From every facet, the game looked like a mismatch. The Steelers were 12–4, edged out of the AFC North title by the Baltimore Ravens on a tiebreaker. The Broncos had been outscored 390–309 in the regular season and won the AFC West with a .500 record—the same as division rivals San Diego and Oakland, only getting to the wild-card round through tiebreakers.

Despite a rash of injuries, including those to tailback Rashard Mendenhall (knee), All-Pro center Maurkice Pouncey (ankle), and Ben Roethlisberger (ankle), the Steelers were installed as 8½-point favorites.

"I'm not sure how many times in NFL playoff history a home team has been a bigger underdog," Logan said.

Intriguingly, the Steelers would be without their top tackler, safety Ryan Clark, who would sit this one out in the Mile High City as a precaution because of a blood disorder that's exacerbated by exertion at high altitude.

About the only thing the Broncos really had going for them was the league's top ground game, but they'd be without their best run blocker in right guard Chris Kuper, who broke his left leg in the regular season finale. Strong safety Brian Dawkins was also ruled out because of a nagging neck injury.

Asked when he last had to defend the option, Steelers defensive guru Dick LeBeau cracked, "Probably when I was playing." (LeBeau is a Hall of Fame defensive back who played for the Detroit Lions from 1959 to 1972.)

The biggest difference in the teams this time around was that the Steelers were the heavy favorites in this playoff game and the Broncos were the big underdogs. Bailey said he liked it that way because he'd rather have people whispering behind their backs saying they have no chance than to be patting them on their backs and talking them up. He liked this role reversal, and he pointed to what the Steelers had done six years earlier: "They came here and beat our butts," Bailey said. "So who's to say what's going to happen Sunday?"

As it turned out, only one of the greatest plays in the history of a franchise defined by comebacks and electrifying Mile High moments in the quarterback-crazed hub of the Rocky Mountains, and with John Elway cheering on the sideline, no less.

One more fantastic finish looked like a pipe dream when Tebow failed to complete even one pass in the first quarter as Pittsburgh safeties Troy Polamalu and Ryan Mundy kept creeping close to the line of scrimmage with just about every snap, leaving wide-open spaces behind them. For the fourth consecutive game it looked like the read option offense the Broncos adopted from the college game to help Tebow adapt to the pro game was as outdated as the Single Wing. The Broncos gained just eight yards in the first quarter and Tebow looked no better than he did in ugly losses to the Patriots, Bills, and Chiefs to close out the regular season.

Things looked even bleaker when wide receiver Eric Decker was knocked from the game with a knee injury on the first play of the second quarter. Yet losing his top target on a day when nothing was working didn't ruffle the unflappable Tebow, who suddenly looked a lot like Steve Young when he began slinging passes near and far, and doing something that hadn't been done in half a century in the NFL, throwing four passes of 30 yards or better in a single quarter.

One of them was a 30-yard touchdown toss to wide receiver Eddie Royal that put Denver ahead 7–6 and energized the Broncos, who took a stunning 20–6 lead into the locker room at halftime.

Roethlisberger rallied Pittsburgh from the two-touchdown half-time deficit with 10 points in the final 10 minutes to tie it at 23, and he drove the Steelers into Broncos territory in the final minute before three sacks and a fumble kept them from getting in field goal range at the end of regulation.

Denver won the coin toss for the first non–sudden death overtime in playoff history. New rules called for both teams to get the ball in the extra period providing there wasn't a touchdown by either the offense or defense first.

Tebow took care of that in a hurry. Just as the Broncos had on 21 of 22 previous first-down attempts on that freezing night in Denver, they came out in a run formation and put a wide receiver in motion. LeBeau had detected the pattern, too, and so, just as they had on all the previous attempts, Polamalu and Mundy started sneaking up to the line. Only Denver offensive coordinator Mike McCoy had drawn up a pass play on the fly at halftime, and he called it on the first snap of overtime. Demaryius Thomas lined up to the left and couldn't believe it when cornerback Ike Taylor lined up on his outside shoulder, leaving a free path over the middle with Polamalu rushing the passer.

Every single Pittsburgh defender was within five or six yards of the line of scrimmage when Tebow took the snap and tucked the ball into Willis McGahee's belly like he'd done all afternoon. Only this time he pulled it back, stood in the pocket for a split second, and delivered a simple slant the way every other quarterback who's ever played the game at the pro level has done. Thomas reached in front of his face to haul in the bullet pass in stride, then, stiff-arming Taylor and outracing Mundy, the backup safety filling in for Clark, he dashed into the end zone for an electrifying touchdown that stunned the Steelers 29–23.

"I knew walking up to the line and I saw the safety come down, I was like, *This is going to be a big play*," Thomas recounted of the game-winning score. "The middle of the field was wide open and all I had to do was beat the corner. And once I beat him, it was like, nothing but green grass. And I knew I was going to score."

Logan figured another run was coming on the first play of overtime. "When the Broncos got the ball, I said, 'They're going to have to knock out two or three first downs. Otherwise, they're going to be punting from their freaking goal line and the Steelers could win it with a field goal," Logan said.

"Polamalu comes down. The other safety comes down as well. So in essence, they have a nine-man box," Logan said. "And on the call, you can hear in my voice that I was surprised it was a pass. I said, 'Tim Tebow from the 20, play fake?' And then he hits Demaryius and Demaryius stiff-arms Ike and the race is on. I screamed, 'Here we go!' Brian Griese, who's my color analyst, just starts laughing. He was laughing all the way from the 30-yard line until Demaryius scampered into the south end zone. He just couldn't believe what he had just seen."

Thomas never broke stride, racing right up the tunnel as the stadium shook. Elway thrust his hands into the air like he used to when he was the one engineering Broncos comebacks and the crowd was going crazy.

Logan and Griese were trying to make sense of what had just happened, but they'd seen this sort of thing all season. "There were like five or six things that happened that season that, as a veteran football guy, I just had to shake my head," Logan said. "I was damn near speechless. And I remember as Demaryius was going down the west sideline, I'm ticking off the yards on the broadcast and as he goes across the goal line I just blurted out, 'It's over in Denver.' But again, I'd seen things like that happen the entire second half of the season."

Daring Tebow to beat them with his left arm backfired on the Steelers and LeBeau, one of the brightest defensive minds the league has ever seen. "He played the percentages and gambled it was going to be a run. And honestly, it was a good gamble. The Broncos had been so run-heavy on first down," Logan said.

Tebow raced after Thomas into the stadium's south end zone, where he took a knee—"Tebowing," as it came to be known that magical season—and pounded his fist on the ground in triumph before hugging teammates and coaches and taking a victory lap following his fourth overtime win of the season.

"When I saw him scoring, first of all, I just thought, *Thank you, Lord*," Tebow said. "Then, I was running pretty fast, chasing him—like

I can catch up to D.T.! Then I just jumped into the stands. First time I've done that. That was fun."

It took all of 11 seconds—the shortest overtime in NFL history—to score the longest overtime touchdown in playoff history—and for Tebow to show everyone once and for all he could be a conventional quarterback.

"Case closed," McGahee said. "They say he couldn't throw."

Tebow threw for a season-best 316 yards and two touchdowns to go with 50 yards and another score on the ground against the league's top defense. And Thomas had a career-high 204 yards on just four receptions against a team that hadn't allowed a 100-yard receiver all season.

Thomas also had receptions of 51 and 58 yards to set up second-quarter touchdowns, and the second one might have gone for a touchdown, too, had he kept racing across the field instead of slowing to cut back, allowing Taylor to catch him at the Pittsburgh 15-yard line.

So, in overtime Thomas never slowed down, running right through the end zone and up the tunnel, followed by cornerback Champ Bailey.

Thomas, however, was confused about the new playoff overtime rules that allowed both teams to get the ball unless one of them scores a touchdown first. He also was thinking back to college, where both teams get the ball in overtime. "I thought the defense had to go on the field," Thomas said. "I actually didn't know. I saw Champ run up the tunnel with me. I was like, 'What's going on?' And then I looked out, I saw everybody on the field, so I assumed the game was over with."

Up next was a trip to top-seeded New England (13–3). The Pats had walloped the Broncos 41–23 in December, sending Tebow into a funk that included seven turnovers and a 40 percent completion clip. It also prompted Elway to implore Tebow to "pull the trigger" and produce something special.

Tebow listened. And he delivered.

# CHAPTER 21
## LAST GASP

Tebowmania ran up against the great Tom Brady, and the man with a playoff pedigree like no other quarterback in NFL history put an end to the unorthodox Tim Tebow's magical, maniacal whiplash of a season.

Brady threw five of his six touchdown passes in the first half of the New England Patriots' 45–10 blowout of the Broncos a week after Denver's shocking, stadium-shaking overtime win against the Steelers. Brady sent the Patriots to another AFC Championship Game and silenced the nationwide frenzy surrounding Denver's quirky quarterback.

Tight end Rob Gronkowski's three touchdown catches helped the Patriots jump out to a 35–7 halftime lead that rendered Denver's deceptive ground game as effective as a poker dealer handing out cards face-up. With derisive "*Teee*-bow" chants ringing in his ears, Denver's quarterback was sacked five times by New England's 31st-ranked defense.

There simply wasn't any more magic left for the quarterback who transfixed the nation with an improbable playoff run that began all the way back when Denver was 1–4 and Tebow replaced Kyle Orton. The onetime third-string quarterback won six games in a row and seven of eight with a string of stirring comebacks before a 41–23 loss at home to these Patriots sent the Broncos tumbling into the playoffs on a three-game skid.

Tebow and the Broncos rebounded in a big way in their first playoff game since the 2005 season with the longest overtime touchdown in playoff history, an 80-yard catch by Demaryius Thomas that stunned the Pittsburgh Steelers 29–23. Against the Patriots a week later, Thomas was as inconsequential as just about everybody else on Denver's offense.

Tebow described his second NFL season as having "a lot of ups and downs," and he suffered bruised ribs that would keep him from playing in the upcoming Pro Bowl, despite his selection. He pledged to double down on his efforts in the off-season to iron out the kinks in his game.

In an interview with the Associated Press a month earlier, in the midst of Tebow's 7–1 run as the Broncos starting quarterback, John Elway said that no matter the highs of Tebow's season, he needed to become a conventional pocket passer to keep playing in the NFL: "I think the big picture with Tim is we've got to see the whole body of work. We've got to get a feel for Tim; you can't really do that after four miraculous runs or five miraculous runs, where things are really going well," Elway said. "And so really what you want to see with him is the improvement that's going to happen over time. Because he's done what we knew he could do and where we've seen his progress is the fact of what he does within the pocket. What we've said, and I said it when I first got here, was we know Tim's a great player and what we've got to do is make him a great quarterback, and what I've learned is you've got to be able to win from within the pocket."

Elway, who went to five Super Bowls that way and won two of them, said Tebow was showing growth in that transformation, albeit in a one-step-forward-two-steps-back sort of way. "He's getting better there," Elway said.

It's just he's never been trained in that. In Florida, he wasn't trained and his first year here he didn't get a lot of training because they were trying to win games and so Kyle was taking all the reps and then we didn't have an off-season [because of the lockout] and then we went right into it. So he's never really been trained on it. So, you know, he's got the work ethic and all those type things. Now, can I sit here and tell you he's absolutely going to get there? I wish I could. But nobody knows that.

But I think that we want it to happen because of the competitor he is and what type of person he is and how he represents not only himself but represents the Broncos and the city. People have been watching him, so he's a draw. But that's where some time in the off-season and getting him a feel and getting him a feel of the offense and what he feels comfortable with, and it comes down to the timing and throwing.

Do I think he'll get there? Yeah, I do. Am I positive? No. Just got to wait and see. And everyone talks about trading Tim Tebow. Tim Tebow's not going anywhere. I mean, he's going to be a Bronco and we're going to do everything we can and hopefully he's that guy.

That was then. But this is the NFL, which players like to say stands for "Not For Long." And Elway would quickly change his mind about Tebow.

The Indianapolis Colts owed Peyton Manning a whopping $28 million bonus in early March as part of a five-year, $90 million deal he'd signed that summer before missing the entire season following multiple neck fusion surgeries. The Colts had plummeted to a 2–14 record without their star quarterback, putting them first in line to select Stanford's standout quarterback Andrew Luck with the first pick in the 2012 NFL draft.

Could Manning actually be hitting the open market? Could Elway possibly talk him into coming to Denver?

And what would all of this mean for Tebow?

# CHAPTER 22
## PEYTON'S PLACE

When Colorado Rockies slugger Todd Helton played the final home game of his spectacular major league career in 2013, Peyton Manning made sure he was there, paying homage to his college buddy who had given him two big assists over the years.

The first came in 1994 when Manning was a scrawny freshman at the University of Tennessee, and Helton, already the big man on the Knoxville campus starring in both football and baseball, took Archie Manning's boy under his wing and helped him adjust to college life. "He was nice to me as an 18-year-old homesick freshman up there in Knoxville," Manning recalled. "Todd was a big star when I got there already, a Knoxville legend, and so he took time to be nice to me and I appreciated that." Although Manning unseated Helton as the Volunteers' starting quarterback, they remained close friends over the years, attending each other's games when they had the chance.

Helton's second big assist came in 2012 when Manning was plotting his comeback from a series of neck operations that nearly ended his NFL career and would lead to his stunning release from the Indianapolis Colts.

With players and owners at loggerheads over a new collective bargaining agreement that spring, Manning was prohibited from rehabbing at the Colts' practice facilities or even seeing his team doctors, so Helton arranged for Manning to work out at Coors Field in downtown Denver. "During that lockout, when I was in a strange and new situation, for him to get on that phone and call me and invite me out here to work out with the Rockies in private and use the Rockies' trainers, I'll always be indebted to him," Manning said later. "Because I was in kind of a weird place, unknown, I had nobody to turn to medically because of the lockout."

It was during this time that Helton legitimately thought his buddy was goofing around one day when Manning threw him a football from a very short distance and it fluttered like a wounded duck and landed at Helton's feet. "He had nothing," Helton recounted. "But I knew he'd come back and be Peyton Manning again because nobody else works that hard."

Manning's father, Archie, said he knew a second act was possible a month before training camp that summer. "By the time we had a football camp he was throwing okay. Three months before that he wasn't," Archie said. "I saw the change February to March to June. But when I saw him at football camp that June I knew he'd be all right. I knew he'd be different. He wasn't his old self. I don't know if he was 70 percent, 80 percent, 90 percent, I don't know where it was. But it wasn't 100." (In fact, four years later, as Manning was preparing for his final NFL season, he revealed that he still had no feeling in the fingertips of his right hand. Yet he managed to replicate a release point consistent enough to throw 140 of his 539 career touchdown passes post-surgery, including an NFL-record 55 in 2013, after trading the blue-and-white horseshoe helmet for the blue-and-orange one with the horse's face.)

Manning was cut loose by the Colts on March 7, 2012. With a shaky voice and tear-filled eyes, he stood at the podium alongside choked-up team owner Jim Irsay, who made the decision to release his injured superstar rather than pay him a $28 million bonus.

The move marked the end of an era, a 14-year alliance between the team that drafted Manning at No. 1 overall and the QB who brought Indianapolis from football irrelevance to the 2007 Super Bowl title and a second Super Bowl appearance three years later.

"The Indianapolis Colts today released quarterback Peyton Manning," read the team's official statement that hit the sporting world like a 300-pound tackle even though the move had been anticipated for some time.

Andy Roddick, the 2003 U.S. Open champion, might have put it best when he tweeted, "The colts cutting Peyton feels like the north pole kicking out Santa."

Manning said he didn't really want to leave the franchise that he'd taken from an afterthought to Super Bowl champion, and Irsay said he wished Manning could stay in the basketball-loving city he'd turned into a football hotbed, one that had hosted the Super Bowl a month earlier.

During that Super Bowl week, the focus was on Peyton Manning, not his younger brother, Eli, who led the New York Giants to the title over Tom Brady and the New England Patriots. Now, the older Manning, the 50,000-yard passer, four-time MVP, 11-time Pro Bowler, and Super Bowl hero who had transformed the very quarterback position itself in the NFL was about to embark on a tour of teams all wanting to serve as his safety net. That was providing, of course, that he could assuage any lingering concerns over the neck operations that forced him to sit out all of 2011.

"I still want to play," said Manning, who would turn 36 two and a half weeks later. "But there is no other team I wanted to play for." So surreal was the notion of the man synonymous with the horseshoe helmet wearing another team's colors that even Manning admitted he couldn't fathom playing for another team. He said he had no idea who might be interested in him and he wasn't even sure how this whole free agency thing worked. Was it like college recruiting, he wondered?

Not at all.

John Elway, who won two Super Bowl rings in Denver after age 37, was the first to reach out to Manning and schedule a meeting with the suddenly available free-agent superstar. Two days after his emotional farewell news conference in Indianapolis, Manning began his free agency tour by jetting to Denver on a chartered plane. He spent the day with Elway, now vice president of football operations for the Broncos, coach John Fox, and general manager Brian Xanders in a scene that included a swarm of television cameras on the ground and helicopters hovering overhead to chronicle the presidential-like visit.

Realizing Manning's emotions were still raw, Elway would later say he made sure to give Manning the space and time he needed, vowing not to pester him for a decision but just laying out what the Broncos had to offer and then going radio silent while he continued on his tour, crisscrossing the country to speak with or throw for the Arizona Cardinals, Tennessee Titans, San Francisco 49ers, and Miami Dolphins.

A few days later, Fox was in Elway's office. "Have you heard back from Peyton?" he asked. No, Elway said, he hadn't. Just then the phone rang.

John Elway was the first to reach out to Peyton Manning and schedule a meeting when he became a surprise free agent. A few days later, after Elway gave him the space he needed to make a decision, Manning was a Bronco.

Manning informed Elway he'd made his decision, and as a courtesy called all the also-rans with the bad news before letting his chosen team know.

Elway's heart skipped a beat. "So am I your last call?" Elway asked hopefully.

Yes, Manning said, he was coming to Denver.

Seeing Elway's reaction, Fox could hardly contain himself. "I almost pulled both hamstrings I jumped out of my chair so high," Fox said.

So, what about Tim Tebow *now*? Elway never sounded all that convinced the southpaw sensation was the Broncos' long-term answer at the sport's most important position, and now that Manning had agreed to a five-year, $96 million contract, Elway could trade the enormously popular but erratic quarterback who was a polarizing figure for both his style of play—as far as possible from a classic, dropback passer—and for his unabashedly outspoken religious beliefs.

Tebow had led the Broncos to the playoffs through a wildly inconsistent season in which he was the main focus in the entire NFL and the most talked-about athlete in sports, one who was frustratingly inconsistent and even obdurate in his insistence on sticking to what made him one of the greatest college players in NCAA history and not adjusting to the pro game that was more suited for pocket passers than an option quarterback.

The cultural phenomenon known as Tebowmania reached its apex in the playoffs, when Tebow threw an 80-yard touchdown pass to Demaryius Thomas on the very first play of overtime to beat the Steelers a week before he and the Broncos were smothered by Tom Brady and the Patriots. Now, Tebow's fans were wondering where he'd go next. Colorado governor John Hickenlooper chimed in, saying he hoped Tebow wouldn't go anywhere but stick around as Manning's backup. "He's a young man, right? And a year or two of working under John Elway and Peyton Manning, you know, I'm not sure any other quarterbacks around the country get that opportunity," Hickenlooper told reporters at the Capitol rotunda.

That wasn't going to happen. "You don't want to bring Manning in and here's Tebow on the bench, and every time Peyton throws an incompletion, you're going to have chants," Dave Logan said. "You just couldn't do that, could you? Couldn't do that. So, I said that on the air. I said, 'That's not going to work.'"

The day after Manning's introductory news conference, the Broncos traded Tebow to the New York Jets, where his football career fizzled. He would rejoin Josh McDaniels, the man who selected him with the 25th pick of the 2010 NFL draft, in New England the next year, but Bill Belichick cut him coming out of training camp and Tebow turned to baseball and broadcasting.

For Manning, it would take a while to feel comfortable with his new team. He'd later say he felt like a visitor in his own locker room for his entire first season in Denver. He won his first game, against Ben Roethlisberger and the Steelers, but lost three of his next four starts. He was getting used to new surroundings, new teammates, new coaches, new schemes, new schedules, a new play caller, a new center, even a new reality that he was a different quarterback after multiple neck surgeries.

Can you imagine if Tebow were on the sideline still when the Broncos fell to 2–3? "Your quarterback is the acknowledged leader of the team. He's got to be the recognized leader of the team in the locker room, period," Logan said. "I've never seen a really good team where that was not the case. And if you keep a guy who was the acknowledged sort of leader the year before and then you bring in the guy who's a great leader, what do you have in the locker room? So that move had to be made."

The Broncos moved on behind Manning's perfectionist personality and precise passes. Tebow's time had come and gone. "But it was a hell of a fun year," Logan said. "Really exciting. Normally in a game I'll have a pretty good sense as to how the game will unfold in two or three ways. But that year, I was just like everybody else sitting at home watching TV and eating popcorn: I never knew. So many times I had the thought during a game, *I have no idea how this thing is going to play out*."

## Dave Logan's Log

Tim Tebow had great leadership skill. Playing quarterback in the NFL—playing in the NFL, period—takes a certain skill set, an elite skill set. But I really think honestly, whatever he puts his mind to do, he's going to be successful at it. He's just that kind of guy.

There are still people in Denver who say Tebow should still have been the starting quarterback. But when you look at his skill set at quarterback, as tough of a kid as he was, and as great a leader as he was, his throwing mechanics were very difficult to replicate. For me, the throwing motion of a quarterback is analogous to the swing of a PGA golf pro. If you look at Jim Furyk, you probably say, "Wow, that's a really unusual swing." But he's able to replicate that and he's able to duplicate that even at stressful times.

And I think you'd watch Tim in practice and he'd make some really good throws. And you'd say, "Okay, okay." But to really do that under duress, where your throwing platform might change a little bit, your arm angle might change because you've got a 320-pound dude in your face—that's hard to do. I don't know if there was a better college football player I ever saw than Tim. But there are many quarterbacks who are really successful in college who don't have great success in the NFL.

Elway looked to silence the skeptics, who at the time didn't know what to expect for the superstar but ailing Manning. "Tim Tebow's a great kid," John Elway said. "If I want someone to marry my daughter, it's him." But to run an NFL offense, to get another Super Bowl trophy, he wanted Peyton Manning. "My goal is to make Peyton Manning the best quarterback that's ever played the game," Elway said of the 50,000-yard passer who redefined the position throughout the 2000s.

While Manning instructed his agent to work out the details on his deal in Denver, Logan reached out to Bob Lamey, the longtime radio play-by-play voice of the Colts. "I said, 'So, what do you think, Bob? He said, 'You're going to love him, but he's not going to do a pregame show, Dave.' I was really surprised. 'He didn't do a pregame show with you?' Lamey was quick to reply, 'Nope.... Peyton will control every single facet of everything he does in the media.' For the most part, he was right about that."

Thirteen days after standing at the podium in Indianapolis alongside Irsay for a tearful farewell news conference, Manning was all smiles as he sat next to Elway, who was flashing that mile-wide grin after landing the biggest prize in the history of free agency, one rivaled only by the Green Bay Packers landing Reggie White in the 1990s and teaming the "Minister of Defense" with quarterback Brett Favre to put the title back in Titletown, U.S.A.

The goal for the powerful pair of Elway and Manning was the same; both talked about hoisting another Lombardi Trophy together. Elway had capped his Hall of Fame career with two titles in the late 1990s and Manning had won a ring in 2007. One more and he'd tie brother Eli.

The Broncos had won just two playoff games since Elway's MVP performance in Super Bowl XXXIII in 1999, one of them coming against Pittsburgh two months earlier, when Tebow delivered his best pass in two years as a pro, a stadium-rocking rocket to Demaryius Thomas who took it 80 yards into the end zone on the first play of overtime for a 29–23 triumph. A couple of large photos of Tebow that had adorned the halls at the Broncos' headquarters were gone by the time Manning was introduced as Denver's new quarterback and Elway famously declared that he had "no Plan B. I'm going with Plan A."

After starting every game for the Colts for 13 seasons, Manning's neck problem kept him off the field in 2011. His deal—the most dramatic for Denver since the Colts traded Elway to the Broncos in 1983—was $96 million over five years and reflected the risk: there was no signing bonus. Manning would get $18 million guaranteed in 2012, but he'd have to pass a physical before each subsequent season to get paid.

"I don't consider it much of a risk, knowing Peyton Manning," Elway said. "I asked him, 'Is there any doubt in your mind that you can't get back to the Peyton Manning we know of?' And he said, 'There's no doubt in my mind.' I believe that he's got a lot of great football left in him."

Manning didn't dance around the questions about his health. "I'm not where I want to be," he answered. "I want to be where I was before I was injured. I have a lot of work to do in getting to where I want to be from a health standpoint and learning this offense. This is going to take a ton of work."

Manning, who would celebrate his 36th birthday that weekend, said he made a quick connection with Elway, who won his two Super Bowls after his 37th birthday, when injuries were taking their toll on him, too.

It's one thing to throw through an entire route tree on a practice field, which he did pretty much to everyone's satisfaction during his frenetic free-agency tour, but it is quite another to take a blindside hit from a 300-pound defender. "There's no question I have work to do," Manning said. "I've been very open with the Broncos, really all the teams, about my medical history, about where I am, about how I feel. I really let them tell me. I've put all the cards out on the table, working out for three teams, going through my entire medical history, not just this past year. I couldn't sell myself when it came to that. I had to let them tell me and decide this was something they wanted to do." Elway was all-in.

The Broncos scrambled that morning of the introductory news conference, where Manning and Elway would hold up his new orange jersey, because Manning's familiar No. 18 was actually retired in Denver, a tribute to the franchise's first quarterback, Frank Tripucka. Associated Press sports writer Pat Graham had written a feature about Tripucka and his retired jersey number and the Broncos reached out to Graham the morning of Manning's introductory news conference as they scrambled to get Tripucka's blessing to unretire No. 18. Happily, Tripucka was glad to let Manning bring it out of mothballs.

As for No. 15's status, Manning said, "I know what kind of player Tim Tebow is, what kind of person he is...and what an awesome year he had this year. If Tim Tebow is here next year, I'm going to be the best teammate I can be to him. He and I are going to help this team win games. If other opportunities present themselves to him, I'm going to wish him the best."

The moment Manning chose Denver as his destination, however, Tebow's days were numbered with the Broncos. Having two entirely different kinds of quarterbacks, it made little sense for the Broncos to keep Tebow as the backup because they were going to install a vastly different offense under Manning. Besides, Manning was going to get almost every single snap at practice as he embarked on his comeback and acclimated to playing at altitude, outdoors, with a new team, and new realities.

After a big false start, the New York Jets pulled off a Tebow-like comeback to acquire the quirky quarterback. The Jets agreed to send a pair of draft picks to Denver but then balked at repaying the Broncos more than $5 million for a salary advance due Tebow. The trade stalled for eight hours, bringing the Jacksonville Jaguars back into the picture as a possible destination, before the sides agreed to split the cost. "I was just kind of watching and waiting—kind of like everybody else," Tebow said on a conference call that night. "It was an interesting day."

Although the Jets saved face by salvaging the deal, they also opened up themselves and starter Mark Sanchez, who has just signed a $40.5 million contract, to pressure from Tebow's relentless fans who would call for their man to start at the first sign of struggles, if not before. Just a few weeks after "Linsanity" swept New York and the rest of the NBA with the Knicks' sensational Jeremy Lin, "Timsanity" was set to take over Broadway.

Jets general manager Mike Tannenbaum said he was well aware of Tebow's "magnetic following" and understood the backup quarterback was often the most popular player on the team, especially when that backup was Tim Tebow. Tebow's legion of detractors would also be out in force in the Big Apple.

"New York is a tough market, right?" said Logan, reflecting on Tebow's struggles there. He still wonders if the quarterback would have been better off going to the Jaguars, where he'd have been hailed as the hometown hero.

Indeed, Hall of Fame quarterback Joe Namath, who led the Jets to their only Super Bowl title in 1969, was among those who were unhappy with the acquisition of Tebow. "I'm just sorry that I can't agree with this situation," Namath said on 1050 ESPN Radio in New York. "I think it's just a publicity stunt. I can't go with it. I think it's wrong. I don't think they know what they're doing over there."

# CHAPTER 23
## A BEAUTIFUL MIND

**T**he Broncos were confident they would get in Peyton Manning a quarterback who could still get so much more out of his body. But they were absolutely certain they had the best brain when it came to NFL quarterbacks. By swapping out Tim Tebow for "the great Peyton Manning," as the late Denver cornerback Darrent Williams called him, the Broncos were going from the most erratic, unpredictable quarterback in the NFL, one whose very style was built on improvisation and gut instinct, to one who rejected anything less than perfection.

Manning revolutionized quarterback play almost from his pro debut in 1998, directing adjustments at the line of scrimmage as he read the defensive formation and deciphered his opponents' intentions, barking out changes to calls and checking out of this play or into that one.

As preeminent as Tom Brady is in the NFL, it was Manning who changed the way the game's most important position is played, Dave Logan said. "Whether it's Tom Brady or any other NFL quarterback, nobody does as much at the line of scrimmage as Peyton Manning," Logan said. "It's not even close. And that's not to say Tom Brady's not a great quarterback. I just don't think anybody has ever done as much at the line as Peyton. I've even heard coaches say he did too much at times."

Manning was the master at finding the soft underbelly of any defensive formation, then delivering the pass to the perfect spot. He also had incredible recall, remembering play sequences on specific drives going back to his days at the University of Tennessee. He could look at a formation that an opponent hadn't run all year, recognize it from several years earlier, and adjust accordingly—all in a matter of seconds.

"One of the things that made him such a special player was his approach mentally," Logan said, "because I think Peyton would be the first to admit that he wasn't the most physically gifted player. He certainly had a good arm at Tennessee, but he worked hard at it and understood what you were trying to accomplish defensively against him."

Logan relayed a story told to him by Josh McDaniels, who was a defensive assistant for Bill Belichick in New England in 2003 when the Patriots were preparing to face Manning and the Colts. In preparing for the game, Belichick instructed his defensive staff to come up with a blitz they had never run before, one that Manning would never be able to find in his meticulous preparation for the Patriots.

McDaniels went on. "It's the third quarter, and we decided to run the blitz. We had two young safeties we'd worked with all week on disguising the look because Peyton was a master of reading your mail [getting a pre-snap understanding of what the coverage is]. I'm watching my safeties and one safety just took a step, I mean, one step toward where he needed to go, before the ball was snapped. As soon as he did that, I looked over and Peyton was staring right at him. He backed away from center and checked to another play. We were on the headset saying, 'Get out of it! Get out of it! He saw it!' But it was too late. The Colts ran the play and it was a touchdown."

"That shows you how good Peyton was," Logan said. "You worked so hard at practice to disguise stuff. You make one false read pre-snap and he sees it, then it tells him what you're going to be in. Peyton saw it, went up, checked it, checked either the protection to take care of the pressure or a route concept, and he throws a touchdown pass."

So meticulous was Manning in his preparation that he demanded full attention and perfection from everyone around him, not just the players.

He despised surprises, too. "My first time that I really heard anything about Peyton was from Bob Lamey," Logan said. "And the two things he told me were he wouldn't do a pregame interview and he doesn't like surprises. He wound up doing a pregame show with me in Denver, but I would say Bob was right in that Peyton did not like to be surprised."

## Dave Logan's Log

I had taken three of my high school coaches and we were down visiting the University of Alabama for spring football practice. We had gone for four days, sat in on coaches meetings, and attended practice. I missed a call while at practice one afternoon, checked the voicemail, and it was Peyton Manning.

So I called him and said, "Hey, I'm down in Tuscaloosa. I just saw one of my former teammates—former Alabama tight end Ozzie Newsome." And Peyton quickly responded, "Well, when you're down there, ask them how the UT-Alabama matchup went back in '98."

I was still standing next to Ozzie when Peyton made that comment. Ozzie responded, "Yeah, well, ask him how it's gone the last four or five years." I didn't have to relay that comment to Peyton. "Yeah, I heard him. I heard him," Peyton said. "It hasn't gone all that well."

So, I got back to Denver, I called Peyton, and he said, "Listen, I'm doing this fundraiser. It's my charity, PeyBack Foundation, and it's going to be at somebody's house and we need an auctioneer. It's like 60, 70 people. Would you do that for me?" I said, "Yeah, I'm happy to do it." I got all the details from him, waited until we were almost finished, and I said, "So, can I talk about my fee?"

Crickets.

There was this really uncomfortable like three seconds of silence before Peyton bellowed, "Your fee?" And I said, "Yeah, my fee." And I'm thinking to myself, *I'd better not play this out too much longer.* So, I said, "Here's my fee: I want to sit down with you for an hour and just talk Xs and Os about some of your no-huddle stuff and other things that I can put to good use from a high school coach's standpoint."

He completely changed from being righteously indignant that I had requested a fee to being really pleased to sit down and talk football. "Absolutely. Absolutely. I'll meet you up there at 1:00 on Wednesday." I got there about 12:45 and was taken to an empty room. Peyton walked in right at 1:00 and shut the door. He had cut-ups prepared, he had stuff that he did back in Tennessee spliced with drills that the quarterback works on and how they helped him over the years. We talked about how important communication was in the no-huddle stuff. But the thing that impressed me the most was how totally prepared he was for the meeting. He brought a notebook with about 10 pages of handwritten stuff in it.

It was a really enjoyable hour for a football nerd like me.

I wasn't huddling with Manning in my role as the play-by-place voice of the Broncos that afternoon but as a former NFL wide receiver–turned–high school football coach. We just went over some of the verbiage that he used, how you change plays, how you condense calls. But I will say this, it illustrated to me what I had always thought about Peyton and had been told by a couple of people who had interacted with him previously: the guy's totally immersed in what he does. He's going to be absolutely prepared beyond 100 percent with every single thing that he does.

And to illustrate the point, when we had the event that I agreed to do for his PeyBack Foundation—I wound up doing it for all three of his years in Denver—he texted me and said "Hey, the event's coming up next week. Can you meet me at 7 o'clock tonight?" I asked where we were meeting and he said, "I want to meet at the house that we're doing the event at...just...to do a dry run."

And I'm thinking, *dry run?* But it was Peyton Freaking Manning, so I agreed. I drove out to the house and he's got the whole script there, I mean, down to every last detail. *So, Dave, you'll come in at 7:15. There will be hors d'oeuvres. At 7:23, there will be this. You'll call people into this room at 7:25. You and I can do a short Q&A. We'll welcome everybody. Then, you do the auction. We'll raise the money.* And he had every single thing detailed by the minute for how things would go. That's just how he's wired.

Just like he was preparing for a football game.

Another time Logan did a Q&A with Manning at the Broncos stadium for about 70 suite holders, which was set up by the team.

"So, he emails a list of questions.... Whenever I do an interview, I never ever go off notes. I formulate ideas about what I want to ask before the interview starts. I may have a couple of topics I want to get to, but I don't ever write out the questions," Logan explained.

On the night of the event, Logan and Manning were about to go onstage.

"Did you get the questions?" Manning asked.

"I got them," Logan replied.

"So, do you have them?"

"Peyton, I've got them. I've got them."

Manning looked perplexed. "I know, but did you get the list of questions I sent you?"

"Peyton, I've got 'em. Trust me, you're in good hands. It's all up here," Logan said, tapping his temple.

Just like Manning poring over the playbook, Logan had memorized the talking points.

Manning nodded. That was something he could certainly appreciate.

"So he is very regimented, to a degree that is highly uncommon even amongst professional athletes," Logan said. "Peyton by far took that to another level."

# CHAPTER 24
# THE MANNING EFFECT

It all began in the spring on local high school football fields during the NFL lockout. The Denver Broncos receivers were working hard at not rounding off their routes, lest they get an earful from No. 18. It continued later on at team headquarters, with cornerbacks picking the four-time MVP's brain to figure out how he was picking them apart.

What began as a season of mystery morphed into one of magnificence as Peyton Manning found his footing and his groove after losing three of his first five games for the Broncos. Behind Manning's 4,659 yards passing—a franchise record and almost 3,000 more than Tim Tebow had the year before—and 37 touchdown throws, the Broncos won their last 11 games, thundering into the playoffs at 13–3 as the AFC's top seed.

Not since John Elway was leading comebacks on the football field had the Broncos gone into the playoffs as odds-on favorites to represent the AFC in the Super Bowl. And it was all because of Manning's arrival.

The "Manning Effect" is what wide receiver Brandon Stokley dubbed it. Stokley traded in retirement that year for a reunion in Denver with Manning, whom he had played with in Indianapolis. Manning sets his standards so high that "it just makes the players work harder and want to do better," Stokley explained. "With Peyton, everything has to be so precise, detail-oriented, it just rubs off on everybody else."

Players see the league's most decorated quarterback working as though he's on the bubble to even make the team, and they take heed. "I think when you have someone of his stature pushing himself to the ultimate level that it makes everyone push themselves to that level too," said Denver tight end Jacob Tamme, who also played with Manning in Indy. "The fact he's had the success he's had but still works so hard still at this point I think shows why he's had the success that he's had in the first place."

In this atmosphere of accountability, highlighted by Manning's miraculous bounce-back from neck surgery that sidelined him for a year, several young teammates blossomed, from receivers Eric Decker and Demaryius Thomas to defensive backs Chris Harris Jr. and Tony

Carter. Von Miller became a bona fide superstar, and veterans such as Stokley looked young again.

With Manning putting to rest any lingering doubts about his health or age, the Broncos' offense rose from 23$^{rd}$ in the league the previous season to fourth, and Denver's defense jumped from 20$^{th}$ to second. They scored 481 points in the season after scoring 309. And their defense allowed 289 after yielding 390.

Champ Bailey said Manning not only proved he's every bit the defensive decoder he's always been but he microwaves young defenders' growth because he had no tolerance for sloppiness or mistakes, and safety David Bruton Jr. said the defensive backs felt they could compete with anyone on any Sunday after facing Manning all week. And with Manning's offense providing so many leads during their 11-game winning streak, Miller and Elvis Dumervil teamed up for 29½ sacks.

This is what Coach John Fox was talking about when he spoke of Manning raising all boats. Even those of the beer and hot dog vendors, because with No. 18 at quarterback, the Broncos' season home attendance of 613,062 was the highest in the team's 53-year history.

The team was confident it would reach Super Bowl XLVII at the Mercedes-Benz Superdome in New Orleans. They even handed out media parking passes to both the AFC divisional round game and the AFC Championship Game together, telling reporters to make sure not to lose next week's passes. Bring on the Baltimore Ravens.

The Broncos had reeled off 11 consecutive wins following a 31–21 loss at New England on October 7, in the process surging past the Patriots (12–4) for the top seed in the AFC playoffs. Coming off a 5–0 December they capped with four double-digit wins to end the regular season, they earned a first-round bye along with the Patriots.

The Ravens earned the fourth seed after slipping from their 9–2 perch with a very different December than the one Denver had. They lost four of their five games that month, including an ugly 34–17 game at home against the Broncos.

They bounced back in the playoffs, however, beating Manning's old team, the Colts—which was now led by rookie quarterback Andrew Luck—24–9 on wild-card weekend, earning a rematch with the Broncos, this time in Denver. The temperature was 13 degrees at kickoff on January 12, 2013, making it the coldest playoff game in the Broncos' history, and the mercury dipped dramatically when the sun dipped below the Rocky Mountains by halftime and the wind snapped the flags atop the goal posts.

The teams would pile up 877 yards and 73 points on that frozen field in the fourth-longest game in NFL history, one that wasn't even decided until the second overtime.

The Ravens seemingly had an answer for every big play the Broncos produced. When Trindon Holliday returned a punt 90 yards for a 7–0 Denver lead, Baltimore countered with a 59-yard pass from Joe Flacco to Torrey Smith to tie it. When Holliday ran into the league record books by taking the second-half kickoff back 104 yards, becoming the first player in NFL history to score on a punt return and a kickoff return in the same game, the Ravens countered with Ray Rice's one-yard run to tie it at 28.

A 17-yard touchdown toss to Thomas midway through the fourth quarter gave Denver the lead again, and when the Broncos stopped Flacco on fourth-and-5 from the Denver 31 with just over three minutes remaining, Manning was about to beat Baltimore for the 10th straight time and prove he didn't need the climate control of a dome to win a big game in January.

But offensive coordinator Mike McCoy decided to put the game in the hands of undersized rookie running back Ronnie Hillman, who took five consecutive handoffs, the last one for no gain on third-and-7 from midfield. Britton Colquitt's 30-yard punt gave Baltimore the ball at its own 23 with 69 seconds remaining.

A misfire to Flacco's tight end brought up second-and-10, and when none of his receivers broke free, he scrambled to his 30-yard line, bringing up third-and-3 as the clock ticked toward 30 seconds.

Exhausted, deflated, and almost defeated, Ravens linebacker Ray Lewis, playing his 17th and final season, slumped on the heated bench behind his teammates. He'd made 17 tackles that night, just one week after collecting 13 tackles against the Colts in his last game at Baltimore and his first game in three months because of a torn right triceps.

Thomas had eluded Lewis' grasp on the go-ahead touchdown minutes earlier, and now the final seconds of his brilliant career were slipping away too.

Flacco took the snap and dodged Dumervil, stepped up, and flung the football high into the cold night and deep downfield. Instead of going for the tackle, safety Rahim Moore went for the interception. Only he mistimed both his leap and the football's trajectory, flopping to the ground and leaving Jacoby Jones with an uncontested catch. Jones pranced into the end zone for a 70-yard game-tying touchdown, silencing the shaking stadium.

"In 30 years of broadcasting Denver Broncos football, it's as close as I've ever come to swearing on the air," Dave Logan said. "I could not believe what I had just seen."

Given the ball at his 20 with 31 seconds, two timeouts, one of the best quarterbacks in the game, and one of the game's best kickers, John Fox decided to run out the clock and play for overtime.

So Manning took a knee, a decision that would be hotly debated after the team that had jelled so well in the regular season wasted an 11-game winning streak and home-field advantage with a 38–35 double-overtime loss that night to the Ravens, a heavy underdog that outplayed, outcoached, and outmaneuvered the Broncos. The second-guessing only intensified the following day when the Atlanta Falcons moved the ball 41 yards in 12 seconds to set up the winning field goal in their 30–28 victory over Seattle in the NFC divisional round.

Fox insisted there was no comparing the two situations. The Falcons were losing and had no other choice. The game was in a dome. The Broncos were outside, freezing in single-digit temperatures. They had just allowed a touchdown pass calculated at 1-in-1,000 odds and were standing on the sideline in disbelief. Besides, Manning had gone deep only twice the entire game.

"You watch a 70-yard bomb go over your head, there's a certain amount of shock value," Fox at the Broncos' season-ending news conference. "A little bit like a prize fighter who gets a right cross on the chin at the end of a round. You're looking to get out of the round."

John Elway agreed with the call. Extracting the Broncos from impossible situations was how Elway built his NFL playing career and his reputation as the king of the comeback, but when asked how he would have responded back then if his coach ordered him to take a knee under those circumstances, Elway the front-office executive sounded nothing like that swashbuckling, go-for-broke Hall of Fame quarterback. "I thought it was the right thing at that time," Elway said. "I think with where the team was mentally and the situation we were in, I thought that it was a good move."

The Broncos stopped Baltimore twice in overtime before Manning threw an interception that set up the Ravens' game-winning field goal 96 seconds into the second overtime. It was an unexpected end to a season they thought would end in a hail of confetti. It was just like that 1996 season that had Super Bowl written all over it, only for the 13–3 Broncos to lose by three points at home to the Jacksonville Jaguars in the divisional round after a bye.

Those Broncos, with Elway under center, bounced back to win the next two Super Bowls. All Elway could do now was hope that this loss would propel this team to those same heights.

"This is something that the players will remember for a long time," Elway said. "They'll never forget what happened...and I think that we'll use that as we did in '96. It was a great incentive for us to come back and have an even better year the following year like we did in '97. Like I said, it's how we approach it, how we use it, how we learn from it. And it gives us an opportunity to be that much better next year."

# CHAPTER 25
## SUPER BLOWOUT

Atop John Elway's to-do list in 2014 was signing off on the next two years and $40 million of Peyton Manning's contract after the quarterback passed his physical in March. Manning had shown no ill effects of the nerve problem in his neck that led to four operations and his departure from Indianapolis. He also up the second-best numbers of his 14 healthy seasons in the NFL.

Then, there was the matter of getting the entire team over the loss to Baltimore in the playoffs, one in which Manning had three costly turnovers, fellow All-Pro Champ Bailey got burned for two long touchdown passes, and coach John Fox made a series of debatable decisions including running underweight rookie running back Ronnie Hillman on third-and-7 while trying to run out the clock and then, after the Ravens had tied it with a most improbable 70-yard touchdown, ordering Manning to take a knee with 31 seconds and two timeouts remaining, choosing instead to take his chances in overtime.

Fox stood by those two strategic choices but acknowledged a post-mortem review. "As a coach—and I know John, as a competitor—you relive it, you redo it, you second-guess, you— I don't know how to explain it, but it stings," Fox said. "They call them scars. You remember it because it doesn't go away, like most scars. And you learn from it. You say, 'I made a mistake.... I'm going to fix it and then not let it happen again.'"

That's precisely what second-year safety Rahim Moore said after he misjudged Joe Flacco's 70-yard prayer to Jacoby Jones in the final minute that tied the game at 35. After the game, a choked-up Moore put the loss squarely on his own shoulders and vowed to atone for his big blunder. "That's definitely going to motivate me," Moore said. "I'm going to keep my head high, and next time the opportunity comes, I'm just going to make it for my team. I'll just make the play. I'm just sorry the way the season ended because it ended all on me.... I apologize to all the fans and people who love the Broncos because this wasn't what they deserved. And I'll get it right."

One of Elway's favorite sayings was, "You make your money during the regular season; you make your legacy in the postseason." The Broncos had some legacy building to do.

Manning's neck was no longer the question, having held up fine in 2013. Now, the concern was whether he could carry the weighty Super Bowl expectations of a franchise on his shoulders with superstar linebacker and defensive leader Von Miller serving an NFL drug suspension to start the season.

Miller's absence was exacerbated by the infamous fax fiasco in the spring that led to the loss of his pass-rush partner, Elvis Dumervil, to the Ravens. On March 15, Dumervil waffled but finally agreed to reduce his 2013 salary from $12 million to $8 million in Denver as part of a renegotiated three-year, $30 million contract. But the paperwork didn't reach the NFL offices in time and the Broncos were forced to release him to avoid having to pay him the full $12 million for the 2013 season. They issued a new proposal to Dumervil and his new agent—he fired his first one after the deadline debacle—but the Ravens swooped in with a better offer and beat Denver for the second time that year.

Dumervil, a fourth-round draft pick out of Louisville in 2006, had 20½ sacks in the previous two seasons, making two trips to the Pro Bowl alongside Miller, the NFL's Defensive Rookie of the Year in 2011 who had 18½ sacks in 2012, breaking the franchise record of 17 set by Dumervil in 2009. Together they were dubbed "Doom & Gloom," and were the most prolific pair of pass rushers in the league over the previous two seasons.

Dumervil's signing eased a sting for the Ravens, who lost several veterans to free agency and emotional leaders Ray Lewis and Ed Reed to retirement. The Broncos, on the other hand, spent big in free agency, acquiring wide receiver Wes Welker, right guard Louis Vasquez, defensive tackle Terrance Knighton, cornerback Dominique Rodgers-Cromartie, and linebacker Stewart Bradley. Plus, Elway re-signed Manning's All-Pro blindside protector, Ryan Clady, to the biggest contract ever for a Broncos offensive lineman.

"Super Bowl or bust, for the most part," Clady said after signing for five years and $57.5 million.

Many fans wondered if Moore would continue playing in Denver after his gaffe in the playoffs, but he maintained his status as the team's starting free safety. "I think he's over it, I think we're all over it," defensive coordinator Jack Del Rio said. "I think we can all look back and see things that we could have done better. We also look back with a great deal of pride in what we accomplished."

Because of a conflict with the Orioles in Baltimore, the Super Bowl champs opened their regular season on the road in Denver. The NFL hung a giant Joe Flacco banner above Denver's stadium for the rematch, but he hardly felt at home in the Broncos' 49–27 victory engineered by Manning, who tied an NFL record by throwing for seven touchdowns.

It was the kickstart to the greatest offensive display in league history, a record 606 points and an unprecedented 55 touchdowns from Manning in another 13–3 season that also included a loss at Indianapolis in Manning's emotional homecoming, an overtime loss at New England, and a home loss to San Diego, all three by a combined 16 points.

Denver's Lamborghini-paced offense, the best of all time, camouflaged an ever-thinning defense that lost young stars Miller and cornerback Chris Harris Jr. to knee injuries along with safety Moore (leg), defensive end Derek Wolfe (neck, seizures), and defensive tackle Kevin Vickerson (hip) down the stretch.

In the playoffs, the Broncos fended off a fourth-quarter rally by the Chargers for a 24–17 win over San Diego that avoided a repeat of their crushing loss to Baltimore exactly a year earlier. Elway said he was "absolutely miserable" watching that game and "it took me four hours to get the pit out of my stomach afterward."

"That was a hump we had to get over because of Baltimore," Elway explained. "So, that was something that we had to put in our rearview mirror, because if we hadn't done it, then we're going to be talking about it for another full year. Then we're dealing with another year of the same thing." That 38–35 double-overtime loss to the Ravens, helped along by Moore's infamous gaffe, haunted the Broncos for a full 365 days before it was finally exorcised.

A week later, Manning threw for 400 yards and two touchdowns in a 26–16 victory over Tom Brady and the Patriots in the AFC Championship Game to send Denver to its seventh Super Bowl. This time, they'd face their old AFC Western Division foe, Seattle.

Manning didn't have one go-to receiver in 2013. He had five. And the Broncos weren't worried if wintry weather at MetLife Stadium in the Meadowlands in Super Bowl XLVIII curtailed his passing prowess because Manning could downshift just as easily as he could dial up deep passes. With the bunch formations and picks and rubs that had gotten under Bill Belichick's skin in the playoffs, the turbocharged Broncos had morphed into a yard-chewing, clock-eating machine on their way to winning the AFC crown for the first time since Elway was their quarterback.

With Manning dinking and dunking his way downfield, Denver's three most time-consuming drives of the season all came in the playoffs: seven-minute masterpieces that rendered Philip Rivers and Brady short-tempered sideline spectators to Manning's magic. He simply had more outlets than defenses have answers for.

No team in the history of the NFL ever had five players reach the end zone 10 or more times on pass plays until Demaryius Thomas (14), Knowshon Moreno (13), Julius Thomas (12), Eric Decker (11), and Wes Welker (10) did it in 2013. This quintet helped the Broncos break the once-unfathomable 600-point barrier in the regular season. And each of them also caught at last 60 passes; no team had ever had five players do that before, either.

"To be honest, as a former wide receiver, I was a little bit jealous," Dave Logan said. "These guys might get 12–14 targets in a game. It was remarkable. It felt like I was broadcasting a video game at times, but the Broncos just seemed to be that much better. They were several steps ahead, they were better athletically. I mean, they just made it look so easy."

Yet it felt every bit like *Madden* football. Manning said his unprecedented 55 touchdown passes and record 5,477 yards through the air were only temporary records which would soon be surpassed by Brady or Drew Brees—or by any number of other quarterbacks if owners get their way and expand the regular season to 18 games. The beauty of this Broncos offense heading into its showdown with Seattle's "Legion of Boom" secondary in the Super Bowl was in its balance.

"Yeah," Seahawks cornerback Richard Sherman said, "but we're pretty good, too."

The elite offense and peerless defense clashed on February 2, 2014. Denver received the opening kickoff, but the Broncos would trail before Manning ever got his hands on the ball because center Manny Ramirez's errant snap went for a safety 12 seconds into Super Bowl XLVIII.

"It was a crazy start," Manning said. And a paradoxical finish to the greatest season ever posted by a quarterback and offense in NFL history.

The Broncos never recovered from that early gaffe. The prolific point producers who scored 606 in the regular season then dominated the AFC in the playoffs managed to muster only Thomas' 14-yard touchdown catch on the final play of the third quarter at the Meadowlands, the only bright spot in a 43–8 drubbing by the Seahawks.

"You've got to play well in this game to win it," said Elway, who knew from personal experience, having been blown out in his first three before winning a close one and another going away to cap his Hall of Fame career at quarterback.

The seeds of Denver's self-destruction in Super Bowl XLVIII were planted in practice earlier that week, when Coach John Fox turned down the volume of the giant speakers simulating crowd noise. "It's not an away game," he reasoned. It was a colossal miscalculation by the veteran coach who also took the Carolina Panthers to the Super Bowl in his second season in Charlotte, North Carolina, a decade earlier only to lose 32–29 to Brady and the Patriots.

Seattle's famed 12th Man indeed showed up on Denver's first play from scrimmage and laid ruin to whatever great game plan the Broncos had cooked up, paving the way for the Seahawks' dismantling of the game's greatest offense in history, the one with the quarterback who had thrown for more touchdowns and yards than anyone ever had and who won an unprecedented fifth MVP award just two years after his throwing arm was weakened by neck fusion surgeries.

The crowd at MetLife Stadium was spirited, as all Super Bowl crowds are at the beginning, and when Manning lined up in the shotgun and called for the ball from his 14-yard line, his center couldn't hear the cadence. Ramirez crouched still and just as Manning stepped up to reset the play, Ramirez's snap sailed past the quarterback into the north end zone, where running back Knowshon Moreno scampered and smothered it for a safety lest a defender fall on it for a touchdown.

"The first snap of the game was like a *what the hell?* moment," Logan said. "You're all geared up for the game and it really looks like a good matchup. Here comes Peyton, here comes Decker, here comes Demaryius, here comes the entire offense—and then the game starts and on the first snap, the Broncos give up a safety! I was thinking at the time, *Have I ever seen a safety on the first play of any game I've played in or broadcast?* I really don't think so.

"As a play-by-play guy you've got to be able to convey to your audience not only the action on the field, but also the overall emotion surrounding the game. And that play was so deflating right off the bat. I was so dumbfounded by the play, it really was a WTF moment."

Of all the mistakes and miscalculations that led to Denver's dud of a Super Bowl XLVIII—including agreeing to hold their player media availabilities and podium news conferences during the week on a docked cruise ship that gave some guys seasickness—this one especially hurt. This team had taken care all season to prepare for every little possibility a year after their blunder-filled loss to Baltimore in the playoffs.

In the quiet locker room afterward, Ramirez said, "None of us heard the snap count. I thought I did and when I snapped it, I guess Peyton was actually trying to walk up to me at the time."

"Nobody's fault," Manning said succinctly. "It was just a noise issue."

Twelve seconds in, the Broncos trailed 2–0, but worse, they never recovered. The end result was a humbling 35-point blowout by the swarming Seahawks, a remarkable rout of the highest-scoring team in NFL history.

The early safety hurt, but the Broncos' self-inflicted wounds never abated. Manning lost a fumble and threw two interceptions, one of which game MVP Malcolm Smith returned for a 69-yard touchdown that made it 22–0 at halftime.

The Seahawks needed all of 12 seconds to score after the break, too. Matt Prater, who led the league by a wide margin with 81 touchbacks on kickoffs, pooched the kickoff in an apparent attempt to keep it out of Percy Harvin's hands. Harvin, however, hauled it in at the 13 and raced 87 yards for the score that made it 29–0.

Several players said they noticed immediately how much fresher the Seahawks were—and not just because they were younger and healthier either. Seattle coach Peter Carroll hadn't broken out the pads for any of his practices leading up to the Super Bowl, while Fox had practiced his guys hard for two weeks.

"It was easy to see while calling the game action how physical Seattle's defense was that day," Logan said. "Every time a Broncos receiver would catch the ball somebody was trying to knock the taste out of his mouth. That's how Seattle had played the entire year. And at least for that game, the Broncos didn't have an answer. They were beat up on defense. Von didn't play. Chris didn't play. So Denver wasn't a dominant defense at that time of the season.

"Even though they were down at halftime, I was trying to remain optimistic, coming up with a scenario to get back in the game: *Okay, you've got to get a stop, get a first-drive stop and then just go down and score.*

*And if you go down and score, you can kind of emotionally get back into this game, right? It's 22–0, get a stop, a quick stop, go on down and score, 22–7. Then you're two scores down.* Well, the second-half kickoff changed all of that. Percy Harvin runs it back for a touchdown and now it's 29–0. And even the most optimistic person would look at that and say 'There's no way they come back on this defense down 29 points. It's just not going to happen.'"

Manning would go on to complete a Super Bowl–record 34 passes and Thomas, the victim of strong safety Kam Chancellor's tone-setting, jaw-rattling, ribs-bruising hit early on, would catch a Super Bowl record 13 of them for 118 yards and a touchdown, Manning's 100th in two years for Denver.

But this loss was like no other.

Manning's defeats with Denver had come by six, six, ten, three, six, three, and seven points—41 altogether, just more than the difference in the Super Bowl itself.

"We worked hard to get to this point and overcame a lot of obstacles to get here, putting in a lot of hard work," Manning said. "It is a really good thing just to have this opportunity, but certainly to finish this way is very disappointing. It is not an easy pill to swallow, but eventually you have to."

Manning stepped off the bus after the game and caught up to Logan as they were walking into the lobby at the team hotel.

"Sorry, Dave," Manning said.

"Listen, you've got nothing to be sorry about," Logan replied. "It was just one of those nights. You had a great year."

# CHAPTER 26
## THE RUBBLE

orty-eight hours after Denver's crushing 43–8 loss to the Seattle Seahawks in Super Bowl XLVIII at MetLife Stadium in East Rutherford, New Jersey, a glum John Elway sat beside flummoxed coach John Fox at his season-ending news conference on a gray Colorado day.

Three times during his Hall of Fame playing career Elway had to slog through the rubble of a Super Bowl landslide before breaking through. First came the 19-point loss to the New York Giants at the Rose Bowl in Pasadena, California, then the 32-point pillorying by the Washington Redskins at Jack Murphy Stadium in San Diego, and finally the 45-point destruction at the hands of the San Francisco 49ers at the Superdome in New Orleans.

How long, somebody asked, did it take him to get over those big blowouts?

"I'm not over them yet," Elway responded. "I just add this one."

With Peyton Manning leading the huddle and Elway in charge of the front office, Denver returned to the big game for the first time since the Broncos won back-to-back titles in 1998 and '99 before retiring.

Elway then tried his hand at running restaurants and car dealerships, but perhaps because those endeavors "don't have scoreboards on Sundays," he returned to his beloved Broncos in 2011 to rescue the floundering franchise after a slow descent under Mike Shanahan and a nosedive under Josh McDaniels. Tebowmania swept through before Manning arrived and threw for 99 touchdowns in leading the Broncos to a 28–6 record over two seasons.

Then came the mauling at the Meadowlands. The highest-scoring team in NFL history self-destructed with Manning, the five-time NFL MVP, throwing just one touchdown pass to go with the 59 he tossed to get his team there.

"It was a great year," Elway professed. "We came up short." For half an hour Elway answered tough questions, mostly about what went wrong at the Super Bowl. (It also would turn out to be the final game for cornerback Champ Bailey, who would join Elway in the Hall of Fame the same summer team owner Pat Bowlen was posthumously inducted in Canton, Ohio, in 2019.)

As Elway rose to retreat to his office, he stopped, leaned back into the microphone, and asked if everyone could take a seat again so he could just add one thing: "Right now the focus is on what happened instead of how we got there and what we did this year, what we went through as a team," Elway said. "But I say that the farther you get away from this, the less you concentrate on just that one game, the more you recognize the whole season and really what we did as a football team and really as an organization. And I'll tell you what, I'm very proud of that."

In the locker room that afternoon, Eric Decker said that like Elway, he wasn't sure he'd ever get over the Seattle loss. "I don't know where or when that corner is," he said. "We were in this similar situation last year, Baltimore, we felt like we had the pieces for a championship season. It sticks with you and motivates you. It never goes away. You learn to fuel your fire from it, to deal with it and to move on."

Decker would move on in another sense a month later, as would Dominique Rodgers-Cromartie, Mike Adams, and Shaun Phillips, three defenders who kept the Broncos afloat during an unrelenting injury epidemic that sidelined Von Miller, Rahim Moore, Kevin Vickerson, Derek Wolfe, and Chris Harris Jr. for the 35-point Super Bowl blowout.

Denver's record-breaking offense wasn't spared, either. After throwing for more yards and touchdowns than anyone in NFL history, Manning had to say goodbye to running back Knowshon Moreno, who combined with Decker to pile up 3,154 yards from scrimmage and 25 touchdowns in the lead-up to the Super Bowl slip-up.

When Elway rejoined the Broncos he said the way to put fans back in the stands was to get good on defense, and watching the best offense in history crumble in the Super Bowl only reinforced his resolve to plug the holes on that side of the equation.

"I will tell you this: it's hard to get things turned around against a great defense like that," Elway said of the Seahawks and their "Legion of Boom" defense, "You can't afford to lose the momentum because to try to flip it on a great defense is always hard."

Richard Sherman, Kam Chancellor, and rest of Seattle's stingy defense hammered Manning into his worst day since he traded the horseshoe of the Indianapolis Colts for the mustang of the Denver Broncos. He was sacked for the first time in the playoffs, threw two interceptions—one of which was returned for a touchdown—lost a fumble, and turned it over on downs another time.

The bumbling Broncos finally found the end zone when Demaryius Thomas made a leaping, twisting grab of Manning's 14-yard pass—his 100th touchdown toss for Denver. But he needed a lot more of those to keep up with the efficient Russell Wilson, who didn't commit any turnovers and kept plays alive with his legs and by making pinpoint passes all night.

"They outplayed us in every facet," tight end Jacob Tamme said afterward.

Denver's five defensive starters who were on IR might have made this a fairer fight. Yet even with so many aging backups on defense facing a younger, fresher team, the Broncos were the popular pick heading in the first outdoor Super Bowl in a northern city, where the NFL dodged a major snowstorm by just 12 hours.

The prevailing wisdom was that if anybody was going to be blowing anyone out, it was going to be Denver doing what it had done all season. But 43–8, Seattle?

"I did not see it coming," admitted Dave Logan, who had predicted a tight game but one in which Denver would prevail. "I thought there was a chance that they might not win, but I thought most definitely they'd be in the game, and I gave them a good chance to win it. They were playing a great defense in Seattle and the Seahawks offense was getting better with a young Russell Wilson, so I thought that was going to be a game that could very well go down to the wire. Then, the first play of the game was somewhat indicative of how the first two and a half quarters would go. I mean, the Broncos couldn't get anything going.

They lost the physical battle. They couldn't get anything going at all on offense. And they were just getting teed off on.

"I really thought the Broncos defense, even with all the injuries, hung in there. They were my biggest concern going in to the game.... But they made a couple of red zone stops, kept the Seahawks out of the end zone, and forced them to settle for field goals. I don't think anybody expected the Broncos defense to go out and shut Seattle out.... That's not how the team that year was built. They won games scoring big points, and it just wasn't going to happen that night against Seattle."

In the end, the final score was difficult to deny. "The best team won the game. There are some times, but very few times, that doesn't happen," Logan said.

Elway knew that, too. The lesson he said he took from the loss was that he needed to do for his defense what he had done for his offense two years earlier, when he lured Manning to Denver.

So he went into free agency determined to build the best defense in the league. But even he couldn't have imagined a makeover so magnificent.

DeMarcus Ware didn't have to meet with him to know how serious Elway was about fixing his defense. Ware was the Dallas Cowboys' all-time leader in sacks, but Jerry Jones let him go in a salary cap move and Ware's first visit was with the Broncos. As Ware boarded a Denver-bound flight in Dallas to visit Elway on March 12, 2014, asleep across the aisle from him was star cornerback Aqib Talib.

Ware had other teams on his itinerary during his first foray into free agency, but Elway won him over with his commitment to defense and the chance to play alongside Manning. So he canceled his other visits. "They're trying to make a statement—a statement *we're a team to be reckoned with*," said Ware, who signed a three-year, $30 million deal on the spot, joining safety T.J. Ward, who signed a four-year, $22.5 million contract, and Talib, who signed for six years and $57 million.

Elway didn't ignore the offense, either, replacing Decker with wide receiver Emmanuel Sanders, whom he snatched away from AFC West rival Kansas City just as the former Steelers speedster was about to sign with the rival Chiefs. Sanders couldn't wait to catch passes from Manning, calling Denver "wide receiver heaven."

What Elway wanted was to make Denver's defense hell on opponents. "I think you see with Seattle's defense last year—definitely defense wins championships," said Ward, who came over from the Cleveland Browns.

Ware, who had 117 sacks in Dallas, said he was also eager to work with Von Miller, who had a rough 2013 season, beginning with a six-game drug suspension and ending with a torn ACL on December 22. Ware was already friends with Miller, a Dallas-area native, and said he would work to get the 2001 rookie of the year back on track by serving as his mentor. "Von is one of those incredible athletes," Ware said. "If you can really hone in on what you do best, and make yourself not think as much when you're out there, he'll be an even better athlete."

Talib hadn't realized he was on the same flight from Dallas as Ware until halfway through the trip. He signed with Denver first and was ecstatic to later hear that Elway enticed Ware to join the Broncos too. "Every year you just want to better your team," Talib said. "Mr. Elway decided to better his team on defense this year, since the offense looks pretty good."

He came over from the New England Patriots, and said there was no bad blood between him and the Broncos after he tweaked his knee early in the AFC Championship Game against Denver two months earlier, when he was bumped by slot receiver Wes Welker on a crossing route. "Wes is a good friend of mine," Talib said. "I can tell you he didn't do it on purpose."

Still, Talib appreciated Patriots coach Bill Belichick sticking up for him after the game. Belichick called it "one of the worst plays" he'd seen in nearly four decades of coaching. The league's officiating chief ultimately ruled it a legal hit by Welker.

Ware, Ward, and Talib brought Denver thumpers on all three levels of defense. And Sanders was a terrific target to team with Demaryius

Thomas and Manning. Logan called it the greatest class of free agents ever.

"You were talking about guys in their prime. DeMarcus was getting up there in years a bit but still had great football left. T.J. brought the toughness that good defensive teams have to have, and Aqib brought the swagger," Logan said. "You have to have somebody who is what I call a tone-setter, the guy to deliver the shot that gets everyone excited. And honestly, since T.J. left, they've sort of been looking for that guy.

"Emmanuel just made big, big plays…. I think he will go a little under-recognized in terms of his true contribution to the team. And I know Demaryius was a heck of a receiver. But Emmanuel was a guy that, even at his size, would go in the middle of the field and put his body in a position where you knew he was going to take a shot and he'd still make the catch," Logan said.

"Just calling games over the years he was in Denver, I developed so much respect for him. Speaking as a former wide receiver, it's not the easiest thing in the world to run as fast as you can in the middle of the field and realize as the ball is in the air, *If I go get that one, I'm going to get blown up,*" Logan chuckled. "But you know what? He did it. I've always respected his toughness and competitiveness as a receiver."

Too many to count were the times fans and even Logan felt, *Emmanuel Sanders isn't getting up this time.* Yet he kept popping up, signaling first down, and running back to the huddle to do it again. "No doubt about it," Logan said. "He's one tough dude."

Later that summer of 2014, Coach Fox, who had open-heart surgery the previous November, signed an extension. He wouldn't be long for Denver, though.

# CHAPTER 27
## WORLDS COLLIDE

Peyton Manning's old team, the Indianapolis Colts, provided the bookends to the Denver Broncos' 2014 season, a third consecutive year filled with high scores and heartbreak.

His homecoming in 2013 wasn't a happy one. He and the Broncos took a 6–0 record into Indianapolis in his first trip back to Lucas Oil Stadium, only to watch Andrew Luck prove himself a worthy successor by beating Manning at his own game. Luck executed a perfect two-minute drill at the end of the first half, threw three touchdown passes, ran for his third score of the season, and kept the Broncos' defense off balance all night in a 39–33 win that snapped Denver's 17-game regular-season winning streak.

Manning admitted his emotions and his old team got the best of him in the most anticipated homecoming since Brett Favre went back to Green Bay in 2009 wearing the dreaded purple uniform of the Minnesota Vikings. After a pregame tribute in Indy, Manning lost a fumble, threw an interception, and was sacked four times, twice by Robert Mathis, one of a handful of holdovers from the Manning era.

Indy's former franchise quarterback arrived to find out the roof and window at Lucas Oil Stadium would be open on a chilly night inside the house he helped build. And a 90-second video tribute interrupted Manning's pregame routine as he stopped to watch some of his most memorable moments with the Colts, including his record-breaking pass to Marvin Harrison, his comeback to beat Tom Brady in the AFC Championship Game, and the night he hoisted the Lombardi Trophy in rainy Miami. When it wrapped up, Manning acknowledged the crowd's standing ovation by stopping his warm-up throws, removing his helmet, waving to the fans, and mouthing, "Thank you." The large video screen then cut to a fan holding a sign that read THANKS PEYTON BUT TONIGHT I'M A COLTS FAN.

A year later, Manning wasn't nearly as distracted or drained when he faced his old team to open the 2014 season in Denver. Jim Irsay wasn't getting under his skin as he had a year earlier with talk about how disappointed he was to win just one Super Bowl with Manning and how he'd traded the "Star Wars" offensive numbers for a more balanced team in his quest to win more rings with Luck (who would retire in 2019 after too many injuries had him on an endless loop of rehab and surgery without having brought Irsay and Indy a single Super Bowl).

In fact, Manning didn't have to deal with Irsay or Mathis this time. Irsay was serving a six-game suspension to start the 2014 season for violating the NFL's personal conduct policy. And Mathis, who finished a half sack shy of 20 the year before, was suspended for the first four games for violating the league's performance enhancing drug policy.

There was no pregame tribute to fuss about, either.

The Broncos started their own season with two prominent players serving four-game banishments: receiver Wes Welker and kicker Matt Prater, who combined to score 210 points a year earlier. Prater violated the NFL's substance abuse policy by drinking alcohol in the off-season, forbidden since his 2011 DUI arrest, and Welker reportedly tested positive for amphetamine use in violation of the league's rules forbidding performance-enhancing drugs.

Still, Manning had weapons. He threw three first-half touchdown passes to tight end Julius Thomas and the Broncos raced out to a 24–0 lead, the perfect test for Elway's blueprint for returning to the Super Bowl, having spent more than $100 million on a defensive makeover in the wake of their loss to Seattle.

The one who saved the day, ultimately, was rookie cornerback Bradley Roby, Elway's top draft pick, who batted away a fourth-down pass in the final minute as Denver finally fended off Luck's furious comeback attempt to preserve the Broncos' 31–24 win.

In his second try, Manning joined Brett Favre as the only quarterbacks at the time to beat each of the NFL's current 32 franchises, with Drew Brees joining them in 2018. When asked what that meant to him, Manning cracked, "It means I'm old."

Manning looked downright geriatric five months later, when the Colts made a return trip to Denver in the playoffs with a trip to the AFC championship on the line.

Manning, the league's only five-time MVP, had extended his quarterbacks record with his 14th Pro Bowl selection, tying center Bruce Matthews, tight end Tony Gonzalez, defensive tackle Merlin Olsen, and quarterback Tom Brady for the most in NFL history. He was one of a league-high 10 Broncos selected to the Pro Bowl, five on each side of the ball, after throwing for 39 touchdowns in 2014, one fewer than league leader Luck. With such a star-studded roster, the Broncos (12–4) had a "Super Bowl or bust" mentality as they sought to return to the title game and atone for their 35-point loss to the Seahawks in the previous season's Super Bowl.

Their 482-point season was more productive than any other team but the Packers, who scored 486. Coming off the heels of their record-breaking offensive explosion the year before, however, it represented a more than 20 percent decline in production.

Denver was the AFC's No. 2 seed behind New England (12–4), which had blasted the Broncos 43–21 in Foxborough in November in the 16th meeting between two of the greatest quarterbacks in NFL history.

But Manning hobbled into the playoffs after injuring his right thigh late in the first half of a 22–10 win at San Diego in mid-December, which he blamed on dehydration from a nasty stomach flu the night before. He missed a handful of snaps to get treatment just before halftime in that game against the Chargers and returned to play the entire second half. He didn't miss any more time with the injury in a loss at Cincinnati and a win over Oakland in the finale to secure a first-round bye and a much-needed week's rest.

Everybody expected another Brady–Manning matchup a week later. But the ailments clearly affected his Manning's play in the playoffs. He had eight overthrows in Denver's 24–13 loss to the Colts, when he also had an incompletion into coverage on a third-and-5 play in which he bypassed the run even though he had a 20-yard gap between him and any of the Colts defenders. The flat performance rocked the organization, leading to a split with Fox. A TV report broke the news to players and fans that Fox wanted out of his contract so he could coach the Chicago Bears as Marc Trestman's replacement.

Manning began to reassess his declaration that he planned to return for an 18th season. Asked after the game if he could say for certain that he'd be back in 2015, Manning, who would turn 39 that March, said no, he couldn't say that because he had to see how his health would be.

Elway met with Manning the next day and asked him not to make a rash decision. He told him he'd check in with Manning during his search for a new head coach but didn't need a decision from his quarterback for a month or more. Then Elway walked down the hall and finalized his separation from Fox, who had everything he could have wanted in Denver: a franchise quarterback, every free agent he asked for, a sparkling new indoor practice facility, an ownership that was all in on chasing Super Bowls....but he still couldn't get it done.

Elway interviewed offensive coordinator Adam Gase and Bengals defensive backs coach Vance Joseph, but he had a preferred candidate in mind to replace Fox: Gary Kubiak, his old backup, who had coached the Houston Texans for eight seasons and revived Baltimore's offense and Joe Flacco's career in 2014 as the Ravens' offensive coordinator. Only Kubiak had just declared he didn't want to be a head coach anymore after a health scare in Houston.

Kubiak was Elway's backup QB from 1983 to 1991 and served as Denver's offensive coordinator from 1995 to 2005 under Mike Shanahan, who helped devise the blueprint for Elway's back-to-back Super Bowl championships in the late 1990s.

"Oh man, if it's Kubiak, that would be great," said Terrell Davis, Elway's copilot on those title runs. "I'd love to see him back in Denver. John Elway said at the podium the other day that he knew what it took to win a championship. Well, who else was there when we won a championship? Kubiak."

# CHAPTER 28
## ONE MORE SHOT

In a promotional appearance at Super Bowl XLIX, the day before Peyton Manning was honored as the NFL's Man of the Year, his father, Archie, said he gave his son space as he pondered his future. "I would never tell him what to do and I don't have an opinion," said the patriarch of America's first family of football. "I want him to do what's in his heart and what he thinks is best. He's pretty good at that. He'll be 39 years old and he's had to make big decisions before and he's usually made a pretty good one.

"So, I know one thing you can count on about Peyton: he will lay it all out there. He will evaluate everything and make a decision. So we're confident whatever that is, it's going to be the right decision."

John Elway was practicing patience too, rolling out the same give-him-some-space approach that he had used to lure Manning to Denver in the first place.

When Manning delivered a shocker in the wake of Denver's 24–13 loss to the Colts in the playoffs by hedging on his pledge to return in 2015, Elway implored him not to rush. Get away from this devastating defeat, he told him, clear your mind, think things over, take a month. Or more.

The strategy worked, again.

Manning, who had been hampered by protection problems and a thigh injury that handcuffed him in the playoffs, worked out in the off-season in New Orleans with trainer Mackie Shilstone, renowned for helping athletes extend the twilight of their careers.

After taking some time to decompress from an arduous season and his latest premature playoff exit, Manning decided he wasn't ready to retire. He still had the health and hunger to play at age 39 and grind through another season in pursuit of becoming the oldest quarterback ever to win a Super Bowl.

There was a caveat in Elway's quiet courtship, though; he wanted the five-time MVP to take a pay cut, and the drama dragged on while the Broncos and Manning's agent, Tom Condon, worked out the details, finally ironing out a $4 million reduction in his $19 million salary, but with incentives to earn back every single penny. Manning would get $2 million of it back by winning the AFC championship and the rest by winning Super Bowl 50.

By almost every measure, the second chapter of Manning's career had been a sensational success in Denver. He'd led the Broncos to the best record in the NFL in each of his three seasons. As was the case in Indianapolis, however, Manning came up short in the playoffs, the Broncos unraveling with a 35-point Super Bowl squelching by Seattle and two stunning home flops coming off a bye.

One was against Baltimore in double overtime, a game the Broncos basically gave away by giving up a 70-yard touchdown pass in the final minute. But the second one cut even deeper, coming as it did against the Colts and Manning's successor, Andrew Luck, whose impending arrival as the top draft pick in 2012 paved the way for Manning's exit from Indianapolis.

Manning flew to Denver to take his physical and sign his revised contract. He huddled with new coach Gary Kubiak. John Fox took play-caller Adam Gase, Manning's co-pilot in Denver's turbocharged offense, with him to Chicago. The new offensive coordinator was another former Bronco, Rick Dennison, although Kubiak would call the plays himself.

On paper, Kubiak and Manning looked like an awkward fit from the start. Kubiak had authored West Coast offenses throughout his career and required the quarterback to mainly line up under center and roll out aplenty. Mobility was never Manning's thing, and the older he got the more comfortable he was making quick decisions and throws out of the shotgun.

Kubiak explained that it's "easy to build a playbook" for Manning and pointed out that Joe Flacco, whom he tutored the year before in Baltimore, had his best statistical season ever and only rolled out maybe two dozen times in 2014. And he pledged flexibility with the five-time MVP.

"The offense Peyton runs, he's tremendous at it, back there in the gun controlling the game, controlling the line of scrimmage. Nobody has ever done it better and he's the master at it," Kubiak said the day he was hired. "Actually, I'm looking forward to learning that style and that system that he has."

Manning said he was good with whatever Kubiak ran, quipping, "Aside maybe from Tubby Raymond's Delaware Blue Hen Wing-T offense, I feel pretty comfortable playing in any offense."

Elway liked that Manning wouldn't have to throw the ball as much in Kubiak's offense, something he noted "gets more helpful the older you get."

Manning had already proven that he knew how to adjust; the last two times he had a new head coach, his teams went 14–2 and 13–3.

The league's most decorated star, Manning already owned most of the significant passing records in the NFL and in 2015 he was closing in on Brett Favre's career yardage record and his mark for most career wins.

Manning's nine one-and-done playoff performances were about the only career blot on No. 18's résumé as he headed into his 18th season. His five MVP awards were two more than Favre, but his single Super Bowl title gave him half as many rings as brother Eli, who twice beat Tom Brady—Peyton's nemesis—and the Patriots in the Super Bowl. Peyton aimed to change that in 2015, with his 17th meeting with Brady on the docket, this time in Denver in November.

"We're just excited to have him back," running back C.J. Anderson said when Manning announced that he had decided to put off retirement. "Of course, he just wants to go out there and win that ring. And we're just trying to go out there and help him win it. If he said he's mentally and physically ready to play, that doesn't mean it's at a subpar level. It means it's at a high level."

Going into his own final season, in 1998, Elway had felt good, too. But he would miss a slew of games with injuries and backup Bubby Brister won four starts in his place and finished up a couple of other games, too. As it turned out, Manning would also have to lean on his longtime backup. Brock Osweiler kept the Broncos pointed toward their Super Bowl dreams while his mentor recovered from a foot injury that for a while looked as though it would end his career short of the finish line.

When training camp started, all eyes were on Manning and Kubiak, but they quickly darted to the star-studded defense. Von Miller was so spectacular that the Broncos essentially decided to hold him out that summer lest he keep blowing up drills and not allowing the offense to get any work done.

Things may have been shaping up as Manning's last hurrah, but it was clearly going to be Miller Time in 2015.

# CHAPTER 29
## GOT YOUR SIGNAL

**B**y the time Aaron Rodgers and the Green Bay Packers visited Denver for a battle of 6–0 teams on November 1, 2015, Peyton Manning finally looked like a five-time MVP and not a creaky 39-year-old quarterback learning a new system. He threw for 340 yards as Denver's defense ransacked Rodgers, whose 77 yards passing were his fewest ever in a game that he didn't leave because of injury. The Broncos powered their way past the Packers 29–10 on the night team owner Pat Bowlen was inducted into the team's Ring of Fame (although it was his family on hand for the halftime ceremonies since the ailing Bowlen no longer was making public appearances).

"It's a good defense, a really good defense," Rodgers said afterward. "They have a good pass rush. They cover well."

And hit hard.

The Broncos offense finally woke up, too, producing the very things coach Gary Kubiak envisioned in his return to Denver: Manning running bootlegs and rollouts, using his tight ends as targets over the middle and watching his running backs race into the end zone. "I've been very determined to get comfortable in this offense," Manning said. "I knew this was not going to be an easy transition. I can't say that a lot of what's happened has been a surprise to me. It was kind of what I expected, there were going to be some rough times, rough patches and rough parts of the transition."

Wearing the same blue jerseys they donned when beating the Packers for their first Super Bowl win in 1997, the Broncos outgained the Packers 500 yards to 140 and Manning tied Brett Favre's NFL record with his 186th regular season win.

With that, the Broncos were 7–0 for the first time since their 1998 team went 14–2 and went on to win the Super Bowl. Maybe this Manning-Kubiak marriage was going to work out after all.

Then Manning had a chance to break two of Favre's passing records in another homecoming, at the RCA Dome in Indianapolis. Manning, however, was left stewing on the sideline when star cornerback Aqib Talib lost his cool and ruined the Broncos' perfect season with a pair of penalties in the final minutes that kept Manning three yards shy of becoming the league's all-time leading passer and one win shy of breaking for record for most victories by a starting quarterback in the NFL.

Talib, arguably the first-half MVP of the league's best defense, cemented a 27–24 loss to the Colts with two inexcusable penalties: a poke in the eye of an opponent that would cost him a one-game suspension and a clap in the face of an official that would cost the Broncos a chance to get the ball back for Manning to break both of Favre's records that night in Indianapolis.

With the two-minute warning approaching and Indy facing third-and-long from the Denver 15, Von Miller and Dwayne Allen starting shouting and shoving when Talib ran up and poked Allen in his right eye with two fingers. Talib later said he meant only to shove Allen in the face. The personal foul gave the Colts a first down, and when Adam Vinatieri nailed a 23-yard field goal with 28 seconds left, linebacker Danny Trevathan, who had a career-best 19 tackles, was whistled for holding, giving Indy another first down. Talib responded by tauntingly clapping at the official, drawing another flag, this one for unsportsmanlike conduct.

Manning was clearly disgusted on the sideline but he wasn't about to denounce the defense that had his back all season while he continued to make mistakes. (He had a league-leading 13 interceptions halfway through the season.)

Despite a sore left foot, throbbing ribs, and an aching right shoulder, Manning insisted on suiting up the following week against Kansas City knowing that Talib was suspended, DeMarcus Ware was hurt, and Emmanuel Sanders was sore. With his first completion, Manning finally supplanted Favre for most career passing yards—but the Chiefs kept him from the record he really wanted: most career wins.

"I thought I felt good enough to play," Manning said after the worst performance of his career in Denver's 29–13 loss. "By going out there and trying to help the team, I ended up hurting the team."

Manning posted an unheard-of 0.0 passer rating by completing just 5 of 20 passes for 35 yards and no touchdowns with four interceptions and two sacks. With his sore left foot preventing Manning from stepping into his passes properly and getting the zip he needed on his throws, Kubiak finally turned to longtime backup Brock Osweiler in the third quarter with Denver trailing 22–0.

Asked whether the benching was for injuries or ineffective play, Kubiak said, "To be honest with you, I was protecting him because I was worried about him," and he went on to say that he regretted even playing Manning in the first place. "But he's a competitor, he wanted to play."

Kubiak said Manning, who had just nine touchdowns and a league-leading 17 interceptions, would remain his starter "if healthy." Coach Kubiak, however, had learned a valuable lesson: from then on, he wasn't going to be swayed by Manning's pleas but by his play.

The only highlight of the day for Manning was his milestone throw, a four-yard pass to Ronnie Hillman. Play was stopped and Joe Horrigan from the Pro Football Hall of Fame secured the football. Manning called it "an awkward situation to have any type of stoppage of play in the middle of a game. I wasn't off to the best start." And he certainly didn't want to keep a memento from this debacle.

Osweiler's first career NFL start came on his 25th birthday, the following week. He threw for two touchdowns, and the Broncos stopped Jeremy Langford on a two-point conversion run in the final half-minute to beat the Bears 17–15 in Chicago with their former coach, John Fox, on the other sideline and Manning back in Denver.

Osweiler completed 20 of 27 passes for 250 yards against the Bears and asserted himself right away with a 48-yard touchdown pass to Demaryius Thomas on Denver's first drive of the game. He added a 10-yarder to Cody Latimer in the fourth quarter that made it 17–9. He stood strong in the face of an aggressive Vic Fangio–led defense—something John Elway would take note of for future reference—overcoming five sacks to get the Broncos to 8–2 with a visit from the New England Patriots looming the following week.

"He does this all of the time in practice, in preseason," linebacker Von Miller said. "I kind of came out here and expected it. What he did is what I expected him to do."

The only question was whether Osweiler was a short-term fix or a long-term solution.

Tom Brady and the unbeaten Patriots were up next, and with Manning in a walking boot on his left foot, the greatest quarterback rivalry in NFL history was on hold. Manning was watching from the cozy indoors at field level the following week as Osweiler and the Broncos overcame a 21–7 fourth-quarter deficit on a snowy night to force overtime.

New England won the coin toss and elected to receive but Miller's sack of Brady forced a three-and-out and on third-and-1 from the New England 48, C.J. Anderson took the handoff from Osweiler and raced around the left sideline into the north end zone with 12:32 left in overtime for a 30–24 win, handing the Patriots (11–1) their first loss since 2014.

"It didn't look good at times, but we figured out a way to get it done," Kubiak said afterward.

Star pass rusher DeMarcus Ware missed the game with a bad back and Denver lost two more members of the league's top-ranked defense on one play in the first quarter when Pro Bowl safety T.J. Ward and nose tackle Sylvester Williams suffered ankle injuries on New England's first run when LeGarrette Blount managed a mere two yards.

Brady threw three touchdown passes, including one to tight end Rob Gronkowski, who would get knocked from the game with a knee injury. Brady's final touchdown toss came on the first play of the fourth quarter, giving the Patriots a seemingly safe 21–7 cushion.

Denver went three-and-out on the next drive on three straight misfires from Osweiler. But Chris Harper muffed the punt and Shaq Barrett recovered for Denver at the Patriots 36. Four plays later, Anderson took it in for a 15-yard touchdown run.

The Broncos got the ball back at midfield after Brady's 51-yard pass was negated by penalty and Osweiler drove Denver to the New England 3. On third down he missed Thomas, but Brandon McManus' short field goal made it 21–17 game with six minutes remaining.

Both teams went three-and-out and the Patriots were moving downfield when Gronkowski was carted off with 2:49 left after injuring his right knee on an incompletion when Broncos safety Darian Stewart sliced across his body and hit his right knee. It was a clean hit, but Brady was furious.

The Broncos got the ball back at their 17 with 2:31 left and Osweiler hit Thomas down the right sideline for a crucial 36-yard gain—Thomas' only catch in 13 targets that night—and then Osweiler found Emmanuel Sanders for 39 yards. A sack was negated by penalty and Denver took its first lead of the night when Osweiler hit Bubba Caldwell for a four-yard touchdown to put Denver on top 24–21 with 1:09 left.

Sixty-nine seconds was plenty of time for Brady, who quickly moved the Patriots into Broncos territory, then found Brandon LaFell for a 14-yard gain to the Denver 29 with four seconds left. Stephen Gostkowski's 47-yard field goal tied it at 24 as time expired.

Anderson's long overtime run handed the Patriots their first loss and put Denver just a game behind New England, a crucial development in their quest to avoid having to play in Foxborough in the playoffs again.

After that came a victory at San Diego before a 15–12 loss at home to Oakland and a 34–27 loss at Pittsburgh. Then came an overtime win at home against Cincinnati that gave Osweiler a 4–2 record as the starter and the Broncos an 11–4 mark heading into the regular season finale against the San Diego Chargers.

Manning returned to practice that week of the Chargers game. After seven weeks, he was finally healthy enough to suit up. Kubiak stuck with Osweiler as his starting quarterback against San Diego, meaning

Manning would serve as a backup for the first time since his freshman year at the University of Tennessee, when he replaced an injured Todd Helton against Mississippi State on September 24, 1994.

In March 2016, at Manning's retirement news conference, Kubiak shared the story about how the two of them had navigated the minefields of the 2015 season to emerge as champions.

Kubiak figured Manning might not want him to tell the tale, but he felt it went right to the heart of Manning's character, so he didn't hold back:

> What I want to do is I want to share a story with everybody. I know I'm sharing it with all of America today but I want to do this. I think it's important, and I'll be real quick. This season was a great one. But it was a tough one, and he and I had some tremendous meetings, interesting moments along the way. I'm going to make it brief, but I want to make a point. We were nine weeks into the season, we were 7–2. We had a rough day against Kansas City. I knew he wasn't feeling good. I knew his foot was hurting. We went in my office and I said, "You're going to get well." He was not real happy with that, not real happy. But we proceeded on that path to getting him well, trying to hang on as a football team. We continued to battle.
>
> So over the next seven weeks, we had many meetings, didn't we? Many meetings, many sit-downs, and I remember him coming out of the cast after putting his foot in the cast for a couple weeks, right? Then he comes out of the cast and we sit down and I said, "Okay, what's the next step? What do we do here?" He said, "Well, it's time to go back to work. I want to come back. I want to play. I want to finish this thing out the right way." And I said, "All right, well we'll step back on the field and go to work next week." And I'll never forget what he told me that day. He said, "Listen, I don't want to be a distraction. I'm not ready to play yet. If I go back on the field with that team, it's going to be all about me. You keep everybody focused on the team. I'll get myself well."

So that's what he did. He devised a plan. Every day we'd come in here, we'd get the team going; we'd have our meetings as a team. Peyton went across the field over there to the Bubble [the Pat Bowlen Fieldhouse, adjacent to the team's outdoor practice fields]. He took three guys with him. "The Famous Three," I would call them. He took "Sunshine"—[wide receiver] Jordan Taylor, for all of you who don't know who that is. He took Coach Harry [assistant equipment manager Mike Harrington], who works in the equipment room and doubles as a quarterback coach. And he took [injured tight end Jeff] Heuerman over there. And he went to work. And we filmed those sessions. And I watched the film and we went through that process for a few weeks. I would deal with the team and he would be over there working in the mornings.

Every Friday, I'd come over there and I'd watch him work out. We went through this process for a few weeks, and as we went through that process, there were some highs and lows. There was one setback, if I recall. But we kept pushing and all of the sudden it was different. I knew he felt like it was time, that he was ready to play, that he was in the right place.

So I think there were two weeks left in the regular season. He and I had talked and I could tell in his voice he felt very good about what was going on and he was ready to come back. So we decided that week that we'd proceed the same way. So we started our Wednesday, had the meeting with the team, he went over and worked out, we went about our business. That evening, I watched his tape and it looked better than ever. Everything was pretty consistent. Thursday was different. We had our work as a team, he had his workout. I sat down and watched the film. As I'm watching the film that day, there was something different about the workout.

During the workout, he sent me a signal to the film. *Hey, we're No. 1.*

You could take it that way. [It was actually a middle finger.]

I took it as "I'm ready to play, Coach." So I was heading home that night, I texted him. I said, "Hey, the workout looked great today, and, oh, by the way, I got the signal."

I said, "I'll see you tomorrow morning at nine o'clock. I want to watch you work out tomorrow. So let me get through with the team in the morning and I'm coming to watch."

So we had our meeting Friday morning, Greek [head athletic trainer Steve Antonopulos] and I walked over to the Bubble, walked in, and they were through. And they were supposed to start at nine, but they were already through. So I walked in the Bubble and I looked at all of them, and I said, "Hey, what's the deal here? I was supposed to watch you guys at nine." And his three buddies, they kind of tiptoed out of the Bubble because they knew something was fixing to take place here. But they all said, "Coach, he said we were starting at 8." So they were through.

So he and I started our conversation, and I'll try to make a long story short: "Why did you all start—" [Manning cut off Kubiak and responded] "I wanted to. I'm ready to play." Before I knew it, the only people left in the bubble were Peyton and I, and a bag of footballs. For five minutes, I proceeded to tell him what I thought was going on with our team and where we were at. For the next 25 minutes, Peyton proceeded to tell me where he was, what he thought our team could do, and that he was ready to lead our team in that direction. And he was right. He was right.

What he proceeded to do over the course of the next month, and leading these players, his football team, and the coaches and push everybody, was the difference in how we ended up as a football team. So I have the utmost respect for this kid, the utmost respect. And on behalf of myself, coaches, players, everybody in this organization, thanks for doing it. I know it was tough, and you were special along the way. So it was only nine months for me, but I'll remember it for a lifetime. I love you, bud. I wish you the best.

Ever the pragmatist, Manning demurred when asked about the signal he'd sent Kubiak from the bubble that day. "I can't confirm or deny that," Manning deadpanned.

Okay then, why, on that day in particular, did he have a message for his head coach? "I'd be lying if I sat here and told you that was not a frustrating time," Manning said.

> The team meets here every morning. I'm a part of those meetings, and then everyone goes on to their individual meetings and goes to practice and I go in the little quarantined sandbox at the far corner. "Hey, don't get near any of the real players. You go over there and you can take Sunshine." It was nice of them to give me a practice squad receiver, an equipment guy, and a guy on injured reserve to throw to. That really helped. I really appreciated that.
>
> It couldn't have been a better guy. Jordan Taylor is going to surprise a lot of people for the Broncos next year, in my opinion. Jeff is going to get healthy. He's an awesome football player. And nobody appreciates a good equipment guy more than I do, and [equipment manager] Flip [Chris Valenti] and [assistant equipment manager] Harry [Mike Harrington] and John Scott and Frog and T. and all the guys that I've been throwing to, there's a special bond there.
>
> But it was a frustrating time because I wasn't getting as healthy as quickly as I wanted to. I'm throwing in that indoor facility and not feeling the same. And then you are starting to make some progress, then you have a little setback, and then of course, you're not playing. I was so fortunate for so many years to have great health and to have played in so many games…. Not to be playing, it was tough. I was starting to feel a little better around that time and maybe getting back to being a little more myself and my signals and my hand gestures and so I think it was the timing of that.

Manning said he appreciated Kubiak's "honest communication and his telling me that, 'Hey, I got you. Stay with me on this.' I trusted him and it was a two-way communication. He and I had a sit-down right after the Cleveland game" on October 18, three weeks before Manning's foot injury. "He said, 'I'm telling you, there's a reason you and I are together this year and I've got a feeling it's going to end the right way.' I remember that. It was Cleveland."

Ultimately, Manning's stint as a backup only lasted a few quarters. He replaced Osweiler in the third quarter of the Chargers game and the Broncos bounced back from five turnovers and an 80-yard touchdown toss from Philip Rivers to Tyrell Williams in the fourth quarter to beat San Diego 27–20.

"It was a pure instinct call for him to put me in there," Manning said later.

No, he didn't lobby for it, either. "Absolutely not," Manning said.

> I told him I'm ready to dress and he said, "That's good to know. Now I have an option." I wasn't wearing my knee brace, which was good. I had not stood there in uniform since 1994. Twenty-two years. And so, with a knee brace, you've got to be stiff. I didn't throw on the sideline because I'm throwing, [and fans would be wondering] *Oh, is he ready?*
>
> So, I'm in the locker room and then Gary and [quarterbacks coach Brian] Callahan were talking and he said, "Are you ready?" At this point, you can't say, "Well, I've had two reps in practice all week and hadn't played in six weeks."

Broncos fans greeted Manning like a conquering hero when he trotted onto the field with 8:18 left in the third quarter. "They were cheering loud, but I'm pretty sure everybody was in their same seats when they were booing my butt off against Kansas City back about six weeks ago," Manning said of his four-interception nightmare that sent him to the sideline with a torn left plantar fascia on November 15.

Osweiler didn't do much to lose his starting job, throwing for 232 yards, including a 72-yard touchdown pass to Thomas on the game's second play. But he was victimized by five turnovers, including one when he failed to recognize the blitz in time. His day was done after Anderson fumbled the second play after halftime.

"I don't think Brock did anything wrong," Kubiak said afterward. "I know as had he turnovers but a couple of them he had nothing to do with. My gut just told me to turn it over to [Manning] and let him lead the football team." And he did just that, leading Denver to 20 points in one and a half quarters, despite completing just 5 of 9 passes for 69 yards. After Manning led Denver to 10 quick points, Williams broke free against the league's best defense for an 80-yard touchdown that put San Diego ahead 20–17 early in the fourth quarter.

"We didn't want them to lay down," Talib, who gave up the long touchdown pass, would quip afterward. "But we wanted them to lay down a little faster than that."

McManus tied it with a 35-yard field goal and Ronnie Hillman's 23-yard touchdown run proved the difference as Denver wrapped up a fifth consecutive AFC West crown and the top seed in the AFC for the third time in Manning's four seasons with the Broncos.

Because he didn't start, Manning didn't break the tie he held with Favre for most regular-season wins, 186; the victory instead went on Osweiler's record, making him 5–2 for the year. "It was tough on the emotions," Osweiler said after the game. "But winning the AFC West is what it's all about."

Denver's defense posted the franchise's first No. 1 overall ranking, allowing just 283.1 yards a game. The Broncos were the NFL's best against the pass—199.6 yards—and third-best against the run at 83.6 yards. They also led the league with 52 sacks and allowed 18.5 points per game. Seattle allowed the fewest points in the league—277—but the Broncos, who yielded 296, could have bested that, too, were it not for a trio of pick-sixes by Manning early in the season.

Shiloh Keo, the most unheralded of Denver's defenders, helped seal it. He atoned for having allowed Oakland's game-winning touchdown in a 15–12 stunner in Denver in Week 13, just five days after joining the banged-up Broncos secondary, with an interception with less than five minutes left to set up Hillman's 23-yard touchdown that broke a 20–20 tie.

Denver's defense allowed just three points off the four first-half turnovers. That was no small feat. Before that game, teams were 2–92 when they were minus-4 or worse in turnover ratio. The last team to win despite a minus-4 turnover ratio had been Atlanta over Arizona on November 18, 2012.

Keo suggested the first-round playoff bye would only help the league's best defense get even better. "It's going to do miracles for our defense," Keo said. "We have a lot of veteran guys, a lot of starters, who are playing on injuries, so this extra week will give them the opportunity to get their bodies back to 100 percent and give us the best shot at going all the way."

Manning said his foot felt fine and he was just glad to contribute again to a big win.

So was Osweiler, who was clearly disappointed in the locker room but said all the right things, including, "As long as this football team is winning games, shoot, I don't care who's playing quarterback."

Good thing, because Manning would get the nod for the playoffs.

It wasn't an easy marriage, Kubiak's West Coast offense with its roots in the run and Manning's revisionist play calling at the line of scrimmage based on his exquisite ability to decode defenses. But they had found a way to make it work for both of them.

With Kubiak as coach, Manning looked a lot like he had with John Fox and Tony Dungy.

Manning had talked Kubiak into letting him play against Kansas City when his foot was bothering him so much he didn't practice until that Friday, but Kubiak had put his foot down after that.

"Father Time gets everybody sooner or later," Logan said. "Some of us sooner than later. But you think of the Kansas City game where he had four interceptions and a zero passer rating. But typical of Peyton, he came back like a mad scientist looking for whatever edge he could find to get back on the field. I also give Gary credit here; he maneuvered through a minefield with plenty of injuries and got that team to the Super Bowl. Gary's a *very* smart guy. He's a people person, and I think one of his strengths is that he understands how guys work, what makes them tick."

When he decided Manning was healthy enough to return, he still started Osweiler. But he didn't hesitate to make a change when he felt the season teetering and a first-round playoff bye slipping away.

It's hard to remember, but the prevailing sentiment back then was that Osweiler was the future in Denver. He'd been drafted with the explicit intent of succeeding Manning one day, and it was apparent that Manning was on his last ride. His longtime apprentice, meanwhile, had burnished his credentials by going 5–2 and keeping the team on track when Manning was injured. Osweiler's contract was set to expire, but Elway was confident he could get him back in 2016 at a reasonable price.

## Dave Logan's Log

We live in a society where if you're out of sight, you're out of mind, and that's definitely how the NFL works. I think nobody could fully appreciate how difficult that was physically for Peyton to get himself back to a position to get back on the field. I also think Kubiak navigated the situation about as well as anybody could. Coaches strategize and they've got to know their Xs and Os, but there's much more to that job.

You've got to know what motivates them, and I think Gary did a really good job with Peyton. Keep in mind he was dealing with a Hall of Famer who thought he was ready to play maybe two weeks earlier, and Gary continued to play Brock at that point. That was a bold move. But he did it in a way that his relationship with Peyton could withstand the process.

Gary, was very cognizant of how important Peyton had been and ultimately would be. And he did a great, great job in that regard. Both of them did.

At that time, there was also a debate within the organization about whether Osweiler wasn't just the franchise's future but its present. "I think there was a belief that given Peyton's deficiencies physically, and even though he's the best there is mentally, our best chance to win right now with Brock. They might never admit that, but that's the sense I got," Logan said. "And then, the last regular season game against the Chargers, the offense really wasn't playing very well and Gary decided to put Peyton back in at quarterback."

Osweiler started the second half against the Chargers in Week 17, but soon it was Manning trotting out to the crowd's roar. He completed his first pass for 14 yards to tight end Virgil Green. Logan remembers the moment vividly: "The crowd as well as the team got really energized. After the game, walking to my car, I remember thinking, *They're going to go back to Peyton. He's a Hall of Fame quarterback. It's Peyton's show for as long as they go.*"

Peyton Manning had started two dozen previous playoff games but was just 11–13 overall. He had also gone one-and-done an NFL-worst nine times, including twice in Denver. That record gave some pause, especially considering his not-so-superlative 2015. In the regular season, he led the league in interceptions with 17 despite missing nearly half the season with a foot injury. And he was just 5 for 9 for 59 yards in his return after a seven-week hiatus.

His backup, Osweiler, was more mobile, athletic, and accurate, but Manning had the pedigree, the panache, and the brainpower. He also had something to prove after playing the season finale as a backup for the first time as a pro.

The Pittsburgh Steelers staggered into Denver on January 17, 2016, with an ailing Ben Roethlisberger (sprained throwing shoulder) and without top rusher DeAngelo Williams (foot) and All-Pro receiver Antonio Brown (concussion), who had burned the Broncos for 189 yards and two touchdowns on a whopping 16 catches in Pittsburgh's 34–27 win at Heinz Field a month earlier.

The Broncos (12–4) swore they wouldn't repeat their mistake from a year earlier, when they were coming off a playoff bye against a banged-up underdog and lost to the Colts 24–13. This time, there was no talk about a possible date with second-seeded Patriots, just the Steelers. "I think we were focused on New England," Talib said about that game, as he looked back at coming up short. "We just knew we were going to tear up Andrew Luck and the Colts, get them up out of here and get ready to go to New England. So when I look back on last year, there was a lot of, *Next week when we go to New England, we've got to play Gronk like this.* There was a bunch of future talk when we didn't even get the Colts yet."

Another thing that they believe bit them a year earlier was a distracted coaching staff. Defensive coordinator Jack Del Rio and offensive coordinator Adam Gase were both interviewing for head coaching jobs elsewhere. And John Fox let it be known even before kickoff that Chicago was his kind of town.

Said Chris Harris Jr., "I think this year [2015] everybody's more focused." From the coaching staff on down to the backup quarterback. "Not a drop of overlooking guys," Talib said. "Not a drop of that."

"All we're worried about now is the Steelers," insisted Thomas, whose 80-yard touchdown in overtime was the difference four years earlier in the last playoff game between the two teams—the best, most memorable, and ultimately the very last pass Tim Tebow would ever throw in Denver.

Just before kickoff in the rematch a strong wind blew over the Rocky Mountains, wreaking havoc on passes and kicks alike. But McManus tied an NFL playoff record by converting all five of his field goal attempts and Chris Boswell made all three of his.

Manning's teammates dropped seven passes, but came through in crunch time on the blustery night. With Denver down 13–12 with less than 10 minutes left, cornerback Bradley Roby, who had been burned time and again, punched the ball from Fitzgerald Toussaint's arms and teammate DeMarcus Ware recovered at the Denver 35-yard line.

Manning went to work, driving Denver to its only touchdown, a one-yard run by Anderson, followed by Thomas' catch on the two-point conversion that put Denver ahead 20–13 with three minutes left.

Ware sacked Roethlisberger on fourth down and McManus added a fifth field goal for a 10-point lead with a minute remaining. The Steelers countered with a 47-yard field goal, but Anderson smothered the onside kick.

That was Manning's 55th game-winning drive in the fourth quarter or overtime, extending one of the dozen NFL records he owned, and Denver improved to 10–3 that season in games decided by seven points or fewer.

It was onto the AFC title game again, against, who else: Brady and the defending Super Bowl champion Patriots.

It was time for Brady-Manning XVII, which was expected to happen two months earlier but Manning was sidelined and it was Osweiler who led the Broncos to a 30–24 win in overtime that ended when Anderson scooted around left tackle for a 48-yard touchdown run in the snow. With both teams finishing 12–4, that outcome ensured the AFC championship would be held in Denver, where Brady has never won a playoff game, and not Foxborough, where he rarely lost.

Manning and Brady had squared off 16 times, a full season's worth of matchups between two quarterbacks whose careers are so intertwined that a conversation about one almost has to include the other, like Bird vs. Magic, Ali vs. Frazier, Jack vs. Arnold.

"I don't know that there'll ever be another rivalry—or has been a rivalry—like it" in football, said Elway, who faced fellow Hall of Famer and Class of '83 standout Dan Marino just twice in his playing career.

"It'll be the Broncos vs. the Patriots," Manning said after the Pittsburgh game. "We'll enjoy this one tonight. I think you knew that answer was coming. To kind of quote Bill Belichick, we'll be on to New England. But I'll be talking about them on Wednesday."

Brady had won 11 of the 16 meetings against Manning's teams, but they had split their four playoff showdowns, including Denver's 26–16 win in the AFC Championship two years earlier.

And for the tiebreaker, Manning would face Brady at home.

# CHAPTER 30

## BRADY-MANNING
## XVII

On the eve of the AFC Championship Game, Broncos coach Gary Kubiak tapped DeMarcus Ware on his shoulder and whispered to him, and the graceful, quiet, hardworking captain stood up and left the room for a few moments.

"The night before the game, I always talk to the guys, but I'll have one player address the football team before we call it a night," Kubiak explained. "I let DeMarcus do that [for this game]. I could sit here all day and talk about it, but he was just tremendous for this team."

Ware wandered into the weight room to gather his thoughts and there on the wall was the phrase Iron Sharpens Iron. He had his theme. He had somebody run and get something for him and he returned to the team meeting room, stood in front of his teammates, and began talking about how much it meant to play with this group.

He spoke about how they all had each other's backs, about how Shaq Barrett had stepped in for him and kept Denver's defense atop the NFL when he missed five games and parts of three others with a bad back and balky knee. He talked about how Brock Osweiler had stepped up and kept things rolling when Peyton Manning missed two months with a tear in the plantar fascia near his left heel. Both Ware and Manning had watched Denver's 30–24 overtime thriller against New England on November 29 from the equipment room adjacent to the Broncos' lockers.

He talked about how others filled in when safeties David Bruton Jr. and Omar Bolden and tackles Ryan Clady and Ty Sambrailo all went on injured reserve. "That was the grit of the whole season," Ware said. "We melted down that metal," he told the team. "The only way you're going to make metal hard is if you get it done."

Ware told his teammates how he'd been playing in the league for 11 years and had never reached a Super Bowl, never gotten this close, and how he wasn't about to let this opportunity—or Tom Brady—slip from his grasp.

"You could see everybody was focused. It really touched everybody who was in that meeting," Aqib Talib said. "That's what D-Ware does. He speaks from his heart, and his message was definitely felt."

"It was very powerful," Kubiak said.

"It was goose bumps," said Talib.

When he was finished, Ware pulled out the first Super Bowl trophy the franchise had ever won, the silver treasure that team owner Pat Bowlen had handed to John Elway on that magical night in San Diego in 1998.

"I sat it on the table," Ware said, "and it just got really quiet."

Ware looked around.

"I saw in all the guys' eyes how they felt, what they felt—because I felt the same way," Ware said. "From that point, I just knew how important it was to those guys."

More silence, some exhalations. When guys got up to leave, Talib turned to safety T.J. Ward and told him what a shame Ware didn't deliver that monster of a motivational speech just before kickoff instead of the night before the game.

"It doesn't matter," Ward replied. "I'm going to feel it in the morning."

Flash back to two months earlier. Manning had watched the Patriots-Broncos showdown on a snowy November night from an equipment room at Sports Authority Field at Mile High alongside injured Ware. The pair of sidelined superstars offered their own commentary and clues on the pivotal showdown. Manning met with Osweiler at halftime that night to talk about Bill Belichick's blitzes, advice his longtime backup credited for helping him lead Denver back from a two-touchdown, fourth-quarter deficit to a 30–24 win in overtime. The triumph broke the tiebreaker that landed the AFC Championship Game between the two teams in Denver, with temperatures in the 40s, instead of frigid Gillette Stadium.

Manning was out for that November 29 game with a foot injury and Ware was sidelined with a bad lower back. The two had already spent a lot of time rehabbing together. They even stayed behind in Denver when the Broncos played at Chicago the week before and Osweiler made his first career start in his fourth NFL season as

Manning's apprentice. While Manning missed midseason games for the first time in his career, excluding the year he sat out following neck fusion surgery, Ware missed a career-high five games and parts of three others.

For the AFC Championship Game, with everything on the line, both Manning and Ware were back on the field. Manning had missed seven starts altogether, relieving Osweiler in the third quarter of the season finale helping secure the AFC's top seed for Denver. Ware returned to the lineup in December and had made huge plays in each of the Broncos' previous three games, including a game-sealing fumble recovery in overtime against Cincinnati and another against Pittsburgh in the divisional round of the playoffs that preceded Manning's game-winning touchdown drive in the fourth quarter.

Brady was less than the GOAT in Denver. In fact, his only victories in Colorado came against Broncos teams led by Tim Tebow in 2011 and Danny Kanell in 2003.

"It's always frustrating for me when we lose," Brady said. "So, yeah, I know we've had a lot of lonely feelings when you're driving out of that stadium. We've had some pretty tough losses there over the years, because they've had really good teams. It's always a challenge going out and playing anybody on the road, especially a team that's as talented as they are. They've just got a lot of great players, really good coaches that put those guys in a position to play their best. It's not easy to go in there and win, but we're going to give it everything we've got. It should be a lot of fun."

It would be, but not for Brady.

"This is Jesse James and Wyatt Earp standing out in the street at high noon for the last showdown," Joe Theismann said before the AFC Championship Game on January 24, 2016. "You've got arguably the two greatest players that ever played the position. Peyton revolutionized the game and Tom, through his championships, has proven he's the best that's ever played the game."

Their respectful rivalry began on a cloudy afternoon in Foxboro Stadium on September 30, 2001, and blossomed into the greatest rivalry in NFL history.

Tony Dungy, the coach of the Colts in Manning's Super Bowl win in Indianapolis, said Brady-Manning was the quintessential quarterback rivalry. "Our sports society is built around stars, and stars draw people to the game. Those are the players they want to watch," Dungy said.

Brady was seeking a seventh trip to the Super Bowl and a fifth championship. His aim was to get past Manning and have the satisfaction of NFL commissioner Roger Goodell handing him another Lombardi Trophy less than a year after being suspended as a part of the scandal over deflated footballs.

At stake for Manning was a fourth trip to the Super Bowl. The league's only five-time MVP had a chance to become the first starting quarterback to lead two different teams on Super Bowl ticker tape parades.

Not to be forgotten, with a win over Brady, Manning would recoup half of the $4 million pay cut he took the previous winter—and he'd have a chance to get the rest of it back with a win in Super Bowl 50, then ride off into the sunset a champion just like Elway did two decades earlier.

Each quarterback was acutely aware that he had to minimize mistakes and magnify the big moments when facing the other. Said Brady, "You can't play anything less than your best," and even that won't ensure you have a shot at beating Manning.

"All I can say about Tom Brady is he plays the position the way it's supposed to be played," Manning said.

Ware declared, "The clash of the titans is here again." The New York tabloids cheekily turned it into "Taintans," a reference to Brady's Deflategate scandal and Al Jazeera's recent report that Manning obtained human growth hormone shipments through his wife from an Indianapolis anti-aging clinic—a claim he vehemently and angrily denied.

They each had each other's back. "Tom has always been in support of me," Manning said, "and I always try to be the same for him."

Brady would get many more chances for championships but it was plain to see Manning's career was clearly reaching its sunset. Almost 40, this was probably the end of the line, win or lose. He'd missed seven games with an injured left foot and threw just nine touchdown passes to go with a league-leading 17 interceptions. Then again, those statistics just happened to be identical to Bart Starr's stats in 1967 when he guided the Green Bay Packers to their second Super Bowl title in his own last hurrah.

Much like Elway in the twilight of his career—when he had Terrell Davis, Shannon Sharpe, Gary Zimmerman and Steve Atwater—Manning no longer need to carry the Broncos himself. Nor did Denver's fortunes reside on his right arm alone.

The stakes were never higher.

The rivalry no longer featured two passers in their prime. Although 38, Brady was as good and healthy as ever, having thrown for three dozen touchdowns and nearly 5,000 yards. But the most dangerous asset for Manning was his mind. He was getting by on guile and grit; his left foot was compromised, his right arm was diminished, and his shoulders no longer hauled the hopes of a franchise and its enormous fan base.

"Peyton's mind has always been at the forefront of this game. The difference in these two is Tom can threaten you down the field, whereas Father Time has taken that away from Peyton, that's all," Theismann said. "That's the difference in these two guys."

That, and the fact that Brady had never won a playoff game in Denver, where he was 2–8 in his career overall.

Two years earlier when these two star quarterbacks and these two teams met in the AFC championship in Denver, the Broncos featured the league's No. 1 offense, a record-breaking bunch that lit up scoreboards at a record rate. This time, they sported the league's No. 1 defense. They had 10 wins by seven points or fewer, tied with the 1978 Houston Oilers for the most ever.

The Patriots tumbled into the playoffs after a tough December that began with the Broncos ending their undefeated season with C.J. Anderson's 48-yard scamper. But they looked championship-caliber again in their 27–20 playoff win over Kansas City during the divisional round.

Denver led the league in several defensive categories: sacks, total yards, passing yards—and gripes about not getting its due as one of the best defenses ever. But linebacker Brandon Marshall said the Broncos realized that to be considered elite like the 1985 Bears or 2000 Ravens, they'd have to do what those teams did: win it all. Sending Brady to his seventh loss in nine trips to Denver would give them that chance.

Manning got the last laugh on Brady in the 17th and final installment of their renowned rivalry.

Elway had Terrell Davis as his wing man on the way to two Super Bowl victories. And Manning had Von Miller, the star of Denver's dizzying defense who had 2½ sacks, an interception that set up a touchdown, and a pass breakup in the Broncos' 20–18 win over the Patriots in the AFC title game.

"Hey, I tell you. I can do it all, baby," Miller joked after what would turn out to be but an appetizer to his heroics two weeks later in the golden Super Bowl in the Golden Gate City.

Miller and the rest of Denver's defense dethroned the defending champions by hitting Brady an incredible 23 times, more than he'd been hit in at least a decade and 16 times more than Aaron Rodgers had been walloped during the worst game of his career—yes, in Denver, on November 1 of that season.

"He was rattled," said Talib, who had played with Brady in New England before joining the Broncos as part of their defensive remodeling after their previous trip to the Super Bowl. "I don't think I've ever seen anybody put that much pressure on Tom—ever. So I think we did a hell of a job getting that pressure on him. That's why we're going to the c'hip."

The championship.

Super Bowl 50.

Along with Manning, who was hit just four times and improved to 6–11 against Brady, half of those wins coming in AFC Championship Games. "I've enjoyed playing on the same team as that defense," Manning said, raising his eyebrows at the thought of Brady having to face this group. "I'm glad I haven't had to face them this season, I'll say that. They've been challenging to go against in practice, going back to training camp, but it is special to watch them work and watch them perform on Sunday."

Denver, which led the league in defense for the first time in franchise history, held on fourth down inside the 20 on consecutive drives, but a bruised and battered Brady wasn't easy to put away. He found his top target, star tight end Rob Gronkowski, in the back of the end zone for a four-yard touchdown pass with 12 seconds left.

Ware, an 11-year veteran who had never reached a Super Bowl, tried to come off the field after Gronkowski's score because he was gassed. Kubiak burned his final timeout instead.

"We weren't going to play another play without him out there, not if I could help it," Kubiak explained.

Gronk was open again on the two-point conversion attempt but Brady tried to thread the pass to wide receiver Julian Edelman over the middle instead, and Talib got a hand on the football, which fluttered into the waiting arms of cornerback Bradley Roby.

The teams lined up for the onside kick and Denver needed one last big play to secure its trip to Super Bowl 50. It was the unlikeliest of heroes who provided it: safety Shiloh Keo, a free agent who had joined the team a month earlier and had given up the winning touchdown in a 15–12 loss to Oakland before making several big plays in subsequent games.

"We're the No. 1 seed," Talib said, "got the No. 1 defense."

The victory was the Broncos' record 11th by seven points or fewer.

Brady misfired 29 times to go with his 27 completions and finished with a paltry passer rating of 56.4, and Derek Wolfe said he knew Brady was bothered after he clobbered him on the game's first series. "That kind of got in his head: *Oh, the D-line's here, they're ready to play,*" Wolfe said. "It sticks in anybody's head when you've got four or five guys that are coming to take your head off."

Wolfe, Miller, and Chris Harris Jr. were sideline spectators in the Super Bowl against Seattle two years earlier. Now they were leading Manning back, with a chance to go out on top.

Two months shy of age 40, Manning had another chance at history: he could become the first starting quarterback to win Super Bowls with two different franchises, and the second one to go out on top.

"God couldn't have written the story any better for Peyton," Harris said. "He gets hurt. Then they said he got HGH. And he loses his spot. He comes back. We're on our way to the Super Bowl. I can see a beautiful ending for Peyton."

Elway thought he could, too. "Hopefully we've saved our best for last," he said.

Had they ever.

## Dave Logan's Log

Peyton's comeback was just remarkable. I think people underestimated the severity of his injury when he went down, I really do. I think people sort of got this notion that it wasn't that big of a deal. It was a big, big deal. He had to work really hard just to get himself in position to get back on the field.

But I think there's no question in the two playoff games, from a statistical standpoint, if you didn't see the games and you wanted to go back and construct a narrative about the game, you'd have a hard time doing it strictly on his passing statistics. But if you saw the game, you would know that there were two or three instances in both of those AFC playoff games where he made the difference. He was so good at getting them out of a bad look and getting them into a situation in which they had a reasonable opportunity to succeed.

I think that's an art that most people don't really understand. I don't know that anyone has ever been better than Peyton at the line of scrimmage.

Peyton checked away from a Steelers blitz late in their playoff game to help seal the Broncos' victory. And let's not forget about his accuracy. Even on a bad foot with his arm compromised a bit, his accuracy in both of those home playoff games was on point. He put the ball where his receivers could handle it.

# CHAPTER 31
## THIS...ONE'S... FOR...PAT!

Upon his arrival in the Golden Gate City for the golden anniversary of the Super Bowl, Peyton Manning made one thing clear: "Our defense is what got us here," he proclaimed on opening night, which had replaced the midweek media day and all its zaniness.

Two years earlier, Manning had brought along the league's top offense—the highest-scoring team in NFL history, in fact—to the Super Bowl at the Meadowlands. Unfortunately, things didn't work out in a 43–8 shellacking by the Seattle Seahawks. This time, Manning was tagging along with the league's top-ranked defense, led by Von Miller, Chris Harris Jr., and Derek Wolfe, all three of whom had sat out Super Bowl XLVIII in New Jersey with injuries.

In the 1970s it was the "Orange Crush" defense that had Denver on the cusp of greatness. Now it was the "Orange Rush," a unit that finished first in the National Football League in sacks, fewest yards per play allowed, pass defense, and total defense. "We got goal boards in our locker room and we see everything that we've done this year," said cornerback Aqib Talib. "But everything will be forgotten by next season if we don't come home with that trophy. So the most important stat is winning this game."

Yes, to earn their place alongside the 2000 Baltimore Ravens defense that featured Ray Lewis, Sam Adams, Tony Siragusa, Pete Boulware, and Jamie Sharper, or the 1985 Chicago Bears D that sported Steve McMichael, William "Refrigerator" Perry, Richard Dent, Otis Wilson, Mike Singletary, Leslie Frazier, and Dave Dueron, Wade Phillips' collection of characters would have to corral NFL MVP Cam Newton and upset the favored Carolina Panthers.

This defense was certainly capable. It featured an all-star list of starters: Von Miller, Malik Jackson, Derek Wolfe, Sylvester Williams, Brandon Marshall, Danny Trevathan, Aqib Talib, Chris Harris Jr., T.J. Ward, and Darian Stewart. And they had a habit of trouncing elite quarterbacks. In October, they held Aaron Rodgers to 77 yards passing in the worst game of his career. They sent Andrew Luck into the hospital in November with a lacerated kidney and torn abdominal muscle.

They pummeled Tom Brady with a career-high 23 hits in the AFC Championship Game.

Cam Newton, though, was another story. He stood 6'5" and weighed 245—bigger than any linebacker trying to hit him. And he was just as effective running the ball as he was throwing it. The Panthers had outscored their opponents 55–7 in the playoffs, beating Seattle 31–24 and Arizona 49–15.

The Broncos knew all too well how a punch to the gut could ruin great game plans. They hadn't been prepared for the noise and the nerves 24 months earlier, when the first snap sailed into the end zone for a safety 12 seconds into the Super Bowl and the Broncos never recovered. That embarrassment prompted John Elway to spend more than $100 million in free agency, then grab first-rounders Bradley Roby and Shane Ray in the next two drafts. Unlike his predecessor, John Fox, who turned down the giant speakers at practice that week of the Super Bowl, figuring the crowd would favor the Broncos, Gary Kubiak pumped up the jams at practice to prepare for the noise of Super Bowl 50.

As running back C.J. Anderson explained, "The goal is don't let them get off to a fast start. Let it be a boxing match, let them keep punching back and forth."

The Broncos' M.O. was to keep it close, because they always came through in the clutch, having won an NFL-record 11 games by seven points or less.

**Week 1:** Broncos 19, Baltimore 13
**Week 2:** Broncos 31, Kansas City 24
**Week 4:** Broncos 23, Minnesota 20
**Week 5:** Broncos 16, Oakland 10
**Week 6:** Broncos 23, Cleveland 20 (OT)
**Week 11:** Broncos 17, Chicago 15
**Week 12:** Broncos 30, New England 24 (OT)
**Week 16:** Broncos 20, Cincinnati 17 (OT)
**Week 17:** Broncos 27, San Diego 20

**AFC Divisional Playoff:** Broncos 23, Pittsburgh 16
**AFC Championship:** Broncos 20, New England 18

These Panthers, though. They'd won 17 of 18, their only slip-up a 20–13 loss to the Atlanta Falcons in Week 16. Worse, Carolina had beaten nine of those teams by double digits, and since the season's midpoint they had outscored opponents 399–180.

Anderson shrugged off the statistic. Should the Broncos fall behind in Super Bowl 50, they wouldn't freak out, he insisted. In addition to winning so many close games, the Broncos were the only team in league history to have overcome two-touchdown deficits to beat three playoff-bound teams in a single season. They did it against the Chiefs in Week 2, the Patriots in Week 12, and the Bengals in Week 16, part of a 7–2 record they posted against playoff teams while playing the toughest schedule in the league in 2015.

"Us being down 14 to some very, very good teams, it lets us know we're battle tested. We've been there before," Anderson said. "We know what we have to do to get back in the games."

The Panthers were bringing the highest-scoring offense to the Super Bowl, just like the Broncos had two years earlier. Manning was creaky and the Panthers were rolling behind Newton, who would be crowned the league's MVP the night before the Super Bowl, and some observers said the Panthers' defense was just as good as Denver's.

"Every time we turn on the TV people are just talking about how we're going to get dogged this game, we're going to get blown out," Harris said with a laugh. "We love that."

Because it was a role reversal from the Super Bowl two years earlier. This time, the Panthers were riding high and the Broncos were the ones quietly confident they'd stop their high-scoring opponent cold on the game's biggest stage.

By leading the Broncos back to the Super Bowl, Manning earned back half of the $4 million pay cut he accepted the previous summer, and a win over the Panthers would allow him to recoup the other $2 million. Not a bad incentive.

So while he and his teammates each stood to pocket $102,000 from the league for winning Super Bowl 50—or $51,000 should they lose—a victory would mean Manning wouldn't have given up a dime in that contentious contract negotiation before the season, when John Elway had initially sought a much larger put cut even though Manning was coming off a 39-touchdown season. (With the pay cut, Manning had still earned $882,352 each week during the regular season, including the ones he spent working with Jordan "Sunshine" Taylor to regain his rhythm.)

Elway's extreme makeover in the wake of Denver's last trip to the Super Bowl meant Manning was leading a much different team this time. The GM had transformed his offensive juggernaut into a defensive powerhouse like Seattle's, in large part because he signed thumpers Ware, Ward, and Talib to free agent contracts worth a combined $109.5 million. Miller and Harris Jr. each visited Dr. James Andrews for ACL surgeries, then rehabbed together, pushing each other back into All-Pro form. And Derek Wolfe recovered from a seizure disorder that had also rendered him a helpless sideline spectator during that nightmare in New Jersey in Super Bowl XLVIII.

The defense that would line up on February 7 against Newton was healthy. It included just three starters from the Broncos' last Super Bowl appearance: hard-hitting inside linebacker Trevathan and linemen Jackson and Williams.

Elway also got gotten lucky in the draft, grabbing two top-15 talents that slipped down draft boards to the Broncos in the two years between their trips to the Super Bowl under Manning. Roby was an All–Big Ten cornerback from Ohio State who was expected to go to a rebuilder as a consensus top-of-the-board talent in the 2014 draft, but he fell to Denver at No. 31 because of a couple of run-ins with the law. (Roby had been suspended for the Buckeyes' first game in his senior season after being accused of getting in a bar fight. He resolved a citation for operating a vehicle while under the influence just before draft weekend by pleading guilty to a reduced charge.) Roby began his NFL career with an assurance to his new team, declaring, "I'm not a bad guy, not a guy you have to worry about off the field." But he was a guy opponents certainly had to worry about on the field. Roby, Talib, and Harris Jr. gave the Broncos the best cornerback combo in football.

A year later, Shane Ray, a pass rusher from Missouri, saw his draft stock slip when a state trooper found weed in his car after stopping him for speeding just four days before the draft. His misdemeanor citation wound up costing him financially after he fell from a projected top-10 pick all the way to No. 23, where the Broncos traded up to grab the SEC defensive player of the year.

Like Roby a year earlier, Ray suddenly found himself in an ideal situation. "If you're going to fall," said his mother, Sabrina Johnson, "who better to catch you than John Elway?"

And who better to learn from than Miller and Ware? Instead of serving as a defensive cornerstone for a rebuilding franchise, Ray was playing in the Super Bowl, teaming with Shaq Barrett to give the Broncos a second wave of pass-rushing pressure that kept Miller and Ware fresh for the kinds of performances Denver provided in the AFC Championship Game, when they delivered such a beating to Tom Brady that Bill Belichick urged his old offensive line coach Dante Scarnecchia to come out of retirement.

Recreational pot shops are almost as common as 7-Elevens in Denver. While that might have seemed like a problem waiting to happen, Elway dismissed any such notion, stressing that while cannabis is cool in Colorado, "it's still illegal in the NFL." Ray, subjected to random drug testing from the get-go, insisted he was no pothead and vowed to put his marijuana mistake behind him. Like Roby, Ray has been a model citizen and teammate.

In the AFC Championship Game, Roby made the game-saving interception of Brady's two-point conversion attempt to tie it with 12 seconds left, sending Denver back to the Super Bowl—this time with a defense that took pressure off Manning.

Also accompanying the Broncos to the Super Bowl this time were Ryan Clady and the six other players on injured reserve. They flew out to San Francisco with the team, a change from two years earlier when Fox left behind all his injured players, including stars Miller and Harris Jr., when the team flew to New York.

"I think it's great," said Clady, the star left tackle who missed the Seattle Super Bowl with a foot injury and was missing this one with a knee injury. "I like the fact that everybody's coming, because honestly I thought it was going to be like last time."

Miller blew out a knee in Week 16 in that 2013 season and said that being left behind during Super Bowl week stung. "That four days, it ate me up, seeing them on TV and not being around them," Miller said.

Harris also had bitter memories of missing out on the media day madness, the team photo and all the other fun stuff, after getting hurt in the playoffs. The two of them arrived with family and friends at week's end, by which time their teammates were focused on football. "I mean, that was so hard to not be in any of that, to enjoy that," said Harris, who injured a knee in the playoffs against the Chargers in the AFC divisional round. "So, for those guys to get to enjoy that this time, I'm happy for those guys. To be able to show the true team aspect that everybody's been needed, I like that approach."

Kubiak said it was all part of his promise he made to the team from the start. "We're all in this together," Kubiak explained. "There are guys that we've lost through the course of the year, but they've been a big part of us. They've been with us. One thing I ask guys to do when they're on IR is stay involved with the team, don't just remove themselves. Guys have done that."

It was a small gesture but a brilliant move in galvanizing the locker room.

"I feel like I had a little bit of a stamp on this season," Clady said, "just being here for a long time and being a part of getting Peyton

Manning here and the success we've had since he's been here. It's exciting. I'm happy for my teammates. Unfortunately, I can't play. But I'm happy for guys I've been working with for years, and we've been grinding. Even last year, practicing with some of the guys, working with D-Ware, I feel like I helped them get a jump on some of the other tackles in this league."

The decision to exclude the injured players was one of several blunders the old Broncos coaching staff made 24 months earlier, along with arduous practices with an older, patchwork roster full of veteran backups past their prime. And who could forget Fox's disastrous decision to turn down the speakers that simulate crowd noise at practice?

This time, they left no teammate behind, the practices would be lighter, and yes, the volume would be cranked up high. "Yeah, we're practicing with noise," Kubiak confirmed before flying out to California. "Peyton mentioned that to me and so we took the approach this week to practice with noise."

Also along for the Super Bowl ride were the practice squad members, including receiver Jordan Taylor, who sauntered into the locker room the day before the Broncos flew to California. A spiffy custom-made charcoal suit was slung over his shoulder.

"Let me see it," Manning asked excitedly. Manning admired the craftsmanship and choice of color when Taylor unzipped the white vinyl bag to reveal the three-piece ensemble along with two crisp shirts and a pair of silky ties.

Manning had sent Taylor his tailor as a way of thanking the 6'5" rookie from Rice for helping him regain his rhythm and reclaim his starting job in time to make this run to the Super Bowl. Taylor served as Manning's dedicated practice partner in December when the five-time MVP began his comeback from a left foot injury that sidelined him for seven games down the stretch.

"I don't think I could have gotten through my rehab and gotten back if it had not been for him," Manning said. "I am very grateful for his help."

The workouts consisted of assistant equipment manager Mike "Harry" Harrington snapping to Manning and Taylor basically running himself ragged. Explained Taylor, "We'd work from the right side first and run all of the route tree: curls, fades, hitches, slants—all that. We'd do 10 routes on the left side, 10 routes on the right side. And then he likes to get into two-minute mode, hurrying up and calling things out. So we would do that up and down the field three or four times. It was exhausting. And then I'd have to go to practice later that afternoon."

Taylor wasn't just a practice squad receiver. He also lined up at free safety on the scout team. He even lost some weight during his very own two-a-days and mornings with Manning. The quarterback said he "felt bad because I was running him into the ground and he hadn't even started practice yet. I have a bad habit of saying, 'Just one more.' And one more can turn into 10 more."

It turned out Manning was no less demanding of his teammates when he was hurt. If anything, his maniacal pursuit of perfection was only heightened during his rehabilitation. Yet Taylor saw it as Manning doing him the favor, not the other way around. He said his route running became crisper, his understanding of the offense clearer. He just had to get over being starstruck first.

"Once you get over the awe of it and actually get to work with him and grind with him, I mean, he's coaching me up on route depths, route techniques, while he's trying to get better, too," Taylor said. "So, it helped me to grow as a receiver."

Taylor had a better view of Manning's progress than did Kubiak, who watched most of those indoor sessions on film. Taylor saw the progress up close from week to week, day to day, throw to throw.

By the time the Broncos played their regular-season finale against San Diego, Manning had progressed enough to suit up and serve as Brock Osweiler's backup. Manning didn't expect to play that day, so he and Taylor worked up a good sweat well before kickoff, doing the same routine they'd done indoors for a month and a half. Then Manning prepared to go stand on the sideline while Taylor showered, dressed, and headed up to the press box with the other practice squad players.

At halftime, Taylor grabbed a hot dog and settled back into his seat for the second half. He'd soon see Manning trotting onto the field and feel the stadium shake. Manning led Denver on four scoring drives, securing the home-field advantage in the AFC playoffs that proved crucial to making it back to the Super Bowl.

Reflecting on that day, Taylor said proudly, "I saw this coming," as he basked in the festivities of Super Bowl week.

The two of them would have one more chance to work together, on Super Bowl Sunday.

When Manning first got to Denver in 2012, he did not warm up on the field before games because he was constantly interrupted to catch up with former teammates who were now playing for his opponent, coaching against him, or broadcasting the game. So he started loosening up his arm in the locker room or the tunnel instead.

That routine changed when he and Taylor hit the field two hours before kickoff against San Diego in the regular season finale for another of their one-on-one workouts. "And we won, so I did it against Pittsburgh, and versus New England," Manning explained. "So we'll be out there Super Bowl Sunday. It's a nice reminder of kind of where we've been this season. I look forward to that."

It was a long road for both Denver and Carolina to get to this point. Five years earlier, in 2011, both the Broncos and the Panthers were picking through the rubble of seasons gone terribly wrong and scouring a draft board that was unusually top-heavy with talent, featuring the likes of J.J. Watt, A.J. Green, Patrick Peterson, Mike Pouncey, Julio Jones, Nate Soldier, Cameron Jordan, and Jimmy Smith. With the top pick in the 2011 NFL draft, the Panthers selected Auburn quarterback Newton, and with the second pick the Broncos chose Texas A&M linebacker Miller.

Now they were meeting in the first matchup of No. 1 vs. No. 2 in the Super Bowl.

"I'm his biggest fan," said Miller.

"I'm a fan of his," Newton said.

Miller couldn't fathom why Newton was such a lightning rod for criticism. "I mean, for what? Dancing after making big plays?" Miller asked. "I do the same thing."

Both seemed to play the game with a child's exuberance, dancing and dabbing to celebrate touchdowns or takedowns. And each took his role as loquacious locker room cutup as seriously as he did his rank as team captain.

Both navigated troubled times to get to this point, too. Miller overcame a drug suspension at the start of 2013 season and an ill-conceived plan to add 25 pounds, which made him stronger but slower and which he now believes led him to tear his right ACL at the end of that season. He reestablished himself as one of the NFL's best outside linebackers with 25 sacks in his two seasons since returning from knee surgery and especially thrived once Ware arrived in free agency.

Newton overcame an automobile accident in 2014 that left him with two fractures in his lower back and imperiled his status as the league's dominant dual-threat quarterback. He set a rookie record for yards passing in a season while earning AP Offensive Rookie of the Year (Miller won AP Defensive Rookie of the Year). No player had more combined yards from scrimmage (21,470) and touchdowns (171) than Newton in his first five seasons in the league.

While Miller found trouble early in his NFL career, Newton navigated his troubled path in college. He originally enrolled at the University of Florida, but would leave after accusations that he stole a laptop. He transferred to Blinn Junior College, which he guided to a national championship. After transferring to Auburn, the NCAA suspended Newton briefly in 2010 while investigating whether his father Cecil had requested $180,000 on his son's behalf from someone acting as an agent seeking Cam to enroll at Mississippi State. However, the NCAA overturned the suspension and Newton went on to lead the

Tigers to a national championship and won the Heisman Trophy in his only season at Auburn.

"We all make mistakes," Newton said. "Yet it's all about how you rebound from that mistake instead of just giving up."

Miller felt the very same way. The league changed its drug policy in 2014. Instead of perpetually being one strike—even a missed urine test—away from a lifetime ban from the NFL, Miller was discharged from the league's drug program altogether the previous summer after staying clean for two years.

So the anvil turned into a carrot, and now the man Elway called "the best football player on the planet" back in training camp was one win shy of becoming a champion, too.

Miller said he had long ago accepted Newton being congratulated first by the commissioner on draft night. What he wanted more than anything was to beat Newton and take to the postgame stage to shake Roger Goodell's hand during the Lombardi Trophy presentation.

On Super Bowl Sunday, the Broncos were methodical in their pregame preparation. Meanwhile, the Panthers looked as if they were expecting a coronation. Newton arrived in golden cleats for the golden Super Bowl in the Golden Gate City—actually Santa Clara, California.

### Dave Logan's Log

I got there about four hours before the kickoff. I remember watching the two teams warm up and I was struck by how different the individual warm-ups for the players were. The Panthers were out just having a great time, very loose. And the Broncos looked like it was all business. And I remember thinking to myself, *Carolina believes this is going to be easy.*

I obviously couldn't get in their minds, but just watching them warm up, they acted like they didn't have a care in the world. It was like they believed the Broncos had no chance to beat them. Even if you're a better team, that's a dangerous mind-set to have. Football's a funny game, and it's got a way of coming back and biting you in the ass when you assume anything.

I thought Denver had to play well, and honestly, I thought they would be better offensively against Carolina than they were. They converted their first third-down opportunity on their opening drive, but they didn't have another third-down conversion the rest of the game! If you looked at their offensive output at the end of the game and nothing else, you would swear that the Broncos lost. But turnovers, obviously, and big, big plays on defense made the difference.

To me, the Super Bowl was somewhat of a microcosm of the season. There were close games and the Broncos ultimately won Super Bowl 50, but it was not an easy season. Plenty of games were nail-biters. There were a handful of games that were in doubt late that could have gone either way. But they developed a confidence in their ability to win those tight games.

You build so much confidence as a team when things like that happen. Your mind-set becomes, *We're going to win every single game we play, no matter the circumstances. We can't be beat.*

Peyton was good at understanding his limitations physically that year. He had a brilliant mind. He didn't put his team in a position where he was going to give the game away. I think he might have been the best in the history of the game at helping his team the most at the line of scrimmage. And he still had enough in the tank that he could make a few key throws, as he did against the Patriots in the AFC championship and against the Panthers in Super Bowl 50. It just was a season when everything came together and the defense really made so many big plays at key times. It was just remarkable.

The Broncos carried Manning across the finish line on February 7, 2016. The five-time MVP was now the first starting QB to win a Super Bowl with two different franchises. As the golden confetti showered down on Manning, he was asked if he'd ride off into that orange sunset a champion, just like his boss Elway had in 1999. "I'll take some time to reflect," Manning said. "I got a couple priorities first. I'm going to go kiss my wife and my kids.... I'm going to drink a lot of Budweiser tonight. Take care of those things first."

No, he wasn't the star in Denver's 24–10 victory over the Panthers—game MVP Miller seemingly was everywhere on every Carolina play, disrupting Newton's rhythm and ruining the Panthers' party plans in the greatest individual defensive performance in the half century of Super Bowls that featured the Steelers' "Steel Curtain" defense, Buddy Ryan's famed 46 defense, and Seattle's "Legion of Boom," among many others.

Denver's destructive defense, the one that ran roughshod over Tom Brady two weeks before, never let Newton get comfortable. Even in the postgame interview, Newton got upset and stormed off when he overheard All-Pro cornerback Harris Jr. on the other side of the heavy-but-not-soundproof curtain talking about how the Broncos had throttled the league's best player and denied him the crown he'd expected would be his.

Miller twice strip-sacked Newton, one that Jackson recovered in the end zone for a defensive touchdown, the second one setting up a game-clinching touchdown by C.J. Anderson in the closing minutes.

The Broncos collected a Super Bowl–record seven sacks, six of Newton and one of receiver Ted Ginn Jr., who went down on an aborted trick play. And if Miller wasn't in Newton's face, Ware was. He hit the quarterback four times, sacking him twice for 24 yards in losses.

Carolina's potent offense, which had led the league with 500 points in the regular season, was held to its fewest points for a single game all year. Denver set an ignominious mark with just 194 yards gained, the fewest ever for a Super Bowl winner.

It didn't matter. The Broncos were champions and Manning, who won his first ring in Indianapolis in 2007, was the first quarterback to win Super Bowls with two franchises. Elway became the first to win a Super Bowl as a quarterback and another as a general manager.

Manning completed 13 for 23 passes for 141 yards against Carolina as he looked every bit of his 39 years: creaky, off-target a lot of the time. He threw his first interception of the playoffs and even lost a fumble. But after setting records his first three seasons in Denver, he capped off his fourth with a championship. So what if his passer rating was 56.6

in the Super Bowl? Or that he handed off on third-and-9 while nursing a lead, something Manning in his prime never would have dreamed of doing?

"This game was much like this season has been, testing our toughness, our resiliency, our unselfishness," Manning said. "It's only fitting that it turned out that way."

Manning had just enough left in that right arm to give Denver small wisps of offense to set up a few field goals and keep the Broncos in good field position most of the night, then got out of the way to let a smothering, historically good defense win it.

Seven sacks, four takeaways, 10 measly points. Any more questions?

"Look man, we're the greatest defense anyone ever faced," linebacker Brandon Marshall professed. "The 2015 Broncos are the No. 1 defense of all time."

Not the '85 Bears.

Or the 2000 Ravens.

Not the 2002 Buccaneers.

Or the Steel Curtain of the '70s.

"You've got to put us right there with them if you ask me, man," Talib said, adding that he was sure people would be talking about this group generations from now after this historic performance. "They should. Why shouldn't they?" Talib reasoned. "Top five in every category. Then, in the biggest game, we played the No. 1 scoring offense against the No. 1 defense. And them boys got 10 points."

With Denver's dominant performance, No. 1 defenses improved to 12–4 in the Super Bowl (and two of those losses were before the AFL-NFL merger, when the No. 1 team from one conference lost to the top defense from the other).

"I'm so proud of my guys," Miller said after accepting the MVP trophy. Miller had 2½ sacks and forced two fumbles that led to Denver's two touchdowns. Trevathan led the team with eight tackles and recovered two fumbles. Ward recovered a fumble and intercepted a pass. Ware had his pair of sacks and four hits on the quarterback. Jackson recovered a fumble in the end zone, then tossed the football into the stands not realizing it was a historic memento: Denver's first defensive touchdown in eight Super Bowls.

After being hit just three times and throwing 15 incompletions in the playoffs coming in, Newton was hit 13 times and misfired 23 passes.

"I remember the Ravens, I remember the Bucs," Talib said, listing the greatest defenses of all time. "I don't really remember the Steel Curtain and all that, but I heard about them. The '85 Bears, I didn't see them, but I heard about them."

And now everybody had heard of the 2015 Broncos.

## Dave Logan's Log

What do I remember specifically about Super Bowl 50? I thought Denver had a really good shot to pull off the win. Quite honestly, I thought the Broncos offense would play much better. I thought they could make some plays on the Carolina defense. And then I thought the Broncos defense would make some plays as well.

They were 5-point underdogs. I liked their chances.

The defense created so many plays. Von's strip sack and the fumble recovered by Malik Jackson for a touchdown, and then Von got another strip sack that set up the final touchdown. So defensively the Broncos just made a bunch of really game-changing plays. I do think Carolina played into their hands a little bit. The Panthers' strength was running the ball and then play-action once they established the run, but the Panthers didn't really run the ball that much at all. Cam threw it 41 times, which really wasn't what they liked to do, and that played right into the Broncos' strength on defense.

Manning stood up in front of his teammates on the eve of the Super Bowl and thanked the defense for bringing him along on this ride. Many players felt certain that it was his farewell address and it galvanized them.

"What impressed me about this team was that only two years earlier they had been shellacked in Super Bowl XLVIII, and here they were in Super Bowl 50 a bigger underdog than they were against the Seahawks. But I think there was a quiet confidence about that Broncos team," Logan said.

The defense would indeed carry Manning all the way across the finish line and help the Broncos avoid another loss on the big stage like the three they had in four years before Elway won two titles with a better supporting cast.

Nobody has ever had a better defensive performance in a Super Bowl than Miller. "He almost single-handedly wrecked Carolina's game plan," Logan said. "If you're Carolina, don't you know going into that game your tackles have been average pass protectors all year? They were pretty darn good in the run game. So wouldn't you think the Panthers would come out and try to run the ball at Denver's defense?

"One touchdown came off the strip sack by Von. Then his strip sack in the fourth quarter is kicked around, recovered inside the 10. That's 14 points, and I think another turnover resulted in 3. So, you gave up 24 points but 14 of those are the Jackson-recovered fumble, then a drive that starts on the Carolina 12-yard line. I'm sure from Carolina's standpoint, they were saying, *We gave the game away.*

"But turnovers are a big part of the game, and the Broncos defense had been great all year coming up with the big plays."

When Commissioner Roger Goodell presented the Lombardi Trophy to the Broncos after the game, Elway flashed that mile-high smile and finally got to holler those four words:

"This...one's...for...Pat!"

# CHAPTER 32
## MANNING'S FAREWELL

**P**eyton Manning came to Denver on March 20, 2012, looking for a chance to win another title in the twilight of his career. General manager John Elway had the blueprint. Four years later, Manning hobbled away a champion.

Like he had when he lured him to Denver, Elway practiced patience with Manning while the five-time NFL MVP contemplated his future. He told Manning after the Broncos' Super Bowl parade in downtown Denver to take his time making a decision about whether or not he would return, to get back to him in a few weeks.

Manning wasn't in any hurry.

"He waited for Peyton," Dave Logan said. "John's smart and also calculating, just like Peyton. Honestly, I don't think John wanted to be seen as the guy who pushed Peyton Manning out the door, at least publicly. So, he waited for Peyton to make up his mind."

The prevailing thought in Denver was that Manning would retire and his longtime understudy Brock Osweiler, who had been groomed to replace him, would re-sign with the Broncos and succeed him. It was going to be Osweiler's team now.

Coach Gary Kubiak said even if Manning decided to play out the final year of his contract in 2016 he wanted Osweiler back on a long-term deal because Osweiler was definitely the future, if not the present, in Denver.

Kubiak didn't want to pressure Manning, either. "There is no hurry here," he declared.

No, but there was a deadline—March 9—when Manning's $19 million salary for 2016 would become guaranteed. Deep down, the face of the league since the turn of this century knew he was finished as a football player. Manning realized he'd no longer have to study an iPad all day. His battered body no longer needed to be submerged for hours in cold tubs. There would be no more defenses to dissect. No more physical gyrations and verbal calisthenics to make at the lines of scrimmage. No more jumpy pass rushers to lure offsides or quick snaps to catch opponents trying to run a 12th player off the field. No more

"Omaha! Omaha!" to holler as he signaled a change in the play call at the last moment upon reading the defense. No more treatment for that torn left plantar fascia near his left heel that had hampered him all the way back to July, which led to his worst statistical season of his spectacular career and sidelined him for six weeks before that fairy-tale finish in Santa Clara, California.

"I think I kind of knew where it was headed, but you want to be sure," Manning said on the day he held his retirement news conference, recounting how Duke University football coach David Cutcliff, who had been his offensive coordinator and position coach at the University of Tennessee, told him, "It's permanent, so understand what that means. So, don't do it if you're not 100 percent ready."

A month shy of his $40^{th}$ birthday, Manning was 100 percent ready for the next chapter in his life. "Maybe you could say I waited because I wanted to be an NFL quarterback for as long as I could," Manning said after his farewell news conference on March 7, 2016, when he officially retired from the league he had transformed over his 18-year career.

Forty-eight hours earlier, Manning picked up the phone and dialed Elway. This time around, he was the first call and not the last. He thanked Elway for bringing him to Denver and told him he was going to retire rather than play a $19^{th}$ season. He called Kubiak next, then Broncos team president Joe Ellis, who was running the team for ailing owner Pat Bowlen.

Manning called the other four head coaches he'd played for during his NFL career: Jim Mora, Tony Dungy, Jim Caldwell, and John Fox, thanking them for all they had done to help him become the quarterback and the man he was.

"I told them all, 'I'd really like you to keep this confidential. There's some other people I'd like to call so they hear it from me first. It's going to get out tomorrow that I'm going to retire on Monday,'" Manning recounted.

"Foxy did not tell Glazer!" Manning marveled. Fox had a close relationship with Fox's Jay Glazer, sometimes having him attend practices and often leaking stories to him.

Manning even called coaches he didn't play for but whom he held in high regard. "I called Bill Parcells. I told him, 'Besides Jim Mora, you were the first NFL coach I talked to.' I talked to him my junior year. I don't think I was supposed to be talking to him as a junior. But I wanted to talk to him because I wanted to see what he had to say and what they might do and so that was kind of important," said Manning.

"And then I called Brady and I called Belichick," Manning said of his New England nemeses, who together teamed up for nine Super Bowls and six championships, numbers that would have been even better were it not for Archie Manning's boys. (Peyton Manning's teams beat Brady and Belichick three times in the AFC Championship Game and Eli Manning's Giants beat them in two Super Bowls.) Were it not for the Mannings, Brady might have had a second hand filled with diamond-encrusted Super Bowl rings. Think of that.

"I had really good talks with them," Manning said. "And then obviously, my family knew at that point, and there were some other people." Manning spent much of that Saturday catching up with old friends, none of whom were at all surprised by his decision.

"It was hard to call John to kind of start that process, but I got to start talking to Jim Mora. I tried to call people that have been a part of all 18 years from the get-go," Manning said. "So I called Bruce [Arians, who was his QBs coach from 1998 to 2000]. Tom Moore, who just learned how to use a cell phone—I could not locate him for my life. So, I said, 'I really want to tell you something but I don't want to do it over voicemail.' I called John Madden, I had a good talk with him. And then I had a really good conversation with Jim Irsay, so I really sort of covered my bases."

Then he called teammates, including Von Miller and DeMarcus Ware, and former teammates including Jeff Saturday and Marvin Harrison.

In his last NFL game, Peyton Manning helped bring the Denver Broncos their third
Lombardi Trophy in franchise history.

Two days later, Manning was choked up as he officially ended his playing career in the league he helped popularize to super-size status during a glittering career as the NFL's all-time leading passer and winningest quarterback, the only one ever to win Super Bowls as the starting quarterback for two franchises.

He retired with an unprecedented five MVP awards and dozens of passing records, including most yards (71,940) and touchdown throws (539). Manning's 73rd career win came in Super Bowl XLI, 29–17 over the Chicago Bears, when he was at the peak of his strength. His 200th win was Super Bowl 50, a 24–10 win over the Carolina Panthers, when his contributions were more cerebral than physical.

"Winning a Super Bowl with his mind impresses me more than winning a Super Bowl with his body," said his father, Archie. "He had to do several things different this last year. Had to take off during the season, which he'd never done before. He ran the scout team, which I don't think he'd ever done, and he dressed out as a backup, which he'd never done."

Archie Manning said that final regular-season game in particular will stick with him, when his son rallied the Broncos to a victory over San Diego. Lose and they're the No. 5 seed. Win and they were the AFC's top seed, with a bye to get healthy and two home games to get to the Super Bowl, the kind of path Brady had so often taken to get his championship rings.

"You may go back and say the second-most-important game Peyton's ever been a part of was his only bullpen game," his father said. "If they don't come back and score and beat the Chargers, I'm not sure Von's going to be MVP of the Super Bowl if they go in as a five seed.

"Olivia and I were at home. [Peyton] had told me, 'I'm not going to play.' Olivia said 'He's warming up.'... Peyton was proud of Brock. I thought Brock played great."

Manning also never before had to submit to being the ultimate game manager like he was during Denver's defense-fueled run to the Lombardi Trophy in that final season. "I'm just glad I was on the same team as our defense," Manning said after Super Bowl 50. Manning had 13 completions for 141 yards, the second-lowest yardage total of his 27 playoff games. But thanks to a defense led by Miller, who was in on three sacks and forced two fumbles that led to 15 points, Manning became the oldest quarterback ever to win a title, a year older than Elway was when he won his second Super Bowl in 1999. (He was supplanted by Brady, who won Super Bowl LIII when he was 41.) Manning went 50–15 in Denver, and that doesn't count the epic comeback he engineered in San Diego relieving Brock Osweiler.

What made the Super Bowl win so special, Miller said, was giving Manning the chance to leave on top of the game he revolutionized with his play under center. "Oh it was very important. The type of friend that Peyton has been for me has been outstanding. When I was going through all my trouble, he was texting me every week and telling me he was missing me," Miller said, looking back on his drug suspension to start the 2013 season. "He didn't have to do that but he did. The list goes on and on and on of things he's done for his team and how he influenced us to play to the level that we have."

Manning also revealed one other bit of the secret sauce that helped him get that Super Bowl ring. He told reporters after his retirement news conference he had an "orthotics guru" who had also helped other NFL quarterbacks take up shop in his garage in November to fit him with some orthotics that helped him get back on the field after he tore a ligament near his left heel. "There's a guru out there for everybody," Manning explained later that afternoon after taking photos with Broncos employees and the Lombardi Trophy. "He works with Brady and Roethlisberger. And I'm not going to put his website out there or anything. But he took a mold of my foot and it's like papier-mâché. And he said, 'Hey, I need a place to work for like a day and a half.' So, I put him in my garage. He had a microwave and he melts it into your shoe. So, I'm kind of thinking it's a little voodoo.... He said 'I might need you every couple of hours.' He had to come mold me, fit me, he had to go work, and then fit me.

"He gave me three pads. I've got them in here," Manning said, pointing to his cowboy boots. "One for my everyday shoes, one for my tennis shoes, and one for my cleats." Manning said his agent, Tom Condon, found the guy. "I rode that pair all the way to San Francisco," Manning said. "I didn't change them."

The summer before his final season, Manning had revealed he still had no feeling in the fingertips of his right hand, and yet he threw 140 of his then NFL-best 539 touchdown passes for the Broncos, including a record 55 in 2013. (Drew Brees would eventually claim the record, with a league-best 547 at the time of this book's publication.)

Manning's college coach, Phillip Fulmer, said it was "almost magical" what Manning was able to accomplish in his four years in Denver following neck fusion surgery that threatened to short-circuit his career. Instead of packing it up for good, Manning won 77 percent of his games and his fifth MVP award, surpassed Brett Favre's records for career yards, touchdowns, and victories, and led the Broncos to two Super Bowls.

"I've said this a lot of times to people, he didn't get better each game. He got better every meeting, every practice, every period in practice," Fulmer said. "He was the most incredible player I've ever seen of taking it from the film room to the practice field and then from the practice field to the game."

Because that last regular-season triumph over the Chargers went on Osweiler's record, not his, Manning tied Favre for most regular season wins with 186. But his victory in Super Bowl 50 was his 14th in the postseason, giving him one more than Favre and making him the NFL's only 200-win quarterback, until Brady joined him in that group.

Manning transcended the sport, making his mark not only on the football field but on Madison Avenue and in pop culture, his dry wit and starpower a staple of late-night television and 30-second commercials for nearly two decades.

Manning would continue being the face of football even when his playing career was done, and his legacy lives on to this day on every

NFL weekend. "He was on the forefront of basically a revolution in the way offenses are run in the National Football League," Joe Theismann said. "His footprint was bigger than just the cities he played in. He transformed the position. The style of offense that he ran in Indianapolis was revolutionary and nobody ever figured out how to stop it there—or in Denver. The only thing that's basically slowed Peyton Manning down was Father Time."

Manning left an indelible imprint on America's most popular sport. When he stepped onto the football field as the top overall draft pick by the Colts in 1998, Manning was equal parts transcendent and throwback. A pioneer in the way he deciphered defenses and directed play at the line of scrimmage, pacing from tackle to tackle, pointing and hollering, he became a model for every quarterback who's come along since. He was at the vanguard of the aerial fireworks shows that light up today's scoreboards.

"I think from the sense of quarterbacks, he's been fast-paced, no-huddle, dynamic offense, score a lot of points, and score quickly," Eli Manning said. "He has won a lot of football games. Now you see that more. More teams are doing it. The Colts kind of started that trend and did it well for a long time."

DeMarcus Ware said Manning was never the best athlete on the field, but his off-the-charts preparation and incredible memory recall made him rise above everyone. "He beat you mentally," said Ware. "That was his guide: physically you might be faster than me, you might be more athletic than me, but I'm going to outsmart you every time."

On the day his son retired, Archie Manning said, "I don't think I've ever brought this up to him. We were riding down the street one day. I was in Indianapolis and he had had a good game and he was able to kind of pick this team apart and he said, 'You know, Dad, I just feel like I know what they're doing. I just got a sense I can predict what they're doing with some defenses and be fairly accurate about it.' I'm not sure I ever felt that way. The game was even simpler in my day. But I...was always proud of him for that. I think coaches admired that about Peyton…. Coaches that he played for [and] coaches that he played against."

Even Osweiler, who spent so much time waiting for Manning to move on, said working with him made him a better quarterback. "There's not a day that's gone by since I've been in the league that I haven't learned something from Peyton," Osweiler said.

The last call Manning made on that Saturday full of phone calls was to ESPN's Chris Mortensen, who was recovering from cancer. He wanted Mortensen to break the story, which he did the next morning.

Once the news was official, Brady tweeted his congratulations to his friend and football foe: "You changed the game forever and made everyone around you better."

Could there be a higher compliment?

"He'll miss it," Archie Manning said. "Peyton, he didn't just love the three hours on Sunday afternoon, he really loved everything about it. He really did. He worked at it. He thoroughly, I've never heard Peyton complain about anything he had to do in relation to football. I don't think he ever complained about doing any interviews. He knew what he was supposed to do and he just kind of lived his life trying to do the right thing and helped people. So, I think he's at peace."

The knock on Manning was that he didn't win more Super Bowls. For a guy with such a great regular season record (186–79), his playoff mark of just 14–13 paled by comparison.

"People don't realize, it's hard to always be the best player," Fulmer argued. "For almost all his years, he had to be the best player. At Indianapolis, he never had a great defense around him. In my opinion, if he had been on teams like this last Broncos team—a team not even as good on defense—the guy might have six or seven Super Bowls."

Miller didn't want to think about the Broncos post-Manning. "It's always sad, but I think it's better that you think about the 18 years he's put into the game. The type of influence he's had on not just the Denver Broncos but the whole sport of football," Miller said. "He revolutionized how you play the position of quarterback. There's been so many greats that have come before him, but he totally changed the quarterback position. You can't say quarterback without Manning. It just goes together. That's on the brighter side of things."

Commissioner Roger Goodell called Manning "a great representative of the NFL both on the field and in his community," adding, "We are forever grateful for Peyton's unmatched contributions to the game and know his success will continue in the next phase of his life."

Manning had to crack a few jokes to help fight back the tears at his retirement news conference, much like Elway did back in 1999, when the words didn't always come as easy as the emotions did. His voice cracking, especially when he mentioned his hero, Johnny Unitas, Manning said good-bye to the game he loved in an auditorium packed with friends, family, and laughter.

"I thought about it a lot, prayed about it a lot...it was just the right time," Manning said. "I don't throw as good as I used to, don't run as good as I used to, but I have always had good timing."

That he did.

"I'm totally convinced that the end of my football career is just the beginning of something I haven't even discovered yet," Manning said. "Life is not shrinking for me; it's morphing into a whole new world of possibilities."

But that day wasn't one to look ahead so much as it was one to take stock of what had been. "When I look back on my NFL career, I'll know without a doubt that I gave everything I had to help my teams walk away with a win," Manning said. "There were other players who were more talented, but there was no one who could out-prepare me, and because of that I have no regrets."

Referencing Scripture, Manning said, "I have fought the good fight and I have finished the race. Well, I've fought a good fight. I've finished my football race, and after 18 years it's time."

Elway thanked Manning for coming to Colorado, saying he made his own job so much easier because with Manning on the team, free agents would visit and basically ask him, "Where do I sign?"

But it was through the eyes of a former quarterback and not those of a general manager that Elway really enjoyed his four years observing the QB who changed the game and the franchise's fortunes. "Peyton Manning revolutionized the game," Elway said. "We all used to think a no-huddle was a fast pace, get to the line of scrimmage and get people off-balance. Peyton revolutionized it, and you know what? We're going to get to the line of scrimmage, take our time, I'm going to find out what you're doing, and then I'm going to pick you apart.

"I can't tell you how many times I said, 'Dang, why didn't we think of that?'"

# CHAPTER 33
## SUPER HANGOVER

John Elway was confident the Broncos would follow in the footsteps of the San Francisco 49ers—who moved seamlessly from quarterback Joe Montana to fellow Hall of Famer Steve Young—and the Green Bay Packers, who replaced all-time great Brett Favre with the game's premier passer in Aaron Rodgers.

Brock Osweiler was no superstar, but he'd served a three-and-a-half-year apprenticeship under Peyton Manning and had gone 5–2 filling in for the starter to help the Broncos become world champions after the 2015 season. But 24 hours after Manning's farewell news conference, the Broncos were saying good-bye to Manning's longtime backup, too, when Osweiler bolted to the Houston Texans, who outbid the Broncos with a four-year, $72 million contract.

"I remember saying this on the air at the time: I thought the Broncos may have underestimated the quarterback market," Dave Logan recounted. "I think they looked at it and said, *Brock's a good player, but he's not going anywhere. Nobody's going to give him more money than we can.* Then came the Houston offer, and I think Brock and his agent may have viewed the Broncos' offer as a bit of a lowball. And we know how the deal played out. Houston brought Brock and his agent in for a visit. He signed the deal, and he never even met coach Bill O'Brien."

The separation would prove a mistake for both Osweiler and Elway. Osweiler would be out of the league by the time his big contract with the Texans ran out, having bounced between Houston, Cleveland, back to Denver, and finally Miami.

Osweiler went 8–6 in his first—and last—season in Houston, guiding the Texans to the playoffs but getting benched along the way. He was traded afterward to Cleveland, dumped by the Browns, and picked up by the Broncos, where he went 0–4 in 2017. He finished up his career with the Dolphins, where he went 2–3 in 2018 before retiring a year later with a 15–15 career record.

Things went even worse for Elway, who would go through a veritable turnstile of head coaches and quarterbacks, two poor draft classes, and several bad free agent signings over the next four seasons, none of which ended with a playoff berth.

There was the coaching carousel. Gary Kubiak stepped down after the 2016 season over health concerns, and his replacement, Vance Joseph, went 5–11 and 6–10. After that first losing season under Joseph, Elway flirted with bringing Mike Shanahan back to coach the Broncos. (Shanahan's son, Kyle, had been a finalist the previous year but instead took the San Francisco 49ers job, where John Lynch joined him as the general manager and led a rebirth of that storied franchise.)

Then, after going into his two previous coaching searches with a preconceived notion of who he wanted to hire, Elway took an open mind into his most recent search, when he landed 60-year-old defensive guru Vic Fangio, who had never been a head coach before.

After draft classes led by first-round bust Paxton Lynch and first-round head-scratcher Garett Bolles, Elway landed the likes of Courtland Sutton and Dalton Risner in two subsequent, solid drafts that gave Broncos fans high hopes for a return to competitiveness in the 2020s. And it wasn't until his seventh starting quarterback post-Manning that Elway finally started to feel good about having maybe found the right guy, Drew Lock, a second-round draft pick out of Missouri in 2019.

Along the way, Elway would go through a confounding array of quarterbacks in search of a suitable replacement for Manning. He traded up to get Lynch out of Memphis in the first round of the 2016 draft and acquired veteran Mark Sanchez only to watch 2015 seventh-rounder Trevor Siemian win the starting job by a wide margin in outplaying both of them that preseason. Sanchez didn't even make it out of training camp, and Lynch would prove the worst of Elway's personnel moves, going just 1–3 over the next two years before getting cut. Siemian had a 13–11 record over two years but he was banged up both seasons. The Broncos even brought back Osweiler in 2017 to serve as a backup when Lynch got hurt in camp. Siemian, Osweiler, and Lynch all ended up starting that season.

Elway acquired Case Keenum in 2017, shortly after the veteran journeyman threw the "Minneapolis Miracle" in the NFC divisional playoffs when the Minnesota Vikings stunned the New Orleans Saints on the final play of the game—the biggest play in a playoff game since Joe Flacco broke the Broncos' hearts with his 70-yard touchdown heave to Jacoby Jones over Rahim Moore in the final minute of regulation back in 2012. Unfortunately, Keenum didn't bring any of the momentum from that iconic play to Denver. He went 6–10 before Elway traded him to Washington after just one season.

In 2019, Elway traded for veteran Flacco from Baltimore six seasons after he'd led the Ravens to that double-overtime stunner in Denver in Manning's first playoff game for the Broncos. Flacco was flummoxed when Elway selected Drew Lock in the second round of the 2019 NFL draft out of the University of Missouri, where he'd thrown for the second-most passing yards (12,193) and the third-most touchdowns (99) in Southeastern Conference history.

When Lock injured his right thumb in the preseason, Elway claimed four-year veteran Brandon Allen off waivers from the Los Angeles Rams. Allen ascended to the starting role after Flacco, who proved even less mobile than the Broncos thought, went on injured reserve with a neck injury halfway through the 2019 season. Allen won his first start 24–19 over the Cleveland Browns, but three weeks later, he was replaced by Lock, who had just 10 practices under his belt.

Lock didn't light up the scoreboard, stack the stat sheet, or thrill many fantasy football players during his NFL debut, a 23–20 win over the Los Angeles Chargers on December 1, 2019, following a three-month stint on injured reserve with a sprained right thumb. He did, however, bring something to the Broncos that was missing at quarterback.

"I knew Drew had a little swag in him," receiver Courtland Sutton said after catching two touchdown passes and drawing a crucial 37-yard pass interference flag with three seconds left that set up Brandon McManus' game-winning 53-yard field goal as time expired.

Lock's saunter was on display even though he threw for just 134 yards, including 11 after halftime. "Drew having that swag, it ultimately rubs off on everyone in the offense," Sutton said. "It ultimately rubs off on the team. Like I said, it's really good to be able to see him go out there and play with that confidence and swag."

Among the congratulatory texts Lock received after his successful debut was one from Archie Manning that read, "You can't win them all if you don't win your first."

"That gave me a good giggle," Lock said. "It was pretty cool to get a text from him and Peyton, as well. Being able to hear from those guys meant a lot." He added, "I thought beating Arkansas my junior year was really cool, but winning your first [NFL] start is definitely a little cooler."

Even cooler was winning his first road start, a shocking 38–24 romp at Houston that made Lock the franchise's first rookie quarterback to win his first two starts since Elway did it in 1983. Moreover, he became the only rookie quarterback in NFL history to throw for 300 yards and three touchdowns in his first road start.

After his debut against the Chargers, his teammates razzed Lock, nicknaming him "Buzz Lightyear" because the large white wristband he wore to help him remember the play calls resembled the Disney icon's forearm laser beam.

"I love that movie, all four of them," Lock said. "The first one's the best, the fourth one's kind of sad." Lock, 23, was born in 1996, a year after the original *Toy Story* hit theaters. "Buzz is older than me," Lock joked. "We've got to bring back some legends sometimes."

So after some of his touchdown throws at Houston, Lock imitated Lightyear firing his laser beam. The buzz was back in Denver. Or, rather, the Buzz was.

Fangio admitted he didn't understand the buzz over Buzz because he had never seen any of the four *Toy Story* movies and didn't know Buzz Lightyear from Buzz Aldrin.

Asked if that surprised him, Lock's eyebrows hopped high. "I actually didn't know that he didn't know," Lock said, laughing. "Yeah, I'm going to have to have a talk with him."

Lock looks to be the quarterback of the future, but the Broncos thought it would be Osweiler. The turnstile at quarterback started with Osweiler's departure, which stunned many of his former teammates. They had watched him fully support Manning throughout the play-offs, then stand atop the fire engines with them during their downtown victory parade only to hear him say he chose the Texans not for more money or a change of scenery but because the Texans offered him a better shot to keep winning.

"I'm very thankful, I'm very appreciative for everything that the Denver Broncos organization has done for me," Osweiler said at his introductory news conference in Houston the next day. "However, in saying that, at this point in time in my career, I feel like the Houston Texans give me the best opportunity to be successful.

"From the top down, starting with the McNair family and then moving on down to the coaching staff, and with [offensive coordinator George] Godsey and Coach [Bill] O'Brien and the offensive attack that they have here, I feel like their offense fits my skill set very well, and I'm very excited to play in that offense," Osweiler said upon his arrival in Houston.

Back in Denver, players were stumped. "I don't know what he means by that, but we've won a lot of games here. So I would think we'd give him the best place to win," Chris Harris Jr. said.

Osweiler ignored the Broncos' invitation later that spring to the Rose Garden to meet President Barack Obama as Super Bowl champions, and to the Super Bowl ring ceremony, both of which were attended by other players who had left Denver behind such as defensive end Malik Jackson, safety and special teams ace David Bruton Jr., and inside linebacker Danny Trevathan.

"Well, the White House was pretty simple. We had an OTA that Monday," Osweiler said. "As we've talked in the past, learning a new offense, a new system, like we went through in 2015 in Denver, it takes a lot of time, it takes a lot of repetitions, and you can even [multiply] that when you're trying to learn a new system and you're trying to learn new teammates and build chemistry."

"So, bottom line, I wasn't at the White House because we had OTAs that Monday when the Broncos visited the president at the White House and I felt like it was very important for me to be here with my teammates and continue to learn this new system," he continued.

Same with the big party to get their gaudy diamond-encrusted Super Bowl 50 rings.

"Ring ceremony, same deal," Osweiler said. "The ring ceremony was Sunday night. We had a practice Monday and if I went to the ring ceremony, I wouldn't have been able to catch a flight to be back for OTAs and bottom line it's the same deal. There are so few OTAs, and when you're trying to learn a new system and learn new teammates and build chemistry with a new team, every single day is extremely important."

Osweiler's departure to Houston also came 48 hours after he skipped Manning's retirement news conference in Denver, the first inkling that there wasn't going to be a passing of the baton in Denver. "I was on vacation with my family when I received the text that he was going to have that press conference," Osweiler said.

> None of us knew when that was going to come, and if it was going to come and how that was going to work.... I was on vacation with my family and I wasn't going to leave the one vacation I get to take with my parents and my brother and my wife to race back last minute.
>
> I have nothing but respect for Peyton Manning. What he accomplished in the National Football League was truly unbelievable. He was always a great teammate to me. He's still a great friend to this day. When I was on vacation and I found out he was going to retire, we were able to share text messages and I left him a voicemail. And he knows how grateful I am for everything he's

done for me, how much appreciation I have for him…. Me not being at the press conference, that's not a story. There's nothing but love and respect for Peyton Manning, the person he is and you know the friend that's he's been to me."

By going cheap at quarterback—Siemian ($435,000), Lynch ($450,000), and Austin Davis ($1.25 million)—Elway was able to re-sign Super Bowl MVP Von Miller to what was at the time the biggest deal ever for a defensive player—$114.5 million over six years, including $70 million guaranteed—and he also gave extensions to line-backer Brandon Marshall and wide receiver Emmanuel Sanders that off-season. Those moves wouldn't have been possible had he paid big bucks to keep Osweiler, who earned a $12 million signing bonus and was due $8 million in 2016.

"I don't think anybody in this locker room cares, honestly, that he left," Marshall said. "I think everybody's happy that he got his money. When you're a player in this league, you're happy when another player gets his money, when he gets what he's due. So everybody in this locker room, nobody has any ill will toward Brock."

However, when the Texans visited the Broncos a few months later, in Week 7 of the 2016 season, the story was a little different. "We want to kill him," Marshall added matter-of-factly.

They smoked the Texans 27–9 to improve to 5–2, but running back C.J. Anderson showed up the next day with a knee injury. That was the beginning of the end for the Broncos' five-year playoff run and domi-nance of the AFC West. They finished 9–7 and didn't even get a chance to defend their Super Bowl title in the postseason.

Osweiler wanted to make one thing clear when he spoke with Denver media prior to that game: he didn't leave because Kubiak benched him in that regular season finale in favor of Manning. "It didn't weigh in whatsoever," insisted Osweiler.

At the end of the day, I really do have nothing but respect for Coach Kubiak and the way he runs that team. If fact, as soon as he got sick and I found out he got sick, I reached out to him right away, we communicated. He continued to wish me nothing but the best. I checked in with him. It's true when I say it, I really have no poor feelings toward Coach or Denver or the organization or anything like that…. Obviously I was a little bit frustrated to get pulled out of a game. You're battling, you're fighting with your teammates, emotions are high. Certainly, I think any competitor would be frustrated in that moment.

But once I got out of the game and I was able to have conversations with Coach Kubiak and John and [passing coordinator] Coach [Greg] Knapp I mean it certainly made sense what Coach Kubiak was doing for the playoff run. At the end of the day, Coach Kubiak always did what was best for the team and I trusted that and I believed in that.

And then the final thing I would say on that topic, in the San Diego game, I got replaced by Peyton Manning to make a playoff run with a great football team. And I think any coach for that matter, or any team in the National Football League, if they had Peyton Manning healthy and ready to play, I mean, I think we all know who's going to play in the game. So, that had nothing whatsoever to do with my decision. I truly just tried to make the best decision for my family and myself.

Osweiler was right about one thing: the Texans did give him a better chance to succeed. While the Broncos missed out on the playoff party, Houston won the AFC South. They had the same 9–7 record but a weaker conference; AFC West rivals Kansas City and Oakland both went 12–4, landing the Broncos third in the division over only the lowly Chargers.

Osweiler had been benched by O'Brien late in the season but came back because of injury to start for Houston in the Texans' 27–14 wild-card win over the Raiders. The Texans were eliminated in the divisional round by the Patriots 34–16.

Afterward, Osweiler was on the move again. The Texans traded him to Cleveland that off-season in a salary dump and Osweiler was subsequently dumped by the Browns on cutdown day at the end of the preseason. In Denver, Lynch sprained his throwing shoulder four days after losing the starting job to Siemian for the second straight summer. The Broncos needed a veteran backup, and suddenly Osweiler was out there. Maybe this was going to work out after all.

The Broncos signed Manning's longtime backup 18 months after he'd bolted in free agency, and they only had to pay $775,000 of his $16 million salary for 2017; the Browns paid him the rest of his salary not to play for them.

Osweiler was so excited to get back to Denver that he swore he'd have signed for a dollar, played in bare feet, or even been their water boy. After reacclimating himself to the team, Osweiler held an extraordinary news conference filled with humility, honesty, humor—and not a drop of heartache.

He said he harbored no regrets over leaving Denver but was "ecstatic to be back here" after an odyssey that included a playoff win, a benching, a blowup, a trade, the birth of his daughter, and a release to go with all those fat paychecks. "It's kind of like that old deal when you're a little kid and your mom tells you, 'Don't touch the hot stove,'" Osweiler said. "So what do you have to do as a curious kid? You have to go touch the hot stove—and you learn real quick how nice that stove is when it's not hot. Needless to say, I'm very thankful to be back here. My wife and I, we miss Colorado every single day. This is a special place, special organization, and a special city."

Elway was excited to have Osweiler back, too. "With everything he went through in Houston and then going to Cleveland, I'm sure he's going to need a little football rehab," Elway said. "We know that. We'll welcome him with open arms and give him some love."

The Broncos' other option was going with undrafted rookie Kyle Sloter, who led the league in passer rating in the preseason but was undressed by Denver's No. 1 defense in practice.

"Sloter played good in the preseason, but you want to go into the season confident in your backup quarterback," Aqib Talib said. "We know Brock knows the system. We've seen him in this system before. We know the worst scenario if something happens to Trev. We're confident in our backup quarterback now."

Once Manning's heir apparent, Osweiler's departure for $37 million in guarantees the same week Manning retired had opened the way for Siemian to rise up the depth chart. And Osweiler was the loyal Broncos backup again.

"I'm prepared and ready to support Trevor with whatever he needs," Osweiler said. "It's funny, I went in to go get cleats today and they asked what cleats I wanted and I said, 'I don't care, just give me something. I'll go out there in bare feet today.'"

He knew some fans were still angry he'd left in the first place.

"I want people to know that decision didn't come lightly," Osweiler said. "I didn't sleep for about a week. I was sick to my stomach every single day. I was a mess. At the end of the day I tried making the best business decision for me and my family. Whether I made the best one or not, that could be argued."

It was a short-lived stay. By the time Drew Lock took over in Denver, Osweiler was retired in Montana with a 15–15 career record and more than $41 million in career earnings.

# CHAPTER 34
## CONSTANT CHANGE

In 1999, John Elway was determined to retire, and Gary Kubiak tried to talk him out of it. Elway's knees were shot after leading Denver to back-to-back Lombardi Trophies, so when Mike Shanahan dispatched his offensive coordinator to try to change his quarterback's mind about retiring, Elway told Kubiak not to waste his breath but to have a seat and chase some beers with him instead.

Eighteen years later, the roles were reversed but the result was the same. "[Gary] put up his hand and said, 'Remember when you did that to me?'" Elway recounted. "I said, 'Yeah, okay.'"

Kubiak stepped down as Broncos coach nine months after Peyton Manning retired, leaving the NFL pressure cooker over season-long health concerns with two years remaining on his contract, a grateful wife and family, and a Super Bowl ring.

Elway hired Kubiak in 2015, a little more than a year after Kubiak suffered a mini-stroke and collapsed at halftime during a game while coaching the Houston Texans. He'd had another health scare in October 2015 when he suffered a complex migraine after a game against the Atlanta Falcons in Denver and had to take a week off work. He lightened the load for a while but he's wasn't wired not to put in 100-hour work weeks as head coach.

Kubiak summoned Elway to his hotel room in Kansas City on Christmas Eve, a day before the Broncos would get bounced from the playoff chase just 11 months after winning the Super Bowl.

"He said, 'I want to talk to you as a friend, not my boss,' and that's how we talked," Elway said, adding that he wasn't surprised when Kubiak told him he was going to step down after the season whether or not they made the playoffs.

"I'm going to find something else to do," said Kubiak, who would eventually serve as a front office consultant for Elway, offering him tips on the draft and other matters.

Players were bummed to see Kubiak go, but they expressed confidence Elway would find the right replacement. "He's the king of the comeback, on and off the field," Von Miller said.

"I can't tell you how many times I thought about putting my boss hat back on and put my selling process back in there so we could try to make it work," Elway said.

The Broncos missed big on Paxton Lynch in the first round of the 2016 NFL draft and their top pick in 2017, left tackle Garett Bolles, was a penalty machine, committing 42 penalties in his first 42 starts, most of them for holding. The Broncos' 2017 draft class also included wide receiver Carlos Henderson, defensive back Brendan Langley, receiver-returner Isaiah McKenzie, running back DeAngelo Henderson, and quarterback Chad Kelly, all of whom flamed out quickly.

And then there were the free-agent classes. After luring the greatest free agent ever in Peyton Manning, Elway had a string of successes in free agency thanks to the best lure in the league. In addition to Manning, he signed safety Mike Adams, wide receiver Brandon Stokley, and tight end Jacob Tamme in 2012. The next year, he landed nose tackle Terrance Knighton, guard Louis Vasquez, and receiver Wes Welker. He hit the mother lode in 2014 with DeMarcus Ware, Aqib Talib, T.J. Ward, and Emmanuel Sanders.

Since then, it's been filled with too many injured, old guys. The likes of Russell Okung, Donald Stephenson, Menelik Watson, Clinton McDonald, Case Keenum, and Ja'Wuan James, among others, all failed to impress.

"Moves out of desperation," Dave Logan said. "It doesn't take much in this league to get yourself in a hole. You miss on two or three of your draft choices and a couple of free agents and mix in a couple of key injuries, and all of a sudden you're in a big hole. It's forced them to make some moves where there's maybe more risk involved."

When the 49ers visited the Broncos for joint practices during Fangio's first training camp, Elway met with his old friend, San Francisco general manager John Lynch, who had served a sort of apprenticeship under Elway in 2013, attending the draft and the combine. When the 49ers approached him about their GM job, Lynch sought Elway's advice again, and Elway told him he could be as great in the front office as he was on the football field for 15 NFL seasons and in the broadcast booth for eight more.

Elway said he knew Lynch had the right temperament, people skills, and football knowledge. "He was a guy that was a great competitor, and so I thought that being a GM for him would be a really good fit," Elway said, before quickly adding: "And I apologized to him a couple of times. I told him, 'I hope you still like it.' Because I don't like it after two losing years."

That was the first time Elway, the notorious competitor, had been so blunt about how losing was affecting him.

Before addressing the roster holes in 2019, Elway needed to find the right head coach. He wasn't in the market for another veteran head coach like Fox or Kubiak, but a young candidate such as Atlanta offensive coordinator Kyle Shanahan—Mike's son—or Miami defensive coordinator Vance Joseph.

"Obviously, there's a lot of young guys out there that have a lot of potential and are very bright, young guys," Elway said. "So hopefully we can get one of those."

Elway ended up hiring Joseph, a decision he would quickly regret after two dismal seasons. In fact, Joseph nearly got fired after one season when Elway seriously considered rehiring Mike Shanahan, an idea that never panned out after team president Joe Ellis told him he'd have to go through a full head coaching search again even if he had a preferred candidate—even Shanahan.

Joseph's first team lost eight straight after a 3–1 start. Worse, most of them were blowouts.

"I liked him personally," Logan said. "I thought he was a bright guy. He had a good understanding of the game. I just think no matter who it is, it's a lot for a young, inexperienced coach to come in and handle everything that you've got to handle in the NFL. Were there things that he could have done differently, for sure. For sure. And you know the quarterback position was unstable and really did not get fixed the two years that he was here.

"I'm not sure Vance was all that comfortable dealing with the media. I think the media today is completely different than what the coaches had to deal with even 10, 15 years ago in press conferences. Everybody's evaluating every single word you say, asking, *What do you mean by this comment?* and then they play it back over and over. It's a tough business for head coaches but especially tough for young head coaches—and even more so for young head coaches who don't win," Logan said.

Joseph had a habit of saying after losses, especially blowouts, that he didn't understand what had happened because the Broncos had practiced so well during the week. Fans started mocking that, saying it was too bad the games weren't played on Wednesday, when the Broncos were undefeated.

"In hindsight, he may have made a mistake in being too much of a player's coach," Logan said. "He didn't want to throw his players under the bus, and I completely understand that. But there's also a certain accountability that I think you have to hold players to, even in the public eye. You have to do it the right way, but to me it has to be done. Vance was always very careful about publicly criticizing his players.

"Players are very aware—even back in the '70s and '80s when I played—of what coaches say in press conferences. And the last thing you want to do is alienate the entire locker room. Because when that happens—and all you have to do is go back and look at Josh McDaniels—guys will literally shut down on you. And then you've got a situation that is untenable and it's almost impossible to get out of.

"Good coaches have great football acumen and Xs and Os, but they're also part psychologist and even part life coach. They have to wear all those hats at different times during each week, and it's a difficult job, it really is. It's tough for a coach to convey to a player, *Listen, I'm trying to help you become better so if I chew your ass it's because I love you and I'm trying to help you become better. So, stay in the saddle and let's work this out together.*

"If you want to play for somebody who's not ever going to critique you or get after you in practice, you're playing for the wrong guy. You almost have to have those conversations at times with almost every single player, and certainly when it comes to particular positions."

While other teams with openings in 2019 were looking for the next Sean McVay and hiring fuzzy-faced offensive assistants, Elway chose the grizzled gridiron lifer, Vic Fangio, a 60-year-old longtime defensive guru who had never been a head coach.

"I really like him. I like his demeanor," Logan said. "He's a no-nonsense football guy that has a very dry sense of humor. And I like guys that love football," Logan said. "I played the game a long time. I've been around the game even longer. There are people who make a living in football that don't necessarily love the game, but they're good at it. Vic Fangio loves football. And you can tell just by sitting down having a conversation with him. He's a bright guy. He's a guy who has other interests outside of football, but you can tell he loves the game. So I think he's perfect for the job in that sense."

Fangio's first training camp in Denver was rather quiet, and that was by design. Mothballed were the huge concert-sized speakers blaring concert-like tunes during practice, because Fangio didn't want to have to yell over the thumping beats to get his points across. He also didn't like his assistants to coach up players on the field; that was for the classroom. So players at practice had to coach themselves up, just like they're on their own on game days.

The sound of silence was among the many things Fangio kept in his mental file folder of things he'd change if he ever got the chance to be a head coach.

The first thing Fangio did at his introductory news conference was call out his best player, saying Von Miller could be even better than he was. Hired away from Chicago, where he'd designed the league's best defense, Fangio proved a mix of old-fashioned and newfangled as he employed philosophies he formulated over four decades as a defensive assistant.

He sports baggy sweats on the sideline at practice regardless of the weather and has his team practice in tight, game-day jerseys, not the larger, looser ones most teams use at practice.

"The whole reason we do that is to cut down on the grabbing," Fangio said. "When you wear the loose shirts, it's very easy, almost unavoidable, for the players to grab each other. Whether it be wideouts, DBs, the interior linemen, it's just so easy to grab those loose jerseys. It's not easy to grab in the game because they're tight. So we want to make it game-like as much as we can."

Fangio only wants to do things that will help him win—thus his philosophy on the music. "Anybody who's been a position coach or an assistant coach, they don't like the music because it makes it hard to talk to your guys, so I don't see the benefit of having music out there," Fangio said. "I was an assistant coach and I don't want to have to drum out the noise to talk to my players."

Besides, Fangio said, there's no music in games. "It will be [crowd] noise. That's what it is in the game. Noise by definition sounds annoying. Music sounds nice. So if we have to deal with noise, let's deal with noise," Fangio reasoned.

What won Elway over was Fangio's "death by inches" philosophy. In his view, inattention to detail was what derailed teams. "I promise you," Fangio told Elway, "we will not kill ourselves by inches."

Defensive end Derek Wolfe said he loved everything about Fangio, from his schemes to the way he rocked his signature sweatshirt on sweltering summer days. "I think he is just an old-school guy," Wolfe said. "I haven't heard him tell a story about an old player post-1990. Everything is from like the '80s."

Yet, here he is, connecting with players who weren't even born then.

# CHAPTER 35
## MEMORABLE BONDS

In 30 years of calling Denver Broncos games, Dave Logan has never missed a single game. He's called more than 600 games in his career, including all three of the franchise's Super Bowl triumphs, but it's the relationships and friendships that stick with him more than the games. Pat Bowlen. Mike Shanahan. Josh McDaniels. Wade Phillips. Dan Reeves. Vance Joseph. Gary Kubiak. Vic Fangio.

Gary Zimmerman. Rod Smith. Ed McCaffrey. Shannon Sharpe. Steve Atwater. Von Miller. Chris Harris Jr. Peyton Manning. Tim Tebow. Elvis Dumervil. Champ Bailey.

Logan has brought all of their insights and stories about football and life to listeners over the years.

"Covering the team for as long as I have, and those guys really being staples of this franchise for as long as they were, you get to know guys," Logan said. "You get to know guys not only as players—and they were great players—but you get to know them a little bit off the field and you get to interview them and you just have an appreciation for them as people.

"I always had an appreciation for how hard the game was…. When you call a game, you've got to be honest, and when they're not playing well, you have to point that out. But I also know how difficult this game can be and how hard it is to prepare for it. It requires a high level of athletic ability and mental and physical toughness in order to succeed."

## Shannon Sharpe

*Tight End; Pro Football Hall of Fame, Class of 2011*

Like most great tight ends, Shannon Sharpe was a late bloomer. A seventh-round draft pick out of Savannah State in 1990, he caught just seven passes as a rookie and had 22 receptions in his second season.

"I remember his first training camp," Logan said. "He was bigger than most wide receivers, and because I was a bigger wide receiver as well, my eyes sort of gravitated to Shannon. It was 1990. And I watched him every day in that camp. We were still in Greeley at that point. And I thought, *He's pretty skilled for a big kid, and he runs pretty well.*

He wouldn't have been a blazer for a guy running outside, but he was athletic.

"I wasn't that surprised he made the team. And even less surprised they moved him inside even though he was a wide receiver in college. And then it was fun to watch his career take off the way it did."

Sharpe caught 815 passes for 10,060 yards and 62 touchdowns during his 14-year career that included eight Pro Bowl berths, four first-team All-Pro honors, and three Super Bowl rings over a four-year span—two in Denver and one in Baltimore.

"He turned into a very good ball catcher," Logan said. "And he was a willing blocker. I don't think Shannon would describe himself as a dominant run blocker, but he was plenty willing…. You could run to his side and he'd give you effort and was strong enough to block you at the point. There have been other tight ends who refused to even engage when they're attached—lined up on the line of scrimmage next to a tackle rather than out wide like a receiver—but that wasn't Shannon. He was a key part of the attack when the Broncos had things really rolling."

When the Broncos had a great line, a great running game, a super-star quarterback, and great wide receivers, it was Sharpe who caused so many of the headaches for defenses. "He was a matchup problem because of his speed…. You couldn't really play him with linebackers because he was too fast for them. He was stronger physically than the safeties you tried to match up," Logan said. "So he presented some real problems for the defense. He gave the Broncos a big weapon that many times was the biggest matchup problem on the field."

Sharpe proved just as integral as a part of the locker room. "His overall demeanor and his sense of humor and sort of how outspoken he was, that was perfect for the team because the other stars on the team were just the opposite," Logan said. "T.D. [Terrell Davis] was quiet, Rod and Eddie were pretty quiet, as well. They just went about their business and turned out to be great players."

While Elway was the face of the franchise, Sharpe was the Broncos' voice. "He was a perfect fit for the locker room.... You could always go to him for a quote. He was more than willing to stand up. He enjoyed it. Whereas I think maybe some of the other guys just sort of put up with it," Logan said.

When Sharpe made it into the Pro Football Hall of Fame in 2011, he had a long list of people to thank. But at the very top was his grandmother, Mary Porter, who raised him and his siblings in rural Georgia and who died at age 89 just a month before his induction. Sharpe so wanted to make it into Canton before she died, but he soon came to see making it in his third year of eligibility was a blessing "because she can hear my speech now."

As usual, he had plenty to say. He thanked his brother Sterling, who motivated him; Dan Reeves, who drafted him; Albert Lewis, who challenged him; John Elway, who believed in him; and Mike Shanahan, who pushed him.

And of course he thanked his grandmother, for instilling in Sharpe a relentless worth ethic. By mixing his uncanny speed and size, he singlehandedly revolutionized the tight end position in the NFL.

Sharpe was presented the Hall of Fame bust by his older brother Sterling, the Green Bay Packers star receiver whose own path to Canton was cut short by a neck injury. (Shannon had given his first Super Bowl ring to Sterling, whose 85-catch average over his seven NFL seasons was 10 more than Jerry Rice averaged in his first seven seasons.)

Hall of Fame tight end Ozzie Newsome called Sharpe the standard-setter at the position, and Shanahan called him "the best."

"He dominated. His work ethic was at the top. He played his best in big games and he did it all over a long period of time," Shanahan said.

Said Elway, "We always got great matchups with him because he was faster than most linebackers and stronger than most defensive backs."

Even though Sharpe made a name for himself as a receiving tight end, former Broncos safety Brian Dawkins said Sharpe's willingness to block was his biggest calling card—followed by his propensity to run his mouth after either a bit hit or a nice catch. "He was one of the best trash-talkers to ever play the game," Dawkins suggested.

One of the best talkers, period. Remember that time he grabbed a phone on the Broncos bench and faked a call to the White House?

"I'm calling the president," he hollered to the crowd. "Mr. President, we need the National Guard. We need as many men as you can spare because we are killing the Patriots.... Send the National Guard, please. They need emergency help. Please, help these folks."

Then he hung up and looked back toward the crowd. "They're coming! Help is on the way," Sharpe said.

For his sense of humor, he also thanked his grandmother, who taught him that laughter could blunt the sharp words of others. As a young boy he saw that if he could crack a joke, maybe his schoolmates would quit teasing him about the way he spoke with a lisp or where he lived.

Elway said Sharpe's work ethic and ability to lighten the mood is what set the tone for the team's two Super Bowl-winning seasons in the late 1990s. "I think you need those guys on every football team, and he was our guy," Elway said. "He kept things light. Things never got too heavy, and that was great because it's a long season, and then the pressure in the playoffs is so great. He had the ability to keep things loose and make the game fun, make practice fun."

## Gary Zimmerman

*Left Tackle; Pro Football Hall of Fame Class of 2008*

Mike Shanahan recalled Gary Zimmerman separating a shoulder against the Raiders one time and refusing to come out of the game. "He said, 'When No. 7 comes out, I'll come out,'" Shanahan recounted. "Old-school. Tough guy. Never said anything to nobody, but just worked his rear end off."

It was appropriate then that his blindside protector was the first Bronco to join John Elway in the Pro Football Hall of Fame. (Tony

Dorsett and Willie Brown played in Denver but they had their best seasons elsewhere.) Zimmerman was chosen for two NFL all-decade teams, earned first- or second-team All-Pro honors eight times, and was selected to play in seven Pro Bowls.

"Gary was the best left tackle I ever saw play the game," Elway said. "His strength and athleticism were exceptional. He understood the game and was as tough as I've ever seen. He practically played his last year one-armed because of a bad shoulder."

Zimmerman began his career with the Los Angeles Express of the United States Football League before spending seven seasons with the Minnesota Vikings. He was traded to the Broncos in 1993 and retired after helping them win the Super Bowl after the 1997 season.

"My loyalty is to the Denver Broncos," Zimmerman said before his induction. "When I went to Denver it's like the dog who gets put in the pound and you get a new owner, and the loyalty is to that new owner and the owner treats you good."

Dave Logan said Zimmerman solidified the line that protected Elway and opened up holes for Terrell Davis when the Broncos ruled the late 1990s. "I remember how excited the Broncos were when they made that deal because you're getting an All-Pro left tackle and the missing piece to what was already a pretty damn good offensive line. And Gary Zimmerman, you talk about a quiet warrior, he probably didn't say three words the whole time he was there," Logan said.

"But you know if you ask anybody in terms of left tackles, that guy was as good as they get. He wound up getting hurt late in his career here in Denver. He played at times with pretty much one arm. The left tackle with a right-handed quarterback is a pretty doggone important position. And I think John felt very comfortable with him out there. Gary was a heck of an athlete, a big man who could move his feet and understood hand placement and leverage. He was a Hall of Fame left tackle, so they hit a home run when they made that deal."

When the Broncos beat the Packers in Super Bowl XXXII, all the talk was about how Denver's offensive line didn't talk. To the media. It was Zimmerman who brought that code of silence to the Broncos offensive line. They had to talk on media day, however, when they explained they'd just as soon go about their business, sit back, and watch Shannon Sharpe hold court instead.

When the Broncos shocked Brett Favre and the Packers 31–24 in Super Bowl XXXII in San Diego, team owner Pat Bowlen approached Zimmerman and asked if he'd be back the next season to help defend the Lombardi Trophy he'd just put his fingerprints on.

"No, Mr. B., I'd be stealing your money," he replied. "I don't feel I can play anymore. I'm retiring."

So he did, after 12 seasons and 197 games.

"It was kind of a storybook ending there for me," said Zimmerman.

Shanahan said Zimmerman was transcendent for one very simple reason: "His man never touched the quarterback. That makes you a great player. He just took great pride in not allowing his man to make plays. His man never did."

Bowlen said back in 2008 that Zimmerman "brought a discipline in here to the offensive line that we'd never seen before. He was the mainstay of that offensive line that won Super Bowl XXXII."

He also brought that quietness to a group that vowed to let its play on the field do the talking, something that made it ironic when he had a hard time trimming his acceptance speech in the weeks before his enshrinement in Canton, Ohio. "For the first time in my life I have too much to say," Zimmerman quipped.

Offensive linemen are usually among the smartest guys on any NFL team, but most O-lines have a little—or a lot—of that code of silence that Zimmerman established in Denver. "Offensive linemen rarely engage too much in the media. I don't know if there's a book that tells them to do that, or what," Logan said. "Back when the Broncos were really good, none of those dudes talked. There was a fine system for offensive linemen who talked too much to the media. I remember our O-linemen had something similar when I played in Cleveland. I don't know why that is. Maybe it's just the position.... I don't know."

Ironically, it's those O-linemen who have little to say in their playing careers who end up talking nonstop when they're through playing. In Denver, the epicenter of the zipped-lip O-line, former linemen-turned-media members include Mark Schlereth, Tyler Polumbus, and Ryan Harris. Even Tom Nalen, the enforcer of the media boycotts, had a couple of drive-time shows in Denver before moving back to Boston.

It's too bad they wait until they're covering the league to speak up, because O-linemen are often the brainiacs of the roster. They're playing 80 of 80 snaps and five of them have to play in unison against wave after wave of fresh defensive linemen. They're the heart and soul of any team.

"No question about that," Logan said. "You ultimately win because you're good up front on both sides. It would be hard to think of a team that had sustained winning without a very good offensive line."

Former Vikings teammate Randall McDaniel said Zimmerman "wasn't the biggest tackle but he did everything right."

Not in Zimmerman's mind. "I hear people who are bulimic, they see themselves as fat," Zimmerman said. "When I was playing I saw myself as not good enough, so I always tried to be better. I could watch people sand think they did a good job but then watch myself and I was kind of embarrassed. So I tried to work harder."

As Shanahan said, a perfectionist out to prove himself everyday gives you "an overachiever with great ability, and then you've got a Hall of Fame player."

## Terrell Davis

*Running Back; Pro Football Hall of Fame Class of 2017*
John Elway credits Terrell Davis with helping him retire a two-time champion. Before T.D. joined him in Denver, Elway and the Broncos were blown out in three Super Bowls. With him, they won two titles.

Davis' career was short but oh so sweet. Their first world championship together came in Super Bowl XXXII against Green Bay following the 1997 season, when Davis rushed for 157 yards and three touchdowns in Denver's 31–24 win despite suffering from a migraine headache that kept him out most of the second quarter.

"There's no doubt, they wouldn't have won Super Bowl XXXII without T.D.," Logan said. "John has said that publicly. They wore down the Packers defense with the running game…. You had two receivers in Rod Smith and Ed McCaffrey who were total team guys, who bought into the importance of blocking downfield and digging out a safety in the run game. You don't get big plays, home run plays, in the running game unless you have wideouts who are willing to do it, who know who they're supposed to block and then go block 'em.

"A lot of guys today don't look at that as their job. But guys like Rod and Eddie were all about being complete receivers. But they don't win Super Bowl XXXII without Terrell and everything that went into that running game."

Davis was just what Shanahan needed to make his West Coast offense work.

"In Mike's offense, they obviously could throw it, but everything was based off the run. *Everything*," Logan said. "That's what his style of offense has always been about. Look at Kyle Shanahan these days. Look at what they're doing in San Francisco. It's based on their ability to attack defenses—different angles, different sets, different splits. But they run the ball first, and then once they've established the run, they'll hit you with the play-action pass. That's a staple of the offense. So, for the Broncos, a guy like Terrell Davis, who was a downhill, powerful, one-cut guy and faster than you think, was the perfect fit for what they wanted."

The 196th player selected in the 1995 NFL draft, Davis was just another late-round rookie trying to make the roster when he made a name for himself in an exhibition game at Tokyo. Davis introduced himself to the league—and even his own teammates—by crushing San Francisco 49ers kick returner Tyronne Drakeford, despite a belly full of junk food. The veterans on the sideline were like those excited NBA players who can't believe a great play made right before their eyes. Fellow future Hall of Famer Shannon Sharpe marveled, "Who was that?"

He was the man who would become the only running back in NFL history to win back-to-back Super Bowl trophies, a league MVP award, a Super Bowl MVP honor, post a 2,000-yard rushing season, and seven consecutive playoff wins in which he topped 100 yards rushing. (In fact, the only other running back to average more than 100 yards a game, including playoffs, was Jim Brown.)

But the hit in Tokyo that heralded his arrival almost didn't happen. Davis didn't play in the Broncos' first exhibition game that season and it didn't look like he would get in this one either. "And I'm hungry, I'm starving," recalled Davis. "So, in the third quarter, I've got hot dogs, I've got chili dogs, I've got French fries, I've got Ding Dongs. I'm thinking I'm not going to play."

Suddenly, he sees special teams coach Richard Smith calling him over to go cover the kickoff. "I was thinking, *'Dude, I just ate all kinds of food. I don't know if I want to go in the game now,'*" Davis remembered. "But I said, 'Okay, I'll go in. And thank God I did. I went in and made that hit."

Davis retreated to the sideline and was vomiting up that junk food when running backs coach Bobby Turner walked up and told him to go in and take some handoffs.

"That's when it all started," Davis said. "I think back to that because if I had said no to Coach Smith that I didn't want to go in, who knows where I'd be today?"

Probably not enshrined in Canton. Or in the hearts of Broncos fans.

"When you're an old quarterback, your best friend is a running game and a running back, and that was T.D.," said Elway. "You can say this about a lot of guys, but we wouldn't have gotten where we did without T.D."

That hit in Tokyo is also seared into Logan's memory. "He'd had a hot dog because he was so down about the fact that he was about the fifth or sixth running back. He wasn't getting playing time, so he just assumed he wasn't going to get into that game. Then he gets put on kickoff coverage, runs down, and just blows up the Niners' return guy," Logan said.

"And you know that was 1995, his rookie season. He didn't even think he was going to make the team. He was getting set to go back home and instead, he winds up being the starting running back and rushing for more than 1,000 yards. It's just a great story and a lesson that young players can learn: never believe you're not going to make the team until somebody comes and takes your playbook away from you."

Davis' brief but brilliant career was marked not only by magnificence and migraines but also by another big hit. Davis was chasing down Jets safety Victor Green after an interception in 1999 when teammate Matt Lepsis made a lunging tackle that also wiped out a trailing Davis. "It was a wild play," Davis said. "Wrong place, wrong time."

Davis, who had averaged an astonishing 1,603 yards and 14 touchdowns over his first four years, missed the rest of that season and would play in just 13 more games and score two touchdowns over the final two years of his career.

Consider this, however, about the play that essentially ended his career: he easily could have saved his health and his chances of putting up more big seasons by pulling up and not chasing down Green. But is that the hallmark of a Hall of Famer?

## Champ Bailey

*Cornerback; Pro Football Hall of Fame Class of 2019*

One of the greatest plays in Denver Broncos history was made by one of the greatest players in the history of the Denver Broncos.

It was January 14, 2006. Tom Brady had already won three of his six Super Bowl rings and all 10 of his playoff starts when he drove the Patriots to the Broncos 5-yard line late in the third quarter on an icy Denver night. Clinging to a 10-6 lead, Coach Shanahan called for a safety blitz from Nick Ferguson, who collected just one sack in his decade-long career in the NFL. Surprised, Brady rolled right and rifled an off-balance throw he'd regret.

"The Broncos never blitzed me, so it probably surprised the hell out of Tom Brady and the offensive linemen," Ferguson recounted. "And truth be told, we ran the same blitz twice. The first time, I didn't go. So the second time I lined up on that particular play, the linemen even said, '25 isn't coming.' And I was like, *Holy smokes, they're not going to block me!*"

Ferguson shot through the line untouched. "Brady saw me at the last second and he started to roll to his right side and he wasn't able to set his feet," Ferguson said. "So he just threw it toward Troy Brown and luckily enough, Champ broke on the ball and we're off to the races."

Scurrying down Denver's delirious sideline after Bailey were teammates John Lynch, Gerard Warren, and Ferguson, who slowed down and stepped in front of Brown to shield Bailey about 25 yards from the end zone.

"I'm just like, *Okay, that's a touchdown*," Ferguson recalled. "Then, *Oh! What was that?*"

*That* was Patriots tight end Benjamin Watson, who had raced from the far side of the field—or as Ferguson said, "from out of nowhere,"—to knock Bailey out at the New England 1.

"It took a fellow Georgia Bulldog to catch me," Bailey cracked after the longest non-scoring interception in NFL playoff history, one that ultimately saddled Brady with his first playoff loss.

Mike Anderson's one-yard touchdown run gave Denver a 17–6 lead heading into the fourth quarter and Jake Plummer's four-yard touchdown throw to Rod Smith would make it 24–6. Jason Elam's field goal capped the 27–13 victory that sent the Broncos to the AFC Championship Game.

"Oh, I think Champ was such a great player. You're talking about one of the elite athletes to ever play in the NFL," said Logan. "And it's a league full of really talented athletes. There were guys like Champ who were just a cut above almost everybody else. Champ had the skill set—and I told him this before, that he could have played wide receiver in the league.

"You could count on one hand the NFL DBs who, if asked to play wide receiver, could do it and make a living at it. That's uncommon athletic ability and even more so it's an uncommon skill set," Logan said. "Champ had great hands….

"One of the other things I admire most about Champ was his willingness and ability to tackle. I've played against and I've seen great corners, some of them Hall of Fame corners, and not all were willing to get involved in the run game. Champ was a great tackler. He was a tough, physical player throughout his entire career. I have so much respect for him…an all-time great player in this league."

He played 15 years, split between Washington and Denver.

Besides his 100-yard return that ended Tom Brady's perfect postseason record, Bailey picked off 53 other passes in the pros.

"That moment was so big because of what the Patriots had done and the kind of run they had going on," Bailey recounted.

In the AFC Championship Game a week later, Bailey had another interception in his grasp and both the end zone and a trip to the Super Bowl in his sights, only to watch Steelers receiver Hines Ward somehow come down with the ball instead. Pittsburgh went on to beat Denver 34–17, denying Bailey a chance to play in the Super Bowl in his prime.

"It denied all of us," Ferguson said. "I still have trouble coming to grips with that years later because you only get a few opportunities and you may get one…. Champ fortunately got another opportunity and he actually went to the Super Bowl. But it would have been great if we could have won that game because we knew for sure Seattle wouldn't have beaten us [in Super Bowl XL, when Pittsburgh beat the Seahawks 21–10]. The NFC didn't have any really good teams that year."

It was nearly a decade later when Bailey again beat Brady in Denver, this time in the AFC title game, to reach Super Bowl XLVIII against a much different Seattle Seahawks team. The "Legion of Boom" crushed

Peyton Manning's record-setting offense 43–8 in what turned out to be the final game of Bailey's career.

"I've settled with the fact I didn't get it," said Bailey, whose dozen Pro Bowl berths are an NFL record for defensive backs. "I did have a shot, though."

Looking back, Bailey said he should have seen it coming. The Broncos were a banged-up bunch, hit hard by injuries to Von Miller, Chris Harris Jr., and others. Even Bailey was on his last legs—or leg. A nagging foot injury limited him to just three starts and only one full game that season.

"I mean, you can't go in there half-stepping on defense and expect to win," Bailey said, although that's exactly what he expected that evening at the Meadowlands. "At least I got to play in a Super Bowl," Bailey said.

Mike Shanahan had sent star running back Clinton Portis to Washington in a blockbuster trade for Bailey in 2004, acquiring a quiet leader in the mold of Jerry Rice and John Elway. "One of the reasons he was such a great leader was that he practiced full-speed," Shanahan said. "Champ set a standard for the rest of the football team that was very high."

Befuddling his opponents was Bailey's versatility, especially in 2005 and 2006, when he collected an astonishing 19 interceptions, including the one that ended Brady's playoff perfection.

"One of the things that made him so good was his ability to match up on so many different types of receivers," Patriots coach Bill Belichick said. "He could handle speed guys, he could handle size guys. He could match up on tight ends. It didn't really matter who he was on; he had a way to match up."

Peyton Manning said Bailey had "as good of hands as any top-flight receiver in the NFL."

Bailey was two years into retirement when the Broncos won Super Bowl 50 behind Miller's performance for the ages and the swarming "No Fly-Zone" secondary that had Bailey's fingerprints all over it thanks to its anchor, Harris Jr. Bailey had tutored a young Harris the same way Hall of Fame cornerbacks Darrell Green and Deion Sanders had helped him navigate the perils of pro football when he arrived in Washington as the seventh overall pick in the 1999 NFL draft.

"I think I would have been great without Deion and Darrell," Bailey said. "Would I have been Hall of Fame good? I don't know. But they actually get a lot of credit for getting me there because I don't know if I would have been as great as I was if I didn't have those nuggets that they gave me early in my career."

Harris, who went from being undrafted to a member of the NFL's All-Decade team of the 2010s, has said he wouldn't have become the star he did without Bailey's assist.

His willingness to share his knowledge was just another thing that made Bailey great, Logan said. "That's how the league works. When young players come into the league, if they're willing to stop talking so much and listen more, there are veteran players who are willing to help those guys. Some guys aren't. Some guys are maybe a bit too insecure for that. That wasn't Champ," Logan said.

## Steve Atwater

*Free safety; Pro Football Hall of Fame, Class of 2020*

The Broncos were loaded on offense when they won their first world championship.

Quarterback John Elway, running back Terrell Davis, left tackle Gary Zimmerman, and tight end Shannon Sharpe would end up enshrined in the Pro Football Hall of Fame, and wide receiver Rod Smith and center Tom Nalen would join that foursome in the Broncos Ring of Fame.

But chances are the Broncos wouldn't have dethroned the defending champion Packers in Super Bowl XXXII were it not for the outstanding play of free safety Steve Atwater.

He spearheaded Denver's dizzying defense with six tackles, a strip sack that turned into a tone-setting takeaway, and two pass breakups in helping the Broncos claim their 31–24 victory.

Mike Shanahan knew he could lean on Atwater to blitz Favre and keep the Packers off-balance: "We actually came after him pretty hard on defense because they were a very talented team and we felt that was the only way we could stay with them is put pressure on them. And Steve made big plays throughout the game. He had an outstanding game, and if Terrell Davis hadn't gotten the MVP, Steve Atwater would have."

The Packers never really adjusted to Atwater, whose strip sack of Favre in the second quarter led to Neil Smith's recovery and a Jason Elam field goal that put Denver ahead 17–7 and showed everyone the Broncos weren't going to go down easily this time.

"Green Bay, people forget how good they were on offense and defense," Shanahan said. "I mean, they played exceptional on both sides of the ball. So, for Steve to have that type of game on that type of stage was very impressive."

And not the least bit surprising.

"He was a difference-maker right from the start because of the size and his ability to deliver a blow," Logan said of the ferocious free safety from the University of Arkansas who ran like a cornerback, hit like a linebacker and, at 6'3" and 225 pounds, was built like today's edge rushers.

"Steve really was a good athlete. I mean, Steve had really, really good speed for a player his size," Logan said. "He was uncommonly big back then for a safety, and then when you look at that combination with Steve and Dennis Smith, who was one of the all-time great hitters in league history, when receivers went over the middle with those two, I mean, there was a price to pay."

While Jack Tatum was known as "The Assassin," Atwater was called the "Smiling Assassin," an homage to his ferocity on the field and friendliness off it.

"Well, I like physical football," explained Atwater, who played in Denver from 1989 to '98, capping his time with the Broncos with a seven-tackle performance in the Broncos' 34–19 win over the Falcons in Super Bowl XXXIII. He played one season with the Jets, then signed a ceremonial one-day contract in Denver to retire a Bronco.

"There have been some really big hitters that have played over the years at safety," Logan said. "You think about Ronnie Lott. You think about Jack Tatum. And there have been many, many others. But Steve was unique in that Steve was a 225-pound safety. I can't think of anybody else really that had that kind of career, that length of career and certainly that Hall of Fame career that was his size. When you looked at him in pregame he looked like a linebacker even though he was wearing No. 27. In terms of his size, he was unique.

"In terms of his overall demeanor, his off-the-field demeanor, we've seen very few players that played the way he did and had that kind of success in the way he played that were so quiet and unassuming off the field."

Shanahan called him the anchor of his defense for those back-to-back championship teams.

"He brought such a physical presence to our football team," Shanahan said. "When he hit you, you were going backward."

Like All-Pro Christian Okoye did on September 17, 1990, at Mile High Stadium.

The Kansas City Chiefs' 260-pound running back known as the "Nigerian Nightmare" was blasted by Atwater just as he stepped into the hole on a handoff.

"Yeah, you tried, baby!" Atwater hollered as he hovered over Okoye.

"He'll be remembered for that hit the rest of his career," Shanahan said following Denver's 24–23 win that night.

"I was just fortunate to come out on the right side of that one," Atwater said, "because that guy had trucked so many people and I'm lucky I wasn't one of them."

## Pat Bowlen

*Broncos Owner; Pro Football Hall of Fame Class of 2019*

Those who worked for Pat Bowlen remember a man who put production ahead of profits, trained tirelessly for triathlons, fostered a winning atmosphere from the lobby to the locker room, and was as quick with a compliment as he was sure to couch his criticism.

Born in Prairie du Chien, Wisconsin, on February 18, 1944, he earned business and law degrees at Oklahoma University before working in his father's oil and gas company and embarking on a successful real estate business in Canada. He and his family purchased the Broncos in two transactions in 1984 and 1985 for a total of $71 million. The franchise is now valued at close to $3 billion, according to the latest Forbes rankings.

Bowlen relished working behind the scenes and shied away from the spotlight. In the words of Shanahan, "Pat just wanted to be one of the guys."

"That's why I think he was so beloved by so many people, including myself," Shanahan said. "And you also knew that he would give anything to make your football team better, or at least get a chance at the Super Bowl. At that time you would say every ounce that he had—I should say every penny he had—he wanted to go into giving the football team a Super Bowl. That was his No. 1 priority. That was it. It was not trying to buy different companies and trying to make more money; his goal was winning a Super Bowl."

Bowlen served as a sounding board for NFL commissioners Pete Rozelle, Paul Tagliabue, and Roger Goodell. He was crucial to the league's growth as a member of 15 NFL committees, including co-chairing the NFL Management Council and working on network TV contracts, such as the league's groundbreaking $18 billion deal in 1998.

Bowlen's death at 75 on June 3, 2019, after a long battle with Alzheimer's disease, came just two months before his induction into the Pro Football Hall of Fame.

At the ceremony, Hall president and CEO David Baker said, "Pat's leadership helped shape the NFL into what it is today. He also transformed the Denver Broncos into one of the finest franchises in the league and gave a winning identity to an entire region."

Bowlen had a deep appreciation for his players, whether or not they were stars, and kept them close, like family. It's still not unusual to see ex-Broncos watching practice. "When I retired, Mr. B. told me I was welcome anytime at team headquarters," said Shannon Sharpe. "He said I didn't need a pass, either. 'Your face is your credential.'"

While Bowlen's competitiveness set the standard for the Broncos, his style set the tone. Think of him on the sideline at games: arms crossed, sporting sunglasses if it was sunny, a mink coat and a stoic look.

It was an image the Broncos embraced, Elway said. "As players we thought, 'This dude is a cool dude as our owner,'" Elway said. "We all thought we were kind of hip because of Pat."

Bowlen was an instrumental figure in the NFL for decades, but many of his accomplishments were unsung.

"He wanted to do the best thing for the league and he didn't want any credit for it," Shanahan said. "He didn't take a whole lot of accolades, but he did a whole lot of work. And I think that was Pat in general."

Bowlen forged Hall of Fame credentials on two accounts: one for what he did in transforming the Broncos from perennial also-rans into NFL champions and another for his key role in helping the league usher in the billion-dollar TV deals that helped pro football become America's most popular sport and a global brand.

He guided the Broncos during his 35 years of ownership with the simple phrase, "I want us to be number one in everything."

The Broncos posted as many losing seasons (seven) as Super Bowls under Bowlen, affectionately known as Mr. B., who was the first team owner in league history to earn 300 victories in his first 30 years. The Broncos averaged more than 10 wins a year during Bowlen's 35 seasons and his .596 winning percentage (354–240–1) was second only to the Patriots in the NFL. Of the 123 major North American professional sports franchises in football, baseball, basketball, and hockey, only the Patriots and the NBA's San Antonio Spurs and Los Angeles Lakers had better winning percentages than the Broncos under Bowlen.

No other NFL owner during his time had more winning seasons (21) or playoff berths (18). He was the first team in NFL history to appear in Super Bowls with four different coaches (Dan Reeves, Mike Shanahan, John Fox, and Gary Kubiak).

Bowlen's footprint in football spread far behind Denver because he not only was driven by doing all he could to make sure his team won but to do everything in his power to help the NFL thrive. Former NFL Commissioner Paul Tagliabue noted that Bowlen was the only team owner who was heavily involved in all four areas of league growth during the 1980s and '90s: broadcast, labor, stadium development, and international play.

Former NBC Sports Chairman Dick Ebersol called Bowlen "the single major force in the creation of *Sunday Night Football*," and Bowlen also played a critical role in the creation and growth of NFL Network, which was launched in 2003. It's hard to fathom anyone having a bigger impact on the sport.

"When you look back at all the things that this franchise accomplished from 1984 until his passing, you're talking about not only one of the best records in the NFL, you're talking about one of the best records in all of sports," Logan said. "That's a credit to the players and coaching staff, but it's also a credit to Pat for putting it all together, for hiring the right people, for empowering those people to do their jobs. You talk to former players, some of them great players, and they constantly talk about how Pat was all about the players, getting to know them and doing whatever he could to help them succeed. Things like that cannot be overstated.

"You also look back at Pat's contributions to the league and the game of football, to *Sunday Night Football* in particular, and also what he did to help grow football outside of the U.S. and being on the rules committee for a number of years. Honestly, Pat was really one of the four or five most powerful and respected owners in the NFL.

"And that's a tribute to him and the kind of man he was and the work he did while sort of taking a backseat in terms of the public eye. It never was about him. And we all know there are owners today where it's pretty clear it's about them and they love the attention," Logan said.

Dallas Cowboys owner Jerry Jones, a fellow Hall of Famer, said in Bowlen he found a kindred spirit, one who recruited him in selecting dark horse candidate Tagliabue as NFL commissioner in 1989, as well as in bringing Rupert Murdoch and Fox aboard as a broadcast partner in 1993.

Bowlen's "leadership of the Broncos and his dedication to the entire league will serve as a template of excellence in sports ownership that will be emulated and admired for years to come," Jones said upon hearing of Bowlen's death on June 13, 2019. "And that's a wonderful legacy."

Patriots owner Robert Kraft said, "There was no owner or person like Pat Bowlen. I loved him.... He was relentless in his competitive desire to win, but he was always a gentleman, a professional, and a trusted partner. He was a leader both in his success and in his kindness and humility."

Bailey suggested that Bowlen had every right to boast but thought better of it: "He had the style for it, he had the charisma for it," Bailey said. "It's just, what does that really bring to the team? Nothing, really. I loved that about him."

A fierce but friendly competitor, Bowlen provided a blueprint for ownership in professional sports, suggested Jaguars owner Shahid Khan.

"A huge reason I came to Denver was I knew Mr. Bowlen was all about winning," Peyton Manning said. "And I knew I was on the clock and wasn't going to be able to play 12 more years. I knew the Broncos were about winning, and winning now."

Zimmerman said that during Manning's whirlwind free agency tour in 2012 he knew all the other teams pursuing the star quarterback were wasting their time once he saw that Denver was in the mix. "I knew he'd be a Bronco before he did," Zimmerman boasted, "because once he visited here and met with Mr. Bowlen, I knew there was no way he could go anywhere else."

Outside the team's locker room is a large image of Bowlen and his signature saying: "I want us to be number one in everything."

Not just on the field or at the turnstiles, but even in community and player relations.

"He ran this football team with his heart and not his pocketbook," Elway said. "He wanted to rip up everybody's contract all the time to give them more money."

Zimmerman, who played for a 13-member ownership group in Minnesota, first realized Bowlen wasn't your quintessential meddlesome NFL owner his first Thanksgiving in Denver in 1993, when he found a sign-up sheet for a free turkey, surely a prank on rookies and newcomers. Figuring he'd play along, he scribbled down his name. A few days later, he came into the locker room after practice "and there's Pat sticking turkeys into our lockers."

Shanahan said Bowlen always asked him what he needed to win. *Was it this player or that? Any new equipment for the weight room? The film room? The classroom? The locker room? It's yours.* And he did everything with the 53 players on his roster in mind.

"He always made it about his players," Logan said. "I just admired the way Pat handled his duties as owner quietly from the background but he was a league leader in so many different ways.

"Pat was a very good listener and could make you feel like your ideas were the single most important thing…. He empowered his people by leading in that fashion. And I think that's…an underappreciated trait of a great leader."

Elway said the greatest thrill of his Hall of Fame playing career was hearing Bowlen holler, "This…one's…for…John!" when the Broncos won their first Super Bowl back in 1997. And the greatest thrill of his career as an NFL executive came in Super Bowl 50, when he was able to return the favor, jab the Lombardi Trophy into the air, and yell, "This... one's...for...Pat!"

"That was my goal when I took the job," said Elway, who considers himself "the luckiest guy in the world to get an opportunity to play for him and also get an opportunity to come back and work for him."

Elway said he and Bowlen were the last ones to leave Qualcomm Stadium for the post–Super Bowl party that night in 1998 after the Broncos won their first championship. "I can remember the hug with him in the locker room" following that first championship, which came after three Super Bowl blowouts, said Elway, who helicoptered his way into history in leading Denver past Green Bay 31–24.

A year later, Bowlen dedicated Denver's 34–19 win over Atlanta in Super Bowl XXXIII to the fans. By the time the Broncos won their third title, Bowlen was homebound, forced by Alzheimer's to step down from his daily duties running the franchise. Team president, CEO, and confidant Joe Ellis took the Vince Lombardi Trophy to Bowlen's house when the team flew back to Colorado.

Three years later, Ellis and Steve Atwater—one of Bowlen's favorite players—informed Bowlen he was a Hall of Fame nominee.

"I strongly believe that he knew that he got into the Hall of Fame," said Brittany Bowlen, the owner's 30-year-old daughter who aims to one day assume controlling ownership of the franchise. "He had a really big smile when he found out. And I find that a real blessing to know that he knew."

Presenting Bowlen at the Pro Football Hall of Fame in the summer of 2019 was longtime head trainer Steve "Greek" Antonopulos, the only full-time employee who worked for the Broncos throughout Bowlen's entire tenure as owner.

Bowlen always entered the Broncos headquarters through a back door and began his day by stopping by the trainer's room for updates from Antonopulos. "Nobody cared more about players than Mr. Bowlen," Antonopulos said. "He liked to communicate with them not because he wanted to rub elbows, but because he cared about them."

Bowlen split his off-seasons between Denver and Hawaii, and every year he'd take his players out canoeing, golfing, and dining at one of his restaurants during Pro Bowl week.

"He was proud of his restaurants," Elway said. "But you know what? He'd walk in that restaurant and he was more proud of the guys he was walking in with. Not too many times did we have a private room. We sat out in the public and he enjoyed that."

Those were the only times Elway ever saw Bowlen show off.

# ACKNOWLEDGMENTS

I didn't play football at the highest level like Dave Logan did, but he and I do share a love of the game and its many nuances, lessons, and experiences. In my 37 years as a journalist, I've been blessed to have covered the Dallas Cowboys of Troy Aikman and Emmitt Smith, the Green Bay Packers of Brett Favre and Reggie White, and the Denver Broncos of John Elway and Peyton Manning, Champ Bailey, and Von Miller.

I'd like to thank my colleagues Pat Graham, Eddie Pells, Barry Wilner, Simmi Buttar, Michael Marot, Dennis Georgatos, and Mike Kelly. And my contemporaries Jeff Legwold, Andrew Mason, Nicki Jhabvala, Mike Klis, Troy Renck, Aaron Lopez, Sandy Clough, Vic Lombardi, Gil Whiteley, Mark Haas, Michael Spencer, Romi Bean, Dave Willie, Brian Madden, John Marshall, John Mossman, and Darren McKee for their insight into the NFL and to this franchise and the many discussions we've had over the years about personnel, performances, and personalities.

Shoutouts to the Broncos' Jim Saccamano, Patrick Smyth, Erich Schubert, and Seth Medvin, some of the best public-relations pros in sports.

Thanks also to Michelle Bruton, my editor at Triumph Books, and to the Broncos for their never-ending ability to move the needle. As Peter King once said, covering a year on the Broncos beat is the equivalent to covering any other team for three years. In that case, I've covered the Broncos for darn near half a century.

—Arnie Stapleton